EGERIA:
DIARY OF A PILGRIMAGE

ANCIENT CHRISTIAN WRITERS

THE WORKS OF THE FATHERS IN TRANSLATION

EDITED BY

JOHANNES QUASTEN   WALTER J. BURGHARDT

THOMAS COMERFORD LAWLER

No. 38

EGERIA:
DIARY OF A PILGRIMAGE

TRANSLATED AND ANNOTATED

BY

GEORGE E. GINGRAS, Ph.D.
Catholic University of America
Washington, D.C.

NEWMAN PRESS

New York, N.Y./Ramsey, N.J.

De Licentia Superioris S.J.
Nihil Obstat
    J. Quasten
       Cens. Dep.

Imprimatur
    Patricius A. O'Boyle, D.D.
      Archiep. Washingtonen.
        die 20 Octobris 1968

Library of Congress
Catalog Card Number: 70-119159

ISBN: 0-8091-0029-0

PUBLISHED BY PAULIST PRESS
Editorial Office: 1865 Broadway, New York, N.Y. 10023
Business Office: 545 Island Road, Ramsey, N.J. 07446

PRINTED AND BOUND IN THE UNITED STATES OF AMERICA

CONTENTS

EGERIA:
DIARY OF A PILGRIMAGE

INTRODUCTION

The *Diary of a Pilgrimage* presented here in translation is variously known in literature as *S. Silviae Aquitanae peregrinatio ad loca sancta, Peregrinatio Aetheriae,*
and *Itinerarium Egeriae.* Very probably written in the
first part of the fifth century, the work is of major significance for the archaeologist and church historian, and
especially for the philologist and comparative liturgist.
The value of the document is unquestioned, though to
this day major questions remain unresolved regarding
who the author was and when she made the pilgrimage
she describes.

It was in 1884 that the historian and archaeologist
G. F. Gamurrini announced his discovery of the substantial but incomplete narrative of a three-year journey undertaken by a devout woman to Jerusalem and to
various places in Egypt, Palestine, and Syria that were
commemorated in Holy Scripture and tradition.[1] The
twenty-two manuscript pages containing the narrative
had been preserved in a codex that also included fragments of the long-lost hymnbook of St. Hilary of Poitiers
as well as Hilary's treatise *De mysteriis.* Found by
Gamurrini in the library of the Brotherhood of St. Mary
in Arezzo, the codex had originated in the monastery of
Monte Cassino and dated from the eleventh century.[2]
The importance of the find was immediately recognized.
Unfortunately, however, the extant pages of the travel-

1

ogue offered no readily discernible clue as to its author, her position in society, her homeland, or the time of her journey and the composition of the text, which apparently had been written in the form of letters addressed to a group of "sisters" in the author's native land.

In the years since Gamurrini's chance discovery, no other copies of the text have been found, except for a few fragments published in 1909 by Dom de Bruyne.[3] It remains to be seen whether further portions of the document will ever be brought to light to complete the narrative and possibly to resolve definitively the questions of authorship and dating.

THE AUTHOR AND THE TITLE

When Gamurrini published the first edition of the text in 1887, he attributed authorship to a St. Silvia of Aquitaine, and he put the probable time of composition in the period 381–388.[4] The circumstances of the journey as described by the unknown writer had convinced Gamurrini that the traveller must have been a woman related to men in high places, and he attempted to identify this woman with the lady mentioned by Palladius in his *Lausiac History* as having accompanied him to Egypt around 388, a certain Silvania, sister-in-law of the Rufinus who was minister to the emperors Theodosius the Great and Arcadius.[5]

But the links connecting Silvania, St. Silvia, and the author of this pilgrimage record proved to be tenuous. Garmurrini had been misled by a Latin translation of Palladius, a version in which Silvania was referred to as "Silvia" and as the sister of the imperial minister, into identifying her with the hazy figure of St. Silvia of Aquitaine, for Rufinus had been born at Elusa (Eause) in southwestern Gaul.[6] This position did not go unchallenged. Dom Cuthbert Butler in fact even suggested that " 'St. Silvia from Aquitaine' is a purely mythical personage."[7] In spite of the many doubts, however, most early editors and critics attributed the work to Silvia for lack of a plausible alternative. In the 1920s, long after substantial proof had been adduced for assigning the work to another author, C. Iarecki tried to salvage Gamurrini's hypothesis,[8] but his arguments found no adherents.

The names of two other persons put forward as possibly being our pilgrim may be briefly mentioned here. Shortly after the discovery of the text, C. Kohler proposed Galla Placidia (d. 450), the daughter of Theodosius the Great and Galla.[9] Much later, in 1924, H. Goussen introduced the name of Flavia, an abbess from Gaul who founded a Latin convent in Jerusalem before the year 454.[10] Neither of these theories has enjoyed any support.

Dom Férotin, meanwhile, had transformed the whole question in 1903 by linking the so-called *Peregrinatio Silviae* to a letter written about 650 by a Spanish monk named Valerius to his monastic brethren.[11] In this letter Valerius praised the intrepid spirituality of a certain *sanctimonialis Aetheria* who many years earlier had recounted the story of an extensive pilgrimage she had undertaken to the East. Valerius, who lived in the district of Vierzo, or Bierzo (*Bergidum*), near Galicia in northwestern Spain,[12] described his pilgrim as having come from the farthest shore of the ocean on the west at a time when the Catholic faith had begun to flourish on the same shores, presumably, where he and his monks lived.[13]

Had Férotin resolved some of the questions surrounding our text, and was the author then a nun or *sanctimonialis*[14] named Aetheria from the western regions of the empire, specifically Galicia?[15] As it so happens, the manuscripts of the Valerius letter—the three that are extant from Toledo (dated 902), the Escorial (954), and Silos (11th century), plus eighteenth-century editions based either on a lost manuscript from Carracedo or on a version of the copy from Toledo[16]—differ on the precise form of the pilgrim's name. In all the manuscripts the name appears in the salutation and recurs twice in the body of the letter; it also occurs in a conclusion appended to the text in the Escorial and Silos manuscripts and in a title added by a scribe to the Escorial copy. Essentially it can be said that the Carracedo manuscript tradition yields the forms *Etheria* (*Aetheria*) and *Echeria*; the Escorial and Silos manuscripts have *Eiheria* (written once *Aeiheria*); and the Toledo copy has *Egeria*.[17] Férotin rejected *Egeria* largely because he knew of no other woman in antiquity who had borne that name, and he concluded that this form had resulted from a slip of the pen by an erudite copyist thinking of the nymph Egeria.[18] Assuming that the first *i* in *Eiheria* should have been a *t*, and with tangible evidence of persons both in Spain and in Gaul named Aetherius or Aetheria, Férotin adopted the latter form; and a whole generation of scholars, such as Cabrol, Heraeus, García-Villada, Meister, Löfstedt, Baumstark, and Bludau, accepted the title *Peregrinatio Aetheriae* (*Etheriae*).[19]

Yet legitimate doubts persisted from the beginning. Férotin himself mentioned that Dom Lambert had called his attention to two independent pieces of evidence which reinforced arguments that our pilgrim was in fact named Egeria.[20] One of these was an index of books compiled from a charter dated around 935 in the monastery of San Salvador de Celanova which mentions an *Ingerarium Geriae*. The other was a thirteenth-century catalogue from the library of St. Martial in Limoges referring three times to an *Itinerarium Egeria abbatisse*.[20]

Defense of the name Egeria, however, was to be slightly delayed. While admitting that that name commanded the best supporting evidence, the Augustinian E. Bouvy believed the original name had been *Eucheria*,[21] a variant of which occurs in the manuscript of Carracedo. Bouvy contended that Greek names were popular in Spain, and he cited specifically that of Flavius Eucherius, uncle of the emperor Theodosius the Great; in fact, Bouvy theorized that Eucheria, putative author of the pilgrimage account, was a daughter of Eucherius, and so a first cousin of Theodosius himself.[22]

Dom Wilmart at first supported Bouvy's position that the correct title should be *Itinerarium Eucheriae*.[23] Shortly afterwards, however, in 1911 and 1912, he reopened the question with the claim that the paleographical and phonological evidence in favor of Egeria as the name of our pilgrim was more substantial and impressive than that supporting the other forms of the name.[24] Though he could adduce no new facts, he subjected the existing evidence to a critical examination from which two key conclusions could be drawn. Of the variants in the copies of the Valerius letter, only *Egeria* was supported by independent documentation—the entries in the catalogues of Celanova and Limoges—specifically referring to the text of the pilgrimage record. Careful examination of the manuscripts of the Valerius letter showed clearly that *Egeria* is the most frequent form. The *Eiheria* of the Escorial-Silos family was judged to be only a phonetic transcription of *Egeria*; furthermore, when the scribe added a title to the Escorial copy, he wrote *Egeria*. Surprisingly, *Aetheria* (*Etheria*) had the least reliable manuscript support, as it appeared only once in an extant manuscript and was otherwise attested only in Manuel de la Huerta's copy of the Toledo text or a reasonable facsimile thereof.[25] Strangely, Dom Wilmart's arguments were generally rejected.[26]

In 1923 J. F. Mountford brought to light further cogent proof for the form *Egeria*.[27] From the *Liber glossarum*, originally compiled at Ansilebus around 750, he culled an entry which was obviously derived from chapter 15 of our text and which was accompanied by a marginal label indicating the source of the item. The entry reads: *Cepos tu agiu Johannis: Graece quod Latine dicitur ortus sancti Johanni.*[28] Although the chief manuscripts give three slightly different spellings of the source in the margin, the evidence is unmistakable: *Egerie, Egeriae, Egene.* Mountford concluded that "the possibility that the name of the authoress is . . . Egeria, is apparently strengthened by this item."[29]

Finally, in 1936, taking advantage of the publication of a monastic charter from Oviedo dated February 15, 899, containing the name Egeria, and thus proof that at least one other person from northwestern Spain had borne that name, Dom Lambert undertook the rehabilitation of the argument put forward by Wilmart twenty-five years earlier.[30] Like Wilmart, Lambert recognized two families of manuscripts, the older emanating from Toledo, the second, from the Escorial. He reasoned from analogous developments in Spanish linguistics that *Egeria*, the form recorded in the Toledo manuscript, was transcribed *Echeria* at Carracedo and *Eiheria* at the Escorial by copyists attempting to reproduce the evolving pronunciation of the guttural *g* in their day; *Heteria* (*Aetheria, Etheria*) he attributed to eighteenth-century scribal errors.[31]

There has since been a rallying of opinion around the form *Egeria*, beginning in 1938 with a brief notice by F. Cavallera in the *Bulletin de littérature ecclésiastique*,[32] and in 1943 with Vaccari's digest of Lambert's arguments in *Biblica*.[33] Scholars of the past two decades have increasingly adopted this form. Although H. Pétré used "Ethérie" (*Aetheria*) in her excellent 1948 edition with French translation,[34] the most recent editions, that of E. Franceschini and R. Weber[35] and that of O. Prinz,[36] have adopted *Egeria*. Short of the discovery of new data, the text appears destined to bear the title *Itinerarium Egeriae*, "the travel memoirs of Egeria."[37]

In selecting a title for the present translation, we have tried to blend the old and the new. The text belongs clearly to the genre of the *itinerarium* or travelogue, but it has always been recognized as more than a mere catalogue of places visited. The religious motivation of the traveller is clear, and her work is a pilgrimage narrative, the diary of her journey cast in the form of a letter. And hence the title we have chosen: *Diary of a Pilgrimage*.[38]

AUTHOR'S STATUS AND HOMELAND

Who, then, was Egeria? Valerius had referred to her as *beatissima sanctimonialis* and *virgo*, while two monastic catalogues that mention the text speak of her as *abbatissa*.[39] K. Meister even suggested that the *Diary* might have begun like a classical letter: *Abbatissa Aetheria dominis venerabilibus sororibus*, "the abbess Aetheria to the ladies, the reverend sisters."[40] Lambert, however, expressed scepticism about this title of abbess.[41] Moreover, there is no certainty that the "sisters" to whom Egeria wrote were nuns, or that the *affectio vestra* whom she occasionally addresses was a religious superior.[42]

Nevertheless, certain aspects of her *Diary* point to a more than ordinary religious status for our traveller. She was very conscious of the monastic milieu, seeking out the monks even in more remote areas such as the Sinai peninsula and the eastern frontier of the empire, and paying a visit to the deaconess Marthana, a friend of hers who was a religious superior in Asia Minor. Moreover, she was familiar with all aspects of the liturgical life at Jerusalem, including the services attended especially by monks and virgins, such as the nocturnal offices. Finally, the text abounds in references to devotional acts which emphasize the uniquely spiritual purpose of the journey. The internal evidence tends to support the affirmation of Valerius that our author was a nun, and strongly suggests that she was writing to fellow religious.

In view of the difficulties of travel in late antiquity, scholars have sought to identify the pilgrim with someone of high rank who would have had ready access to imperial

favor in obtaining military escorts and the obliging service of officials along the way.[43] Most such speculation
has centered on the family and entourage of Theodosius
the Great, emperor from 379 to 395. Mention has already
been made of the various names proposed—Silvia, Silvania,
Galla Placidia, Eucheria. Férotin suggested our author
may have been the daughter of some Spanish-born official
who held a lesser position in the imperial court.[44] The
text will neither confirm nor rebut these various hypotheses, all of which are predicated on the assumption that
Egeria travelled to the East late in the fourth century
or early in the fifth.

It is striking that our pilgrim never mentions the names
of any contemporaries, except that of Marthana; but
equally striking is the fact that no direct reference to her
can be traced to the Christian community at Jerusalem.
For this reason, both Dom Morin and Dom Lambert
sought for some clue to her identify in the letters of
St. Jerome.

In a letter written by Jerome to Furia around 394
there is a brief passage evidently referring to the ostenta-
tious behavior of a wealthy party travelling through the
East. Morin took this as a reference to Egeria.[45]

Lambert turned to a much later letter, one addressed
by Jerome to Ctesiphon around 415,[46] in an effort to
find some new link between our author and the family
of Theodosius, and he concluded that a much-discussed
passage of the letter contained the answer: *Priscil-
lianum . . . cui juncta Galla non gente sed nomine
germanam huc illucque currentem alterius et vicinae
hereseos reliquit heredem.*[47] He interpreted the passage
to mean that Galla, who was a Galician and related to

the family of Theodosius through the empress Flacilla, had a younger sister who was involved in an Origenistic heresy resembling the Priscillian heresy, and who was well-known for her travels.[48] The younger sister was supposed to be Egeria. The textual evidence that Lambert cites to buttress the theory that Egeria had Priscillian tendencies will be found in the notes pertaining to the particular passages. Lambert suggested that Egeria had left Spain to live in the imperial court under the empress Pulcheria, her cousin, and that she later undertook her long journey in the company of Avitus of Braga, who served as her chaplain.[49] Although the arguments of Lambert are inviting, his views on "Egeria, sister of Galla," remain an inconclusive theory.

Discussions regarding our author's homeland have been dominated by two main theories. The earlier critics, generally following Gamurrini, favored a French locale, either the province of Aquitaine or that of Gallia Narbonensis. But since Férotin's decisive study, the weight of criticism, drawing its principal support from the Valerius letter, has shifted to northwestern Spain, specifically Galicia.

K. Meister has presented the most serious defense of the first hypothesis, citing in its favor topographical and linguistic evidence gleaned from the text.[50] In his opinion, the language of the author best fits the Latin of the region adjoining the Rhone and the Mediterranean Sea, the neighborhood of Arles or Marseilles, a judgment which he believes is reenforced by Egeria's comparison of the Euphrates to the Rhone and by a reference, in a passage considered to be based on lost pages of the *Diary*, to the clear cool waters and the savory fish of the

Italian Sea,[51] as that area of the Mediterranean bordering
southern France was then called. Assuming Egeria to be
a religious, he asserted that before the middle of the
sixth century monastic centers were more likely to be
found in southern Gaul than in the remote districts of
Galicia.[52]

Meister's arguments are inconclusive. As Férotin,
Anglade, García-Villada, and Bludau have pointed out,
certain features of our pilgrim's Latin have greater affinity
with Ibero-Romance linguistic developments.[53] Even
Löfstedt, who otherwise endorses Meister's conclusions,
considers his examples of words or syntax peculiar to
the Latin of Gaul to be too few and of dubious certainty
to justify situating her homeland in southern France
primarily on linguistic grounds.[54] However, the most
compelling evidence against Meister remains the statement of Valerius that Egeria came from the farthest
shore of the ocean on the west (*extremo occidui maris
oceani litore*),[55] which García-Villada has shown to
be a phrase used by other Hispano-Latin authors to
refer to Galicia.[56]

It is the consensus of contemporary scholarship that
Egeria was a consecrated virgin, writing most probably
to a group of fellow religious, and that her homeland
was originally Galicia. As to her age, her family connec-
tions, her theological opinions, her education, and even
the general level of her culture, there is little evidence
on which to base conclusions.[57] We have reserved
comment on whatever the text itself reveals regarding
her cultural background to the discussions of the style
of the *Diary*.

Date of the Pilgrimage

In 1954, seventy years after Gamurrini chanced upon the text, J. G. Davies stated that "short of the discovery of further unambiguous evidence, the determination of the date of the *Peregrinatio* must rest upon a delicate balance of probabilities."[58] Every date suggested has ultimately been based on internal evidence and rests on comparisons of information supplied by the text with contemporary historical and religious data. J. Deconinck long ago defined the limits of the period in which the work could have been written: after A.D. 363, when the emperor Julian ceded to the Sassanian King Sapor II the Mesopotamian city of Nisibis, which our author could not visit because access there was forbidden to Romans; but before 540, the year the Persian armies of Chosroes destroyed Antioch, where our author was able to spend a week.[59]

Most scholars accepted the original hypothesis of Gamurrini that the *Diary* was written late in the fourth century, with the earliest critics dating it between 378 and 388.[60] K. Meister tried to shift the date to the sixth century, and to put Egeria's journey within the period 533–540.[61] We have incorporated the details of his arguments in the notes that bear on particular items in the text. In general Meister asserted that specific historical references and the overall picture depicted of church life, such as the state of monasticism and the fasting practices, fit better in a sixth- than in a fourth-century milieu. His conclusions, although favorably received by many,[62] were almost immediately rejected by Deconinck, Baumstark, and Wiegand.[63] It is impossible to discuss here all aspects of the problem of dating the text. We will confine ourselves to an outline of those "probabilities" that have persuaded recent scholars to propose a date somewhat later than that originally suggested by Gamurrini.

If Dom Morin's hypothesis identifying Egeria with the object of St. Jerome's satire in his letter to Furia could be proven, the pilgrimage would have occurred between 393 and 396.[64] Internal evidence strongly indicates that this is the earliest dating that can be assigned the text. It has been demonstrated that Egeria quotes verbatim from Jerome's Latin translation of Eusebius' *Onomasticon,* and that translation was published after 390.[65] Chapters 18 and 19 of the *Diary* refer to the relics of St. Thomas the Apostle in the basilica dedicated to him in Edessa. The transfer of these relics from a small shrine to the newly restored basilica occurred on August 22, 394.[66] Chapters 18 and 19 also speak of the apocryphal correspondence between Christ and King Abgar the Black of Edessa. This correspondence is mentioned by Eusebius in his *Ecclesiastical History,* where he provides a Greek translation of the Syriac versions he had found in the library at Edessa. Egeria states that she had a copy of these letters at home. Presumably the first Latin version of this correspondence that she could have read would have been in Rufinus of Aquileia's translation of the *Ecclesiastical History* in 403.[67] Certain quotations or paraphrases of Holy Scripture that appear in the *Diary* resemble the text of Rufinus' Latin translation of Origen's *Homilies* on the Old Testament, a translation that appeared in 404.[68]

Can the date of Egeria's pilgrimage be put even later

in the fifth century? This was the contention of Dom Lambert, who, on the basis of his interpretation of Jerome's letter to Ctesiphon mentioned above, suggested that Egeria's journey could very reasonably have been made in the years 414–416.[69] The most striking evidence thus far to bolster Lambert's hypothesis has been that provided by Dom Dekkers on the basis of his interpretation of chapter 42 of the *Diary*.[70] In that chapter Egeria describes how the feast of the fortieth day after Easter, presumably the Ascension, was celebrated in Bethlehem, although in the next chapter she mentions a commemoration of the Ascension at services on Pentecost Sunday in the church marking the historical site on the Mount of Olives. For Dekkers, the celebration in Bethlehem was the result of a unique coincidence; he cites a Georgian liturgical calendar indicating that in 417 the Ascension fell on May 31, which happened also to be the feast of the Dedication of the Basilica of the Nativity,[71] and he concludes that the pilgrimage took place in 415–417. Dekkers' arguments, however, have been disputed by F. L. Cross and J. G. Davies.[72]

We seem to have rather firm proof precluding a date later than 448, the year in or before which Basil of Seleucia composed his *Life and Miracles of St. Thecla, Virgin and Martyr of Iconia*.[73] In that work a certain Marthana is mentioned among the titular guardians of the shrine of St. Thecla. The convent of Egeria's friend, the deaconess Marthana, was at the shrine of St. Thecla, and it is presumed that Egeria's friend and the Marthana noted by Basil are the same person. There is no indication that Marthana was still living at the time Basil was writing, and so Egeria's visit to her probably took place before 448. Further negative evidence is seen in the fact that although Egeria visited Chalcedon and proposed to go to Ephesus, she does not mention the Ecumenical Councils held in those cities in 451 and 431.

It seems clear that Egeria's *Diary* was written after 394; it is very probable that she could not have written it before 404; and there is reason to believe the work may not have been composed until 417. Suggestions of any later date are almost certainly to be rejected. The consensus of scholars is that the picture of church life which emerges from the narrative best describes the ecclesiastical and liturgical milieu of the early fifth century.[74]

THE TEXTUAL PROBLEM

We do not know how much of the original text has been lost. The manuscript of Arezzo begins with Egeria's account of her arrival at Mount Sinai, and breaks off in the middle of her description of the Feast of the Dedications. There are also at least two pages missing in the body of the text,[75] and several chapters have shorter lacunae. Evidence as to what was described in the lost pages of the conclusion is totally lacking; however, we have some indication of the contents of the missing introductory chapters.

Presumably Valerius was acquainted with a more complete text than the one preserved in the manuscript of Arezzo.[76] Thus he speaks of a journey lasting many years to different provinces, cities, and isolated spots inhabited by solitaries. Specifically, he mentions visits by Egeria to the Thebaid, to the other provinces of Egypt, and to various sites in Judaea and Galilee.[77] Egeria may also have given an account of the journey from her homeland to Constantinople, and from there to Jerusalem, along with a description of the Holy City and its environs.[78]

A partial reflection of the initial chapters of the *Diary* may be contained in the twelfth-century *Liber de locis sanctis* of Peter the Deacon, librarian of Monte Cassino, whose work is a compilation based on the Venerable Bede's earlier digest of travelogues recording trips to the East and on other anonymous sources.[79] Gamurrini had recognized that the final pages of Peter the Deacon's book were composed of extracts from the first seven chapters of Egeria's narrative as we have it; but how much of the preceding material could reasonably be considered a summary of the missing chapters? Although Peter the Deacon does add considerable information to his borrowings from Bede, he slavishly follows the structure of the latter's text until he begins to speak about places in Egypt connected with the Exodus of the Hebrews. After a brief mention of Memphis and Heliopolis, he launches into a very detailed description of Clysma, near the present-day port of Suez, where according to the Christian tradition of late antiquity the Israelites' crossing of the Red Sea had occurred.[80] He then describes the places a pilgrim would visit who wished to follow faithfully each stage of the Children of Israel's journey from the Red Sea to Mount Sinai. These passages blend smoothly into those extracts that can unmistakably be identified as borrowings from Egeria.

The extant pages of the *Diary* also give us some idea

of the contents of the lost initial pages. Egeria had visited the great monastic center of the Thebaid in Upper Egypt and the metropolis of Alexandria prior to her pilgrimage to Mount Sinai, and she indicates that she had already written about the places lying between Clysma and the sacred mountain. It does not seem unreasonable to accept the substance of Peter the Deacon's remarks on Egypt and the route to Sinai as an accurate, although impersonal, summary of Egeria's words.

Accordingly, we can assume that after describing Clysma, Egeria spoke of crossing the vast desert of Sur and of arriving at the fountains of Mara by the shores of the Red Sea.[81] A three-day journey across another desert region would then have brought her to Arandara, the biblical Elim, a pleasing oasis with abundant water and vegetation.[82] From here she would have entered the narrow valleys that led to the town of Pharan, the biblical Raphidim, a little over thirty miles from her immediate destination.[83] The text we have today begins as Egeria is on her way from Pharan to Mount Sinai.

Contents and Historical Significance[84]

The text has two major sections. The first twenty-three chapters are devoted to several pilgrimages and the return journey to Constantinople; the remaining twenty-six chapters describe the liturgy of the church of Jerusalem. Written primarily in the first person, the *Diary* provides an eyewitness account of what the pilgrim Egeria observed in the course of three years of residence in Jerusalem and travel in the Near East. As such, it is a primary document for the archaeologist, the geographer, the church historian, and the student of the liturgy. But the wealth of information it contains will be best appreciated if understood within the milieu in which its author moved and in terms of the literary genre in which she wrote.

Each of the journeys undertaken by Egeria was a true pilgrimage motivated by a specific religious objective. The relationship of man to God in both the Old and the New Testament is generally existentialized in a particular historical site, and the religious pilgrim wishes to realize anew, for himself and in his own time, the truths of faith commemorated in a specific place. With increasing frequency throughout the fourth century, men and women from both the Greek and Latin worlds travelled eastward to look upon the sites of the Nativity, the Mission, the Passion, and the Resurrection of Christ, and to visit the numerous churches and shrines built since Constantine's day.[85] Except insofar as those scriptural events were relived in the ritual of the liturgical year that Egeria witnessed in Jerusalem and its environs, these primary objectives of the Christian pilgrim are not mentioned in the extant text of the *Diary;* we can assume that Egeria spoke of them in her account of her first days at Jerusalem, that is to say, in a part of the *Diary* now lost.

The surviving text describes four journeys taken by Egeria. Because of the isolated, rugged, inhospitable, and perilous regions into which she ventured, the unusual distances she travelled, and the infrequency with which the average pilgrim could reach the particular sites she visited, Egeria's journeys stand out from among other pilgrimages of her time. Recorded in her *Diary* are a pilgrimage to Mount Sinai and a retracing of the route of the Exodus (chapters 1–9); a trip to Mount Nebo, the traditional site of Moses' death (chapters 10–12); a visit to the tomb of Job at Carneas in Hauran (chapters 13–16); and an extensive detour to the tomb of St. Thomas the Apostle in Edessa and to the house of Abraham in Carrhae, the biblical Haran (chapters 17–21). Egeria's description of her return trip to Constantinople includes accounts of visits to the tomb of St. Thecla at Meriamlik near Seleucia in Isauria and to the Basilica of St. Euphemia in Chalcedon (chapters 22–23).

The facts Egeria presents in recounting her journeys are always subordinate and incidental to her central purpose, which was to vivify and confirm her faith in the truths of Scripture through personal contact with those places marked by the action of God on man,[86] and to meet and pray in the company of those who she considered best exemplified the Christian life, the monks of Sinai, Palestine, Mesopotamia, and Isauria.[87] Unlike the authors of other early *itineraria*, especially the earliest known example of the genre, the *Itinerarium Burdigalense* written by an anonymous pilgrim from Bordeaux around 333,[88] Egeria pays scant attention to distances between places. Occasionally she gives the number of days it required to reach a certain destination; very rarely does she give the actual Roman mileage. By her own testimony she was very curious;[89] but on the four journeys described in her text her curiosity had a special orientation—she wanted to be shown the physical sites of biblical events, particularly those recorded in the Pentateuch. The modern reader should not expect numerous precise topographical details, or indeed anything more than the most general descriptions. For Egeria, all places are very beautiful and pleasant to the traveller.[90] In specifying the locations of places or in providing additional information about them, Egeria borrows from both Holy Scripture and St. Jerome's Latin translation of the *Onomasticon* of Eusebius;[91] her own comment on a biblical site is often merely a paraphrase of Scripture or of the *Onomasticon* instead of a personal observation or the information she must have received from guides and the local inhabitants.

Despite these limitations, the first section of the text represents an important addition to the oral tradition that had developed over four centuries concerning the location of sites mentioned in Scripture. Moreover, it publicizes much local tradition that had grown up to satisfy the need of believers to have concrete "proof" of the reality of the events narrated in Scripture. Finally, it offers valuable information on the state of Christianity, and especially of the progress of monasticism, in various areas.

Egeria's testimony is frequently cited among the earliest documentary evidence pointing to the identification of the Djebel Musa massif with the Mount Sinai of the Exodus.[92] She provides a valuable link between the first allusions to a Christian presence at Mount Sinai around 378 and the period of greatest prosperity there under the emperor Justinian, when the monastery-fortress of St. Catherine was built. Egeria speaks of an intermediary stage, when four small churches had been built and numerous cells of anchorites dotted the landscape.[93] However, an elaborate local tradition had already evolved, and the solitaries of Sinai were ready to point

out to the traveller where God had appeared in the
burning bush, where the golden calf had stood, and
so forth.[94]

Partisans of the southern route of the Exodus find
further confirmation in this text that early Judaeo-
Christian tradition generally situated the crossing of the
Red Sea at Clysma, near Suez. Of greater importance,
the *Diary* serves as a guide for the contemporary
archaeologist and biblical exegete attempting to locate
the "mansions of the children of Israel"[95] prior to the
crossing. One of the first archaeologists to utilize this
text was E. Naville, who cited it in 1885 to substantiate
his identification of the biblical Phithom and the Graeco-
Roman city of Heroopolis, and later in locating the city
of Arabia, an Egyptian administrative and episcopal
center in late antiquity. [96] C. Bourdon has used the *Diary*
to support the prevailing view of those favoring a
southern route that the crossing took place at the
southern edge of the Bitter Lakes, while A. Servin has
utilized data from it to revive the older tradition of a
crossing near Suez.[97]

Egeria's account of her visit to Mount Nebo has
focused attention on the legends that had developed
around the death of Moses and on the general location of
Sodom and the cities of the Pentapolis. In the small
church on the Ras Siagha (Egeria's Nebo), the ruins of
which have been excavated since the 1930s, monks
showed her the reputed site of Moses' grave. Apparently
she was told an earlier version of the legend with which
by 430 Peter the Iberian was acquainted, that is, the
story of a shepherd who saw in a vision the place where
Moses was buried.[98] Sodom and the other cities of the

Pentapolis are generally believed to have stood on the southern shores of the Dead Sea. In her description of the panorama to be viewed from the summit of the Ras Siagha, Egeria presumably was reflecting the general opinion of her day on the location of these cities. The testimony of the *Diary* is considered crucial both by those who favor the more traditional southern site and by E. Power and A. Mallon, whose excavations point to the regions north of the Dead Sea.[99]

Although the *Diary* does nothing to dispel the confusion about the location of Job's land of Hus or the location of Melchisedech's city of Salem,[100] it has added much to the already rich legends that had identified Job with the Hauran district to the northeast of the Sea of Galilee, and it indicates how rooted in popular tradition may have been one of the hypotheses reflected in Jerome's letters and in the *Onamasticon*, namely, that Melchisedech's Salem should be sought in the upper Jordan valley. One consequence of Jerome's hypothesis is the *Diary*'s identification of Salem with the Salim mentioned in the New Testament and near which stood Ennon, one of the sites of the mission of John the Baptist.[101] Through Egeria we also learn of a tradition associating Elias with this area. From her account it is apparent that there were numerous monks in this area, and we have the one extant reference to Carneas as a bishopric.[102]

Chapters 17–23 of the *Diary* provide concrete illustrations of the vitality of the monastic life in Syria and Asia Minor at the time of Egeria's travels. The bishops she met in Mesopotamia were all former monks.[103] The desert regions around Carrhae, the biblical Haran, were inhabited by numerous solitaries, while at Meriamlik, the site of the shrine of St. Thecla, there seem to have been several flourishing monastic communities. We are given a vivid picture of the importance of the legendary correspondence between Christ and Abgar in the religious life at Edessa; we learn of the devotion to a certain St. Helpidius in Carrhae; and we become aware of the interest an early traveller took in the veneration of Sts. Thecla and Euphemia. Finally, the importance of the Apocrypha to the spiritual life is reflected in the role accorded them in prayer. At Edessa passages from the *Acts of St. Thomas* and at Meriamlik a reading of the *Acts of St. Paul and Thecla*[104] constituted integral parts of the ritual of prayer and scriptural readings that marked each visit to a religiously significant site.

The Liturgy of Jerusalem

The second section of the *Diary*, consisting of chapters 24–49, deals with the daily liturgy and the cycle of the liturgical year in Jerusalem. It is this portion of the text that has received the greatest attention in recent years.[105]

In general these chapters yield valuable information on the ecclesiastical topography of Jerusalem and its environs. Both Dom Cabrol and H. Pétré introduced their studies of the Jerusalem liturgy with a survey of the churches mentioned by Egeria in which the chief ceremonies of the daily, Sunday, and seasonal liturgy took place.[106] Cabrol emphasized the essentially stational character of the services, since each of the churches was often allotted the celebration of a particular office of the day or a particular feast of the year: "Suivant les solennités, on se transportait du Calvaire au Golgotha, du Golgotha à la Croix, de la Croix à l'Église de Sion ou au Mont des Oliviers."[107] A brief description of these edifices will facilitate comprehension of the text of the *Diary*.[108]

Six churches played the greatest role in this liturgy—the Basilica of the Holy Sepulchre and the Church of Sion, both within the walls of Jerusalem; the two churches on the Mount of Olives, the Imbomon and the Eleona; the Basilica of the Nativity in Bethlehem; and the Church of the Lazarus, or Lazarium, in Bethany. Egeria never refers by name to the Basilica of the Nativity, but in chapters 25 and 42 she mentions services held in the Bethlehem church "where the grotto in which the Lord was born is located."[109] The Lazarium served as a stational church particularly for the solemn service of the Saturday before Palm Sunday, the Lazarus Saturday.[110]

A reader could almost reconstruct the plan of Constantine's Basilica of the Holy Sepulchre from Egeria's references to the various services held in the individual churches composing that structure. Moving from west to east, we find first the Anastasis, or sanctuary of the Resurrection, a church in the round, in the center of which was the grotto of the Holy Sepulchre.[111] The divine office was celebrated there daily. Next there is the atrium of the Holy Cross, an inner courtyard that was enclosed on three sides by porticoes and on the fourth or east side by the chevet of the Martyrium, the chief church. In the southwest corner of this large, open-air courtyard, called the Ante Crucem,[112] there stood a cross, on the reputed site of the Crucifixion. The rock of Calvary, which rose to a height of about twelve feet and which was surrounded by a grille, was called the Ad

Crucem. The rock of the cross, along with the area of the courtyard that stretched out before it, comprised the church called the Ad Crucem, which was the stational church for certain seasonal rituals and for the elaborate rites of dismissal from daily vespers.[113] Behind the cross was a chapel called the Post Crucem, where Mass was offered on Holy Thursday and the "sacred wood of the cross" was venerated on Good Friday.[114] The Martyrium, the chief or so-called major church (*ecclesia maior*) of Jerusalem, where Sunday Mass was celebrated, was a five-aisled church with an apse on the west end. Frequently called the church on Golgotha, the Martyrium was built over the grotto of the Finding of the Holy Cross.[115] Egeria does not mention the courtyard on the east front of the Martyrium, and only once, in chapter 43, does she refer to the main portals that constituted part of the propylaea, the colonnaded entrance situated on the eastern end of the basilica and opening from the middle of the market street, which was called the *quintana*.[116]

The Church of Sion was the stational church for the Wednesday and Friday liturgy throughout the year. A small chapel had been erected on Mount Sion, the southwestern hill of Jerusalem, around the year 130, and between 335 and 347 this original structure had been enlarged by the addition of a basilica. Referred to by St. Cyril of Jerusalem as the Upper Church of the Apostles, the Church of Sion stood on the traditional site of the upper room in which the Eucharist was instituted and the apostles received the Holy Spirit. It was the church reserved for the chief liturgy of Pentecost.[117]

On the summit of the Mount of Olives stood the Imbomon, marking the site of the Ascension,[118] and down the slope from there was the Eleona,[119] built over the grotto where Christ taught His apostles during the first Holy Week. In these churches the Palm Sunday procession began, the events of Holy Thursday were commemorated, and important liturgical offices during Eastertide and on Pentecost Sunday afternoon took place.

Whoever reads this second section of Egeria's *Diary* will quickly grasp the dramatic quality with which she invests the liturgy of Jerusalem. It is not to her that we should turn for specifics on the prayers recited, the Psalms and hymns sung, or the precise rubrics followed. Frequently she tells us that the hymns and prayers were appropriate to the day and the place,[120] but only rarely does she even tell us what scriptural passages were read at the various services.[121] However, for anyone seeking an overall view of the liturgy celebrated in Jerusalem, and especially for a panorama of the great feasts, her descriptions are unique.

A picture of the general religious life of Jerusalem, particularly the degree of participation of the people in the rituals, may also be gleaned from these pages. If nocturns and the daily morning office were essentially monastic services, a multitude, including many children, attended daily vespers.[122] On Sundays, the crowds were as large as at Easter.[123] On the great feasts, particularly Palm Sunday, Holy Thursday evening, and Pentecost, vast throngs moved from the Mount of Olives in procession to the city. Egeria states that on Pentecost not a single Christian remained at home. [124]

The twenty-six chapters that treat of the Jerusalem liturgy deal with ten major topics—the daily order of the divine office and the Sunday liturgy (chapter 24 and the first half of chapter 25); the Epiphany and its octave (the conclusion of chapter 25); the feast of the Presentation (26); Lent, the nature of the Lenten liturgy, and the fasting customs, particularly the continuous fasting practiced by the rigorous ascetics (27–28); the liturgy of Holy Week, beginning with the Lazarus Saturday liturgy and concluding with the Easter vigil (29–38); the liturgy of Easter and Eastertide (39–41); the feast of the fortieth day after Easter (42); Pentecost and the liturgy of the time after Pentecost (43–44); the instruction of catechumens preparatory to baptism (45–47); and the feast of Dedication of the Basilica of the Holy Sepulchre (48–49).

It has been suggested that in opening her account of the Jerusalem liturgy with a description of the daily offices of prayer held at the Anastasis, Egeria was putting first that aspect of the ritual which she felt would find the most sympathetic echo in the hearts of her fellow religious, namely, the hours of the divine office.[125] However, her order of presentation possesses an inner logic of its own. She begins with those ceremonies which were performed *daily*. Next she turns to what was done *every Sunday*. There is a lacuna in the text at this point, but very likely she next reported what occurred *weekly* on Wednesdays and Fridays. Finally she discusses the great feasts and the seasonal cycle of the liturgy that recurred *yearly*. Certainly her *Diary* significantly illuminates what the structure of the church worship in Jerusalem was like and to what extent the formation of the major patterns of the liturgy had been completed at the time of her pilgrimage.

Apparently five distinct services constituted the weekday liturgy in Jerusalem when Egeria was there—nocturns, the morning office, sext, nones, and vespers. The most striking omission in this list is that of a liturgical office at tierce. The *Diary* does report that an office for the third hour was incorporated into the order of services during Lent; but from the second century on, in the lists of times to be especially observed by Christians, the third hour was always linked to the sixth and ninth hours as one of the traditional times of the day for prayer.[126] The restriction in Egeria's account of such an office to Lent is even more surprising in view of the testimony of contemporary writers to the incorporation of tierce into a well-defined order of prayer in Jerusalem and Syria during the fourth and fifth centuries. The *Apostolic Constitutions* speak of six hours of prayer—in the morning, at the third, sixth, and ninth hours, in the evening, and at cockcrow.[127] The monastery of St. Paula (d. 404) in Bethlehem observed these same hours, as we learn from Jerome: *Mane, hora tertia, sexta, nona, vespera, noctis medio per ordinem psalterium canebant.*[128] Cassian, who provides expert testimony on the customs of the East, also refers to six regular hours of daily prayer.[129]

For the offices that she does name, Egeria employs only a semitechnical terminology. The night office, which closely resembles the later matins or nocturns, bears no specific name; it is variously referred to as observing the vigil at cockcrow, the service at cockcrow, or, simply, the vigil.[130] The morning office, which is the equivalent of lauds and which originally bore the name of *matutini*,[131] is obliquely given a proper name, for Egeria labels its hymns *matutinos hymnos*, and the dismissal from the service is referred to as *missa matutina*. Occasionally Egeria refers to the morning office as the service which begins at dawn or in the morning.[132] In speaking of sext and nones, she employs slightly varying constructions, thus indicating that these offices were not as yet designated by fixed liturgical phrases (i.e., the *ad sextam* and *ad nonam* that we find in St. Benedict).[133] Vespers or the evening service is called candlelight (*lucernare*).

The Jerusalem vigil service and morning office were juxtaposed one to the other. The first was essentially an office for "monks and virgins," and was attended by only few of the laity and by only two or three priests and a like number of deacons who were assigned to recite prayers after each hymn or Psalm. The vigil service was followed without interruption at daybreak by a completely public office presided over by the bishop and attended by the clergy, the faithful, and the catechumens. Formerly, liturgists were unanimous in considering the origin of this vigil to lie in the middle section of the Easter *pannychis*, or all-night vigil. There is a growing tendency to view this vigil either as a transformation of the early Christian's private midnight prayer into a public office or as a sort of pre-lauds, a service of psalmody and prayer prefixed to the morning office. The direct relationship of the cathedral morning service in Jerusalem to the night office lends support to this second view.[134]

The services at the sixth and ninth hours were both cathedral offices, for the bishop presided, offered prayer, and bestowed the blessing. The church of Jerusalem's daily corporate act of prayer was most fully realized in vespers (*lucernare*, candlelight), when a large crowd, including many children, gathered in the Anastasis for a service similar in structure to, though more elaborate in

detail than, the parallel morning office.[135] The singing
of hymns, Psalms, and antiphons, a series of commemorations, and prolonged rites of blessing and dismissal
characterized both services. The vespers commemorations,
however, had developed into a full litany with a con-
gregational response of "Lord, have mercy," while the
initial rite of dismissal at the Anastasis was duplicated first
before the Cross, then behind the Cross, following a
procession of the whole congregation to the adjoining
Church of the Cross.

The structure of the Sunday morning vigil has both
intrigued and divided liturgists. Long before cockcrow,
the normal hour for the vigil to begin, a multitude of
the laity gathered in the forecourt of the Anastasis, the
doors of which remained shut until the first cockcrow.
The people sang hymns and Psalms and were led in prayer
by the deacons and priests who were on hand, ready to
hold the vigil. This gathering, then, had assumed the
proportions of a liturgical office. Duchesne called it a pre-
matins and considered it a relic of the primitive church's
all-night vigil before a Sunday or a martyr's feast day; but
Cabrol relegated it to the status of an unofficial service to
occupy the waiting faithful.[136] J. Mateos calls it a pre-
vigil and finds a parallel for it in the Sunday *Lelya* of
the Chaldean rite.[137]

At cockcrow the bishop arrived, the Anastasis was
opened, and there followed a full public office. Three
hymns were sung, each followed by a prayer; the
Resurrectio Domini was read; and then there was a procession to the Cross, where the dismissal rites took place.[138]
There is no agreement on the proper classification of this
office. Cabrol and Bludau see it simply as the Sunday

vigil service, but Hanssens states that it may either be
the Sunday lauds or the solemn conclusion of the vigil
that had already begun outside the Anastasis.[189] Mateos
compares the structure of this office to the Chaldean
Qale d-sahra, the formal vigil service which occurs after
the *Lelya* but before the morning office or *Sapra*.[140]

The question of a Sunday lauds is also in dispute. For
Cabrol, there is no lauds in this Jerusalem Sunday ordo;
for Bludau, it is constituted by the chant of the monks at
the Anastasis after the bishop's withdrawal; for Mateos, it
is assimilated to the divine service which began at dawn
in the Martyrium.[141]

Apparently Mass was celebrated twice in the Basilica
of the Holy Sepulchre on Sundays, first at the Martyrium,
then at the Anastasis. At least, such a conclusion seems
warranted on the basis of a careful examination of the
text. Several critics—notably H. Leclercq[142]—have maintained that there was only a *missa catechumenorum* at
the Martyrium, while Bludau contended that the subsequent service at the Anastasis was simply an act of
thanksgiving.[143] The uncertainty stems from Egeria's terse
and even ambiguous description of the services at the
two churches.[144] However, references in her account of
the Pentecost Sunday liturgy established clearly that Mass
was offered in the Martyrium every Sunday morning, and
that a second Sunday Mass, albeit at the Church of Sion,
was offered on Pentecost.[145] The absence of catechumens
from the second service on ordinary Sundays at the
Anastasis points to a eucharistic sacrifice, a *missa
fidelium*, and a recent emendation of the manuscript
proposed by E. Wistrand would offer textual support for
such an inference.[146] Further support for the view that

there were two successive Masses on Sundays, one at the Martyrium, the other at the Anastasis, may also be found in Egeria's description of the Easter vigil service.[147] The Martyrium service was by far the longer, and was characterized by numerous sermons, whereas the service that followed at the Anastasis probably was limited to the offering of the sacrifice.

From references in chapters 27, 41, and 44 we can reconstruct one additional regular feature of the Jerusalem liturgy, the celebration of Mass at the Church of Sion every Wednesday and Friday except during Lent. The hour for this Mass varied. On a regular ferial day, it occurred at the ninth hour, that is, in mid-afternoon; but during Eastertide and on the feast day of a martyr, the Mass was celebrated in the morning. The customary Wednesday and Friday fasting on ferial days accounts for the afternoon Mass, since the eucharistic sacrifice marked the end of the fast. It is Wistrand's contention that Egeria described these services in the missing part of the text in chapter 25.[148]

What distinguished the rites of the church of Jerusalem from liturgical action elsewhere was the essentially representational nature of its festal cycle. Sunday was primitive Christianity's unique feast day, on which the Church dwelt on the full depth of the motif of redemption eternalized in the timeless celebration of the Eucharist.[149] The festal cycle evolved through an extension of the nontemporal commemorative action of the Mass to its cyclical representation in the greater dimension of the full year. Easter emerged first as an accentuated Sunday, what St. Ambrose called the sacred triduum during which Christ suffered death, was buried, and rose from the tomb;[150] and there followed the division of the total motif into its chief parts, with the creation of separate feasts for the Nativity, Ascension, and Pentecost.[151] A. Baumstark emphasizes that in their original conception such feasts were not historical commemorations of this or that episode of sacred history, but rather the expression of theological truths.[152] By the fourth century, however, the historical nature of many feasts was being emphasized, and, as Jungmann notes, "in Jerusalem we meet the manner of celebration which picks out and reproduces details, a method which made sense in the places where those events actually happened."[153]

The creation of many parts of the liturgy described by Egeria may be explained by O. B. Hardison's principle of coincidence: "When an historical event of major importance coincides with a regular liturgical service, a representational ceremony is likely."[154] It is this "coincidence of historical and liturgical space"[155] which exercised incalculable influence on both the conception of certain feasts and the amplification of others through the creation of certain extraliturgical forms.

The *Diary*'s description of the liturgical year begins with the Epiphany, celebrated in the East as the Feast of the Nativity.[156] Because there is a lacuna in the manuscript here, we do not know what Egeria might have said of the beginning of the Church year. The stational and representational nature of the Jerusalem liturgy is, however, immediately apparent. A throng of clergy, religious, and faithful had accompanied the bishop from Jerusalem to Bethlehem, where the vigil service was held in the grotto church of the Nativity, and the text resumes as the returning procession nears Jerusalem.[157]

Baumstark[158] states that Egeria provides evidence that Mass was celebrated twice on the feast of the Nativity, first at the Basilica of the Nativity in Bethlehem, then in the Martyrium. Egeria stresses the rich decoration of the churches, which accentuated the pomp surrounding the celebration of the feast. The liturgy of the Epiphany octave had a stational character, being celebrated on the first three days at the Martyrium, then on successive days at the Eleona, the Lazarium, the Church of Sion, the Anastasis, and the Cross.[159]

The creation of a feast to commemorate the Presentation of Jesus in the Temple provides a second example of the impact of the historical surroundings on the formation of the liturgical cycle. Egeria's *Diary* apparently provides the earliest evidence for the existence of this feast.[160] The church of Jerusalem observed it as the Christ-centered feast of *Hypapante*, the meeting of the Messiah with Simeon, and not as the Marian feast of the Purification. There is no allusion in the *Diary* to a procession of lights, a ceremony introduced into the Jerusalem rite in the middle of the fifth century by a Roman matron, Ikelia.

At the time of Egeria's visit an eight-week Lent was observed in Jerusalem. The order and type of service that unfolded in the first seven weeks differed from the normal weekly ritual on only three points. A service was held at the third hour (mid-morning) each weekday; the customary afternoon Mass on Wednesdays and Fridays in the Church of Sion was replaced by a liturgy of the word— sermons, prayers, and psalmody; and each Friday night an all-night vigil, culminating in a pre-dawn celebration of the Eucharist, was held.[161]

Holy Week, a period marked by numerous representational ceremonies, was in fact inaugurated on the Saturday before Palm Sunday, the Lazarus Saturday, called the "Great Saturday" by St. John Chrysostom.[162] In the seventh week of Lent the site of the Friday night vigil was shifted from the Anastasis, where it was held in the first six weeks of Lent, to the Church of Sion, and on Saturday morning after Mass the procession to Bethany was announced. Egeria affirms that the intention to commemorate the events at the locale of their occurrence gave rise to the procession of the bishop and the people to the Lazarium.[163] In this rememorative rite two distinct events of Christ's ministry were relived, His recall of Lazarus from the dead and His coming to Bethany on the eve of His triumphal entry into Jerusalem.[164] The procession observed a station at a small church on the site of the meeting of Lazarus' sisters with Christ,[165] and then proceeded to Bethany, where a great multitude, reminiscent of the crowds described in the Gospel of St. John 12.9, overflowed into the fields. The ceremony culminated in the re-creation of the historical incident in its spatial and temporal setting, as a priest read St. John's account of the events in Bethany the day before Palm Sunday and proclaimed the Pasch.[166]

Egeria is the first author to describe the dramatic imitation of Christ's entry into Jerusalem that was to become one of the church of Jerusalem's most significant contributions to the liturgy.[167] The emphasis was clearly on *imitatio*, for the bishop re-enacted the role of Christ, being led "in the same manner as the Lord once was led" (*in eo typo quo tunc Dominus deductus est*).[168] The eleborate ritual began at the seventh hour (early afternoon) when "all the people" assembled at the Eleona on the Mount of Olives. At the ninth hour they moved to the Imbomon, the site of the Ascension, where at the eleventh hour there was a reading from St. Matthew's account of Palm Sunday.[169] A procession then formed and slowly descended the mountain with the people chanting the refrain, *Blessed is He who comes in the name of the Lord*, and with the children bearing olive branches and palm fronds. The procession moved through the entire city and terminated at the Anastasis, where vespers was celebrated. No account is given of a blessing of the palms, and the procession existed as a rite independent of the Palm Sunday Mass to which it was later attached.[170]

Certain departures from the usual Lenten ritual occurred on Monday, Tuesday, and Wednesday of Holy Week.[171] Both the ninth-hour service and vespers were celebrated in the major church, but the services there were prolonged until after nightfall, and were continued afterwards for a time at the Anastasis. On Tuesday a representational ceremony was enacted on the Mount of Olives at the Eleona, commemorating the eschatological sermon of Christ given in the Gospel of St. Matthew 24.3-25.46. This sermon was delivered privately to the disciples on the Mount of Olives two days before the Pasch, or, according to tradition, on Tuesday of Holy Week.[172] Christian tradition fixed the betrayal of Judas on Wednesday,[173] and a commemorative ceremony was held on Wednesday of Holy Week in the Anastasis. While the bishop stood within the grotto of the Resurrection and a priest read the Gospel text, much "moaning and groaning" was heard from the people.[174]

Egeria emphasizes two features of the Holy Thursday

rite, namely, the celebration of Mass at the major church and again at the Cross, and the elaborate all-night vigil observed at various stations on the Mount of Olives, culminating in a pre-dawn procession through the city and to the Church of the Cross. Most remarkable in a historically oriented liturgy is the absence of a commemorative station at the Church of Sion, traditionally associated with the site of the Last Supper. The fifth-century Armenian Lectionary mentions a station at Sion at which the chief scriptural reading was St. Paul's account of the institution of the Eucharist.[175] Does Egeria's failure to describe such a station indicate the lack of a tradition at her time linking the institution of the Eucharist with Sion? Thibaut prefers another explanation, suggesting that the commemoration at the Cross was motivated by a desire to accentuate the union of the sacrifice of the altar and that of the cross.[176]

The vigil on Holy Thursday night was marked by a selective re-enactment of the events described in the Gospels. The vigil began at the Eleona on the Mount of Olives with a commemoration of Christ's discourse to the apostles.[177] At midnight a procession formed to ascend to the Imbomon for a service of prayer, Psalms, and readings. Shortly before cockcrow all moved down to where Christ fell into agony, and subsequently to the place in Gethsemani associated with Christ's arrest. The vivid reliving of these scenes is apparent in Egeria's reference to the loud "moaning and groaning" of the people.[178] The procession then returned to the city and the Church of the Cross, where Christ's appearance before Pilate was commemorated with the reading of appropriate scriptural texts. A departure at this point from strict adherence to the historical route of Christ is apparent. The seventh-century Georgian *Canonarion* prescribes stations at the Church of St. Peter on Mount Sion, where Caiphas' palace stood, at the Church of St. Sophia, where Pilate's palace was located, and at Golgotha.[179] Egeria does mention a station at Sion to commemorate the Scourging at the Pillar; this followed the dismissal from the Cross and concluded the vigil.

The Good Friday liturgy was characterized by a striking representational ceremony and an extensive service of the word. The four hours before noon were devoted to veneration of the cross, the *adoratio crucis*, in the chapel behind the site of the Crucifixion. Egeria's description is the earliest account we have of this rite. It is not known how long a time elapsed between the finding of the True Cross by St. Helena, in the third or fourth decade of the fourth century, and the incorporation of a ceremony of veneration into the Jerusalem Good Friday liturgy.[180] At noon a three-hour service began before the Cross; this consisted largely of readings from the Old and New Testaments bearing on the Passion and concluded with a reading from the Gospel according to St. John.[181] There was a vespers service at the Martyrium, which was followed by a procession to the Anastasis, where the entombment of Christ was commemorated by a reading from Scripture at the site of the Holy Sepulchre itself.[182] An all-night vigil then ensued.

In fifth-century Jerusalem the Easter vigil apparently began in mid-afternoon with the unfolding of the elaborate ritual of baptism, on which the whole service was focused.[183] The preparation of adult candidates for baptism constituted an important aspect of the Lenten liturgy, and in chapters 45–47 Egeria sketches the rites that accompanied their instruction before formal baptism at the vigil. On the first day of Lent the catechumen who had given his name was formally accepted as a *competens* after a public examination by the bishop.[184] Every morning on fast days (Mondays through Fridays) there were three hours of catechetical instruction, exorcisms, and scrutiny or examination.[185] After five weeks of instruction centered on the Scriptures, the *traditio symboli* rite was held,[186] followed a fortnight later by the *redditio symboli* ceremony.[187] Egeria does not say whether there was a final scrutiny on Holy Saturday.[188]

She also omits all detail on the rites immediately preceding the administration of baptism, stating merely that "the Easter vigil is observed here exactly as we observe it at home." According to the fifth-century Armenian Lectionary, the vigil began in the Anastasis with the lighting of the Paschal candle and the chanting of the *Exsultet*.[189] The congregation then proceeded to the Martyrium for the reading of twelve scriptural lessons, each followed by a Psalm.[190] Then ensued the administration of baptism, for which we have a description from a fourth-century source, the *Catecheses mystagogicae* attributed to St. Cyril of Jerusalem. In the forecourt of the baptistery the candidates faced to the west and renounced Satan. Then they turned to the east and recited the Creed. After entering the baptistery, they undressed and were anointed from head to foot. Each candidate then descended into the baptismal font, where he was immersed three times. At this point confirmation was administered, and the neophytes, vested in white robes, were led to the Anastasis, where the bishop offered a prayer on their behalf at the site of the Resurrection.[191] According to Egeria, the neophytes and the bishop then returned to the Martyrium, where Mass was celebrated. Other sources from the period indicate that the newly baptized communicated at this Mass, although no reference to their receiving the Eucharist is found in the *Diary*.[192] Following the vigil Mass there was a procession of the whole congregation to the Anastasis, where Mass was offered a second time.

The Easter octave liturgy had a stational character. On Sunday, Monday, and Tuesday, Mass was celebrated in the morning at the Martyrium, and on successive days thereafter at the Eleona, the Anastasis, the Church of Sion, and the Cross. On Low Sunday, the octave day, Mass was again offered at the Martyrium. According to information supplied in chapter 47 of the *Diary*, on each of the eight days the newly baptized came in procession to the Anastasis after Mass for instruction in those mysteries of faith not fully revealed to the catechumens.[193] Every afternoon there was a procession to the Mount of Olives, where a service of prayer and Psalms was held at the Eleona and the Imbomon. This was followed by vespers at the Anastasis. Finally, two representational ceremonies commemorated events that Scripture localized on Easter and its octave day. After vespers on Easter Sunday the congregation proceeded to the Church of Sion, where there was a reading from the Gospel of St. John describing Christ's first appearance to His disciples in the upper room after the Resurrection and the incredulity of St. Thomas. On the octave of Easter there was a similar ceremony in commemoration of Christ's second appearance and His reproval of the sceptical disciple.[194]

From the evidence provided by Egeria's *Diary* it appears that the mysteries of the Ascension and Pentecost were closely associated in the Jerusalem liturgy. The question of whether there was a separate feast of the Ascension is left unanswered by Egeria's account of two distinct rites, one in Bethlehem on the fortieth day after Easter, the other on Pentecost Sunday afternoon at the Imbomon, the site of the Resurrection.

Surprisingly, it was in Bethlehem that the church of Jerusalem observed the feast of the fortieth day after Easter.[195] On the Wednesday which was the eve of the feast, after the office of the sixth hour, the Jerusalem congregation proceeded to Bethlehem, where the vigil was celebrated in "the church where the grotto in which the Lord was born is located."[196] On Thursday Mass was offered and sermons "appropriate to the day and the place" were preached. On Thursday evening everyone returned to Jerusalem. Is this feast, described by Egeria in a terse and almost cryptic account, that of the Ascension of Christ, and, if so, how does the liturgist explain the celebration of it in Bethlehem? Cabrol originally suggested that the feast of Ascension had not as yet been detached from that of Pentecost, and consequently commemoration of the Ascension was still incorporated in the Pentecost Sunday afternoon liturgy; the ritual of the fortieth day in Bethlehem would then pertain to a totally different feast, perhaps the Annunciation.[197] Both Bludau and J. G. Davies, however, have attempted to demonstrate from the testimony of the Fathers that even in a historically oriented liturgy, such as that of Jerusalem, a commemoration of the Ascension at Bethlehem, though unusual, would not be inconceivable.[198] Another possible solution of the problem posed by this part of the *Diary* has already been referred to above and is that suggested by Dom E. Dekkers, namely, that in 417 the formal observance of the feast of the Ascension was transferred to Pentecost Sunday, because in that year the fortieth day after Easter coincided with the feast of the Dedication of the Basilica of the Nativity.[199]

On Pentecost the scope of liturgical action exceeded that of any other feast day described in the *Diary*. The regular Sunday morning ritual unfolded at the Anastasis and the Martyrium, but the dismissal was given early enough to allow the congregation to assemble at the third hour (mid-morning) at Sion. There, at the hour and in the place traditionally associated with its occurrence, the church of Jerusalem commemorated the Descent of the Holy Spirit with special scriptural readings and the celebration of Mass.[200] Up to this point in the liturgy, then, Pentecost appears to have been celebrated as a historical feast. However, as Baumstark has emphasized, the afternoon and evening liturgy, marked by lengthy processions and stational services at every major church in Jerusalem, reflected the original concept of Pentecost as an "idea feast,"[201] going beyond the commemoration of a single mystery to become the manifestation of fulfillment of the total act of redemption. It was in the context of the closure of the seasonal cycle that Baumstark sought to explain the afternoon station at the Imbomon, for which scriptural readings clearly alluding to the Ascension were designated. From early afternoon until midnight services were held at churches built on sites associated with the history of the redemption—the Imbomon, the Eleona, the Martyrium, the Anastasis, the Cross, and the Church of Sion.

The last feast of the Church year to be described by Egeria is the double commemoration of the Dedication of the Basilica of the Holy Sepulchre and the Finding of the Holy Cross. Called the Feast of the Dedications, it was celebrated with a solemn octave beginning most probably on September 13. The description unfortunately is incomplete, for at this point the manuscript breaks off.[202]

EGERIA'S SOURCES AND STYLE

Although the *Diary* is a firsthand account of what Egeria saw in the course of her travels, her quotations from Scripture and many of her topographical descriptions, as well as many characteristic features of her style and language, have their source in two works, a pre-Vulgate version of the Bible, one very much indebted to the Septuagint, and St. Jerome's translation of the *Onomasticon* of Eusebius. While many earlier commentators had called attention to these sources,[203] it was J. Ziegler who presented a detailed analysis of Egeria's biblical quotations, comparing them with various passages from the *Vetus latina*, and who correlated many of her topographical comments with the *Onomasticon*.[204] A surprising number of verbatim quotations from Jerome's version of the *Onomasticon* appear in the first section of the *Diary*. It has not been determined whether Egeria used other literary sources.

Aside from its importance for the liturgist, Egeria's *Diary* has been a text of greatest interest for the philologist. It is impossible here to do justice to the wealth of information that the *Diary* has supplied to students of Vulgar Latin and Primitive Romance. J. Anglade, E. Bechtel, P. Geyer, E. Wölfflin, and E. Löfstedt have contributed the major works in the interpretation of the Latin of the text.[205] Their interest was primarily in distinguishing those features of Egeria's Latin—vocabulary, morphology, and especially syntax—that differed not only from the Latin of the Golden and Silver Ages, but also from the generally accepted norms of her period.

Although Bechtel in particular attempted to classify those words of the text which were peculiar to Ecclesiastical Latin,[206] it has remained the task of more recent scholars to study the role of a specifically liturgical vocabulary in the *Diary*. Among these investigators, A. Bastiaensen of the Nijmegen School has produced the most extensive study thus far.[207]

The use of the term "Vulgar Latin" to describe Egeria's language may prejudice some readers in their conception of Egeria's style and, to the extent the style is considered to reflect the author, of her general cultural level. It is clear that, except for a few words and phrases that she picked up during her three years in the Near East, Egeria knew no Greek.[208] She lived, however, at a time when there had been a precipitous decline in the knowledge of Greek in the West. Moreover, her grammatical errors in Latin, her lack of precision in the use of cases and tenses and moods, are insufficient grounds for concluding that Egeria was an ignorant woman.

Perhaps the most imaginative attempt to situate this

text in its proper genre and to interpret its style in terms
of that genre has been that made by L. Spitzer. In
an article entitled "The Epic Style of the Pilgrim
Aetheria,"[209] he attempts to treat the text "from the point
of view of the literary genre it purports to represent."[210]
This is, of course, the pilgrimage genre, which has a style
of its own. Thus Spitzer can interpret favorably certain
features of the text which have appeared "barbaric" to
others—the numerous repetitions, the excessive use of
demonstratives, the lack of descriptions, the lack of a
single quotation from a classical author. For Spitzer, the
author's unique purpose was to emphasize the concrete
reality of all that she had been shown by her guides and
all that she had witnessed in Jerusalem. Thus the importance of repetition, of words that point out, of extended
phrases introduced by the verb *ostendere*, emphasizing
what was seen.[211] Though the *Diary* is a first-person
account, Spitzer interprets the text as an attempt at
idealization, in which the individual is subordinated to the
truth he represents.[212] Thus no proper names of contemporaries save Marthana are given in the *Diary*, which
leaves the guides, the monks, the bishops, all Egeria's
informants, anonymous; much of the action in the narrative is described with impersonal passives that focus on
the acts, not on the actors; things are not described
individually, but in terms of their eternal value. Spitzer
thus sees the work as possessing a distinct, nonclassical
style, perfectly representative of its genre and anticipating
the style of certain medieval literary forms.

One final observation should be made. The superior
quality of this text can be fully appreciated only by
comparing it to the other *itineraria* of the fourth to the

eighth centuries, such as the *Itinerarium Burdigalense*, the *Breviarius de Hierosolyma*, Anthony of Piacenza's *Itinerarium*, and many others.[213] Whereas Egeria's *Diary* has a distinct style, the others are little more than endless catalogues of places visited.

EDITIONS AND TRANSLATIONS

A complete list of editions and translations is given below in the bibliography on pages 135–142. In the preparation of the present translation I have used as my primary text of the *Itinerarium Egeriae* the edition prepared by E. Franceschini and R. Weber for the *Corpus christianorum* series and published in 1965. That edition incorporates in its critical apparatus all the major textual corrections that have been proposed since Gamurrini's first edition; moreover, it cites in their appropriate places the fragments of the text discovered by Dom de Bruyne, as well as those passages from Peter the Deacon which are summaries of Egeria's narrative. I have also utilized the 1960 edition of O. Prinz (which replaced the older editions by W. Heraeus in the *Sammlung vulgärlateinischer Texte* series) and the earlier editions of P. Geyer in the CSEL series and H. Pétré in the *Sources chrétiennes* series. Other editions were also consulted.

The present translation is the third to appear in English. The first was published by J. H. Bernard in 1891 for the Palestine Pilgrim's Text Society, and the second by M. L. McClure and C. L. Feltoe for the SPCK series in 1919. A new translation, accompanied by an introduction and detailed commentary, is amply justified in view of the abundance of new scholarship bearing on the work. I have benefited greatly from the French translation of the *Diary* by H. Pétré and the paraphrase of the text given by A. Bludau.

* * *

Note: At many points in the *Diary* various times of the day are indicated by such terms as "at the third hour," "at the sixth hour," "at the fifth hour of the night." It is not possible to give exact modern equivalents, nor has it been considered necessary to footnote each instance of such usage. The "hour" in Egeria's time varied according to the season of the year; the day between dawn and sunset was divided into twelve equal "hours," as was the night between sunset and dawn. Thus, "at the third hour" was roughly equivalent to today's "at 9:00 a.m.," while "at the ninth hour" was roughly equivalent to "at 3:00 p.m." Noon was "at the sixth hour," while midnight was "at the sixth hour of the night."

Chapter 1

. . . were shown according to the Scriptures.[1] As we moved along, we came to a certain place where the mountains through which we were travelling opened out[2] to form an immense valley, vast, quite flat, and extremely beautiful;[3] and across the valley there appeared Mount Sinai, God's holy mountain.[4] This place where the mountains opened out adjoins the spot where the Graves of Lust are located.[5] When one reaches this place, "it is customary," said the holy men who were guiding us[6] and so advised us, "for those who are coming to say a prayer when, for the first time and from this place, the mountain of God comes into view." And that is what we did.[7] From this spot to the mountain of God it was about four miles[8] in all across the valley, which, as I have said, is vast.

Chapter 2

This valley is certainly vast, extending to the slope of the mountain of God.[9] As far as we could judge with our eyes and as the guides told us, it is around sixteen miles long; and they said that it is four miles wide.[10] We had to cross this valley in order to be able to climb the mountain.[11] This is the vast and very flat valley where the children of Israel tarried during those days when the holy man Moses climbed the mountain of God; and he was there for forty days and forty nights.[12] This is also the valley where the calf was made, and to this day its location is shown, for a large stone set there stands on the very spot.[13] Furthermore, at the head of this same valley is the place where God spoke twice from the burning bush to the holy man Moses as he was grazing his father-in-law's flocks.[14]

And here was our route: first, we would climb the mountain of God, because on the side from which we were approaching the ascent was easier;[15] and from there we would descend then to the very head of the valley where the bush stood, because the descent from the mountain of God was easier there. And so it was agreed that, once we had seen everything we wished, we would descend the mountain of God and come to where the bush stood, and from that point we would resume our journey all the way down through the center of the valley in the company of the men who were showing us each place in the valley mentioned in Scripture. And this is what was done. We then set out from the place where, on arriving from Pharan,[16] we had prayed, and we took a route crossing through the middle of the head of the valley, and in this way we approached the mountain of God.[17]

This seems to be a single mountain all around;[18] however, once you enter the area, you see that there are many, but the whole range is called the mountain of God. However, the one specifically so-named, on the summit of which is the place where the Glory of God descended,[19] as it is written in Scripture, that one is in the middle of them all. These mountains, which are all around, are as high, I think, as any I have ever seen; yet this one in the center, where the Glory of God descended, is so much higher than all the others that, once we had climbed it, then all the mountains which had seemed so very high were as far beneath us as if they were very small hills. Surely here is something very wonderful, and without God's grace I do not think that it would be possible, namely, the central mountain, which in particular is called Sinai because the Glory of God descended there, although higher than all the others, still cannot be seen until you come up to its very base, just before you climb it. Once all your wishes have been fulfilled and you have come down from there, then you can see it in the distance,[20] which you cannot do before climbing it. I already knew this before coming to the mountain of God, because of what the brethren[21] had said; but after I had been there, I recognized that it was obviously so.

Chapter 3

On Saturday[22] evening we proceeded onto the mountain, and, arriving at some monastic cells,[23] we were received very hospitably by the monks dwelling there, and they offered us every courtesy.[24] Since there is a church there with a priest,[25] we stopped there for the night. Early on Sunday morning, accompanied by that priest and the monks who lived there, we began climbing the mountains one by one. These mountains are climbed with very great difficulty, since you do not ascend them slowly going round and round, in a spiral path[26] as we say, but you go straight up all the way as if scaling a wall. Then you have to go straight down each of these mountains until you reach the very foot of the central mountain, which is properly Sinai. By the will of Christ our God,[27] and with the help of the prayers of the holy men who were accompanying us, I made the ascent, though with great effort, because it had to be on foot, since it was absolutely impossible to make the climb in the saddle.[28] Yet you did not feel the effort; and the reason it was not felt was because I saw the desire which I had being fulfilled through the will of God. And so at the fourth hour we reached the summit of the mountain of God,[29] Holy Sinai, where the Law was given, at the place, that is, where the Glory of the Lord descended on the day when the mountain smoked.[30]

In this place there is now a church,[31] though not a very large one, because the place itself, the summit of the mountain, that is, is not very large. Yet this church has great charm all its own. When through God's will we had reached the mountain top and had arrived at the church door, there was the priest who was assigned to the church coming forth from his cell to meet us. He was an old man, beyond reproach, a monk from his youth, and, as they say here, an ascetic;[32] in a word, he was a man worthy of being in this place. Then the other priests and all the monks who dwell there by the side of the mountain, that is to say, at least those who were not impeded either by age or by infirmity, came forth. Indeed, no one lives on the very top of that central mountain, for there is nothing there save the church alone and the cave where the holy man Moses was.[33] All of the proper passage from the Book of Moses was read, the sacrifice was offered in the prescribed manner,[34] and we received Communion. As we were about to leave the church,[35] the priests gave us gifts[36] native to this place, that is, some fruit[37] which grows on this mountain. Now this holy Mount Sinai is itself all rock, without even a shrub. Down at the foot of these mountains, however, either around this one which is in the middle or around those which encircle it, there is a small piece of ground.[38] There the holy monks carefully plant bushes and lay out little orchards and cultivated plots,[39] next to which they build their cells, and the fruit which they have seemingly raised with their own hands they take from, as it were, the soil of the mountain itself.

After we had received Communion, then, and the holy men had given us gifts, and we had come out the church door, I asked them to show us each place. At once the holy men consented[40] to point out each one. They showed us the cave where the holy man Moses was[41] when he ascended the mountain of God a second time to receive anew the tables, after he had broken the first ones because the people had sinned.[42] Moreover, they consented to show us whatever other places we desired and with which they were very well acquainted. Ladies, reverend sisters,[43] I would like you to know that we were standing around the enclosure of the church on top of the central mountain, and from this place those mountains which we had first climbed with difficulty seemed, in comparison with the central mountain on which we now stood, as far beneath us as if they were hills. Yet they were so high that I do not think I have ever seen any higher, except for the central mountain which towers very much above them. And from there we saw beneath us Egypt and Palestine, the Red Sea, and the Parthenian Sea[44] which leads to Alexandria, and finally the endless lands of the Saracens.[45] Hard as this may be to believe, the holy men did point out each of these things to us.

CHAPTER 4

Having satisfied every desire for which we had
hastened to make the ascent, we now descended from
the summit of the mountain of God, which we had
reached, to another mountain which adjoins it. This
place is called In Horeb,[46] and there is a church there.[47]
Horeb is the place to which the holy prophet Elias came
when he fled from before the face of King Achab,[48] and
where God spoke to him, saying, as it is written in the
Books of Kings, *What are you doing here, Elias?*[49] To
this day they show the cave where the holy man Elias
hid,[50] in front of the door of the church which is there,
and also the stone altar which the holy man Elias himself
set up to offer sacrifice to God.[51] And the holy men
therefore consented to show us each site. We offered the
sacrifice there, and recited a very fervent prayer, and the
proper passage was read from the Book of Kings. For
this was always very much our custom, that, whenever
we should come to places that I had desired to visit, the
proper passage from Scripture would be read.[52]

After the sacrifice had been offered, we set out for
another place not far from there which was pointed out
by the priests and monks, that is, the place where the
holy man Aaron had stood with the seventy elders[53] while
the holy man Moses received from the Lord the Law for
the children of Israel. Although it is not mentioned in
Scripture,[54] there is in this place an enormous rock, circular in shape, with a flat surface, on which the holy men
are said to have stood. In the center of it there is a sort of
altar made of stone.[55] And there the proper passage from

the Book of Moses was read, and a Psalm fitting to the
place was sung. After reciting a prayer, we came down
from there.

It was now getting on toward the eighth hour and we
still had three miles to go before we would pass out of
those mountains which we had entered the preceding
evening.[56] However, as I mentioned before, we were not
to come out on the same side as we had entered, for we
had to go to all the holy places and visit whatever
monastic cells were there; and so we had to come out at
the head of that valley I mentioned before, the valley,
that is, which lies below the mountain of God. We had to
come out at the head of the valley for this reason as well,
because there are many cells of holy men and a church
on the spot where the bush stands; and this bush is still
alive today and gives forth shoots. So, after descending
the mountain, we reached the bush around the tenth
hour.[57] It is from this bush, as I have already said, that
the Lord spoke in the fire to Moses; the bush is in a place
where there are many monastic cells and a church at the
head of the valley.[58] In front of the church there is a very
pleasant garden, with a large supply of good water. It is
in the garden that the bush stands.[59] They also show
near-by the place where the holy man Moses stood when
God said to him: *Loosen the strap of your shoe,* and so
forth.[60] When we came to this place, it was already the
tenth hour. Since it was already evening, we were not able
to offer the sacrifice. However, a prayer was said in the
church as well as in the garden beside the bush. Then the
proper passage from the Book of Moses was read in
accord with our custom. Because it was evening, we ate a
light meal with these holy men right in the garden in

front of the bush, and we stopped there for the night.[61] On the following day we arose early and asked the priests to offer the sacrifice. And this was done.

CHAPTER 5

We took a route by which we would go down the length of the center of the valley, which, as I mentioned before, is the valley where the children of Israel camped while Moses was ascending and descending the mountain of God. As we proceeded through the valley, the holy men continually pointed out to us each place. At the very head of the valley, where we had camped and had seen the bush out of whose fire God spoke to the holy man Moses, we saw the place where he stood before the bush as God said to him: *Loosen the strap of your shoe, for the place on which you stand is holy ground.*[62]

And as we set out from the bush, the guides began to show us all the other places. They pointed out[63] first the place where the camp of the children of Israel stood in the days when Moses went up the mountain, and then the place where the calf was made, for a large stone is set there even today.[64] As we went along, we saw at a distance[65] the summit of the mountain which looks down over the whole valley; from that place the holy man Moses saw the children of Israel dancing in the days when they made the calf.[66] Next they showed an enormous rock, at the very place where the holy man Moses came down from the mountain with Josue, the son of Nun;[67] on this rock, Moses, in anger, broke the tables he was carrying.[68] Then they showed how each and every one of them had had dwellings, the foundations of which are still visible today throughout the valley, and how they had been built in circular shape, out of stone. Then they showed the place where the holy man Moses, on his return from the mountain, ordered the children of Israel to run *from door to door*.[69] Next they showed us where the calf which Aaron had built for them was burned at the command of the holy man Moses.[70] Then they showed the torrent from which he gave drink to the children of Israel, as it is written in Exodus.[71] Next we were shown the place where the seventy had received of the spirit of Moses,[72] and then the place where the children of Israel had lusted for food.[73] Moreover, they also showed us the place called The Burning, where a certain part of the camp had burned, and then the fire stopped because of the prayer of the holy man Moses.[74] We were also shown where manna and quails had rained on them.[75]

And so we were shown everything written in the holy books of Moses that was done there in that valley which lies below the mountain of God, the holy Mount Sinai. It was too much, however, to write down each one individually, because so many details could not be retained; besides, when Your Charity[76] reads the holy books of Moses, she will perceive, carefully written, all that was done there. This is the valley where the Passover was celebrated,[77] one year after the children of Israel had gone out of the land of Egypt, for they tarried in that valley for some time, while the holy man Moses twice climbed the mountain of God and came down again. Moreover, they also dwelt there long enough for the tabernacle to be made, and for all things shown on the mountain of God to be accomplished. Accordingly, we were shown the place where the tabernacle was first set up by Moses,[78] and where everything was accomplished which God on the mountain had ordered Moses to bring about. We saw anew at the end of the valley the Graves of Lust,[79] at the place where we once again returned to our route. It is here that on coming out of that large valley we took up the road by which we had come through those mountains about which I spoke earlier.

On the same day we also visited other very saintly monks, who, either because of age or because of infirmity, were unable to go up to the mountain of God for the offering of the sacrifice, but who, when we arrived, consented to receive us very hospitably in their cells. Once we had visited all the holy places we desired, especially the places the children of Israel touched on their journeying to and from the mountain of God, and after seeing the holy men who dwelt there, in the name of God,[80] we returned to Pharan. Though I must always give thanks to God for all things, I shall not speak about the many favors which He deigned to confer upon me in spite of my unworthiness and lack of merit, in allowing me to travel through all these places, which I did not deserve.[81] Yet I cannot sufficiently thank all those holy men who so willingly consented to receive my humble person in their cells and above all to guide me through all the places which I was forever seeking out, following Holy Scripture. Many of the holy men who dwelt on the mountain of God and around it, that is to say, those who were more robust in body, were kind enough to guide us as far as Pharan.

CHAPTER 6

Once we had arrived at Pharan,[82] which is thirty-five miles from Sinai, we had to stop there for two days in order to rest. On the third day, after an early morning departure,[83] we arrived once again at the resting station which is in the desert of Pharan, where we had stopped on our journey down, as I mentioned earlier.[84] Then, on the following day, after replenishing once again our water supply, we proceeded a short distance through the mountains and arrived at the resting station which was right above the sea.[85] This is the spot where one comes out from among the mountains and once again begins to walk right beside the sea, so near the sea that at times the waves strike the animals' feet; yet at other times the route is through the desert at one hundred, two hundred, and sometimes as many as five hundred feet from the sea. There is no road there at all,[86] only the sands of the desert all around. The Pharanites, who are accustomed to move about there with their camels, place markers for themselves here and there. It is by aiming for these markers that they travel by day. At night, however, the camels follow the markers. To be brief, from force of habit, the Pharanites move more skillfully and securely about this place at night than it is possible for other men to travel in places where there is an open road.

It was here on our return journey that we came out of the mountains, at the same spot where we had entered them on our way down. And once again we approached the sea. On their way back from Sinai, the children of

Israel followed the route by which they had gone to the mountain of God as far as this same place, where we came out of the mountains and where we once again reached the Red Sea. From here on we now retraced the way by which we had come. From this place, however, the children of Israel went their own route,[87] as it is written in the books of the holy man Moses. But we returned to Clysma by the same route and by the same resting stations by which we had come.[88] When we arrived back at Clysma, we had to rest there once again, because we had travelled a very sandy route through the desert.

CHAPTER 7

I was, of course, already acquainted with the land of Gessen from the time when I first went to Egypt.[89] It was, however, my purpose to see all the places which the children of Israel had touched on their journey, from their going forth from Ramesses until they reached the Red Sea at a place which is now called Clysma, because of the fortress which stands there.[90] It was, therefore, our wish to go from Clysma to the land of Gessen, specifically to the city which is called Arabia. This city is in the land of Gessen, and this territory takes its name from it, that is, the "land of Arabia" is the "land of Gessen."[91] Though this land is a part of Egypt, it is nevertheless far better than the rest of Egypt.[92] It is a four-day journey across the desert from Clysma, that is, from the Red Sea, to the city of Arabia. Though the journey is across the desert, each resting station has a military outpost[93] with soldiers and officers who always guided us from fortress to fortress.

The holy men who were with us on this journey, the priests and monks, that is, showed us all the places which I was always seeking out, following the Scriptures. Some of the places were to the left of our route, some were to the right; some were far off the road, some were close up. I hope Your Charity will believe me that, as far as I was able to see, the children of Israel marched along in this manner, going a certain distance to the right, then going an equal distance to the left, going ahead a certain distance, then backtracking an equal distance.[94] And they marched along in this way until they reached the Red Sea. Epauleum[95] was pointed out to us in the distance,[96] and we went to Magdalum.[97] There is a fort there now which has an officer and a garrison which exercises the authority of Rome in these parts. As is customary, they escorted us from there to another fortress, and there we were shown Beelsephon;[98] indeed, we were at the very spot. This is a plain above the Red Sea by the side of the mountain which I mentioned above, where the children of Israel cried out when they saw the Egyptians pursuing them.[99] They also showed us Etham, which lies on the edge of the desert,[100] as it is written in Scripture, as well as Soccoth,[101] which is a small hill in the middle of a valley. Next to this hillock the children of Israel fixed their camp, for this is the place where the Law of the Passover was received.[102]

We were also shown along the same route the city of Phithom,[103] which the children of Israel had built. It is here that we crossed the frontiers of Egypt, leaving behind the lands of the Saracens.[104] Today this same Phithom is a fortress. Heroopolis,[105] which existed at the time when Joseph went forth to meet his father Jacob, who was coming to Egypt, as it is written in the book of Genesis,[106] is today a village, but a large one, one which we would call a little town.[107] This little town has a church, shrines of martyrs,[108] and many cells sheltering holy monks. In accord with the custom which we observed, we made it a point to dismount there to visit each place. This town, which is called Hero today, is located sixteen miles from the land of Gessen and is within the frontiers of Egypt.[109] This place is quite pleasant, for a branch of the river Nile flows here.[110] We then left Hero and came to the city called Arabia,[111] which is a city in the land of Gessen. For this reason it is written that Pharaoh said to Joseph: *In the best land of Egypt, gather your father and brothers, in the land of Gessen, in the land of Arabia.*[112]

CHAPTER 8

Ramesses[113] lies four miles from the city of Arabia. In order to reach the resting station of Arabia, we passed straight through Ramesses. Today this city of Ramesses is a barren plain with not a single dwelling place standing there. It is clear that it was extensive in circumference and had many buildings, for its enormous ruins are visible even today, just as they fell. There is nothing there today except a single enormous Theban stone on which are two very large carved figures, which are said to be of the holy men Moses and Aaron.[114] It is said that the children of Israel placed them there in honor of them. In addition, there is a sycamore tree, which was planted, it is said, by the Patriarchs;[115] the tree is very old now and therefore rather small, but it still bears fruit to this day. Those who are ill go there and take away twigs, and it helps them.

We learned this from the holy bishop of Arabia who spoke about it. He told us the name of the tree, that it is called in Greek *dendros alethiae*, or, as we would say, "tree of truth."[116]

This saintly bishop graciously came to meet us at Ramesses. He is an old man, very devout indeed, a former monk,[117] a gracious man who receives pilgrims very hospitably; and he is very learned in the Sacred Scriptures. Since he had kindly taken the trouble to come to meet us there, he pointed out each place there, and he spoke about the figures which I mentioned as well as the sycamore tree. The holy bishop also told us that Pharaoh, on seeing that the children of Israel had deserted him, entered Ramesses with his whole army and, before setting out after them, burned it completely, though it was very large;[118] and then he set out after the children of Israel.

CHAPTER 9

A very pleasant thing happened to us quite by chance, for the day on which we arrived at the resting station of Arabia was the eve of the most joyful day of the Epiphany, and on that very day the vigil was to be held in the church.[119] And so we were detained there for about two days by the saintly bishop, truly a holy man of God and well-known to me from the time when I had gone to the Thebaid.[120] This saintly bishop is a former monk, who had been raised from childhood in a cell, and is therefore as learned in the Scriptures as he is above reproach in his way of life, as I mentioned above. At this point we sent back the soldiers who, through the authority of Rome, had escorted us as long as we were travelling through unsafe places; now, however, it was no longer necessary for us to trouble the soldiers, since there was a public highway through Egypt, passing by the city of Arabia and running from the Thebaid to Pelusium.[121] We set out from there, and we travelled through the whole land of Gessen, constantly passing among vineyards which produce wine and other fields which produce balsam, past orchards, heavily cultivated fields, and numerous gardens along the banks of the river Nile, past many estates which were formerly the properties of the children of Israel.[122] What can I add? I do not think I have ever seen a more beautiful land than this land of Gessen.

From the city of Arabia we travelled for two whole days through the land of Gessen, arriving at Tanis,[123] the city where the holy man Moses was born.[124] This same city of Tanis was once the capital of the Pharaohs. I had already become acquainted with these places, as I have mentioned, on my journey to Alexandria[125] and the Thebaid, but I wished to become more thoroughly acquainted with those places through which the children of Israel had passed, as they went all the way from Ramesses to Sinai, the holy mountain of God. And so I had to return once again to the land of Gessen, and from there to Tanis. We left Tanis, and I travelled along a road already known to me until I came to Pelusium.[126] Setting out anew from there, I reached the frontiers of Palestine via the same resting stations of Egypt by which we had come.[127] From there, in the name of Christ our God, I travelled still some distance through Palestine and I returned to Aelia,[128] that is, to Jerusalem.

CHAPTER 10

Some time afterwards it was once again my desire to travel, this time, God willing, as far as Arabia, to Mount Nebo,[129] which God had commanded Moses to climb. For He had said to him: *Climb up Mount Arabot, Mount Nebo, which is in the land of Moab, over against Jericho, and look upon the land of Chanaan, which I will give to the children of Israel; and you will die on the mountain which you will ascend.*[130] And our Lord Jesus, who does not desert those who trust in Him,[131] deigned to accomplish the fulfillment of my will even in this matter. We set forth from Jerusalem in the company of holy men, of a priest and deacons from Jerusalem and some of the brothers, by which I mean monks, and we travelled until we came to the place on the Jordan where the children of Israel made their crossing.[132] The holy man Josue, the son of Nun, led them over the Jordan, as it is written in the Book of Josue, son of Nun.[133] A little farther up we were shown the place where the children of Ruben and Gad and the half-tribe of Manasses had built an altar,[134] on the same side of the river where Jericho stands.

After crossing the river, we came to the city of Livias,[135] which is on the plain where the children of Israel had pitched their camp in those days. Even today the foundations of the camp of the children of Israel and the houses where they dwelt can be seen here, in this immense plain beneath the mountains of Arabia, above the Jordan.[136] It is this place of which it is written; *And the children of Israel mourned Moses for forty days in*

Arabot, in Moab, beside the Jordan, facing Jericho.[137]
It was here, after the passing of Moses,[138] that Josue,
son of Nun, was immediately filled with the spirit
of wisdom, for Moses had laid his hands upon him, as
it is written in Scripture.[139] Here Moses wrote the Book
of Deuteronomy;[140] here he chanted within hearing of the
whole assembly of Israel from beginning to end the words
of the canticle written in the Book of Deuteronomy.[141]
Here Moses, the holy man of God, blessed the children
of Israel, each in his turn, before his death.[142] On arriving
in this plain we proceeded to this very place; there we
said a prayer and read a certain passage from Deuteronomy, as well as the canticle and the benediction which
Moses had said over the children of Israel.[143] We said a
second prayer after the reading from Scripture, and,
having given thanks to God, we moved along. Whenever
we were empowered to reach our destination, it was
always our custom first to say a prayer, then to read a
passage from the Bible,[144] sing a Psalm fitting the occasion,
and finally say a second prayer. We always observed this
custom whenever, God willing, we were able to reach
our destination.

And so to complete the work we had begun, we hurried
on to reach Mount Nebo. Along the way, a priest of that
place, I mean from Livias, advised us, for we had asked
him to accompany us as we set out from the resting station, because he was very well acquainted with these
places. This priest said to us: "If you wish to see the
water which flowed from the rock, the water which
Moses gave to the children of Israel when they were
thirsty, you can see it, if you wish to take the trouble of
turning off the road at the sixth mile."[145] When he had

said this, we were very eager to go, and we immediately turned off the road and followed the priest who was guiding us. In this place there is a small church[146] at the foot of a mountain which is not Mount Nebo, but another one nearer at hand, though not far from Nebo. Many monks dwell there, very holy men indeed, who are called ascetics here.

CHAPTER 11

These holy monks consented to receive us very hospitably, and they permitted us even to come in to greet them. When we had entered their cells and after we had prayed with them, they graciously gave us gifts, for they are in the habit of bestowing gifts on those whom they receive hospitably. There, midway between the church and the monks' cells, there flows out of a rock a large stream of water that is very beautiful, clear and very good to taste. We then questioned those holy monks who dwelt there as to what this water of such fine quality and taste was, and they replied: "It is the water which the holy man Moses gave to the children of Israel in the desert." In accord with our custom, we prayed, read the proper passage from the books of Moses,[147] and sang a Psalm. Then we proceeded toward the mountain with the monks and the holy clergy who were with us. Many of the holy monks who dwelt there beside the water, and who were physically able to undertake the task, kindly agreed to ascend Mount Nebo with us. We set out from there and arrived at the foot of Mount Nebo. Although it was very high, the greater part could be climbed by donkey, but a small portion was so steep that it was necessary to climb on foot and with great effort. And this is what we did.

CHAPTER 12

We had now reached the top of the mountain. On the very summit of Mount Nebo there is today a small church.[148] Within the church, on the spot where the pulpit stands, I saw a somewhat elevated place which was about the size graves generally seem to be. I then questioned the holy men as to what it was, and they answered: "Here the holy man Moses was placed by the angels, for, as it is written in Scripture, *no man knows his sepulchre*;[149] and so it is certain that he was buried by the angels. But his grave, where he was placed, is shown to this day.[150] Since where he was placed was shown to us by the older monks who dwelt here,[151] we therefore can show it to you; and the older monks themselves said that such a tradition had been handed down to them by their predecessors." We then said a prayer, and everything was done here that we customarily did in a set manner in every holy place. And we began to leave the church.[152]

Those who were acquainted with the place, that is, the priests and holy monks, then said to us: "If you wish to see the places which are described in the books of Moses, go outside the door of the church and observe attentively from the summit, because they are visible from here; and we will identify for you each place which is located there and can be seen." We were overjoyed at this and went immediately outside. From the door of the church we saw where the Jordan flows into the Dead Sea, for this place appeared right beneath where we were standing. We next saw in the distance not only Livias,[153] which was on this side of the Jordan, but Jericho as well, which lay across the river. That is how high the place where we were standing outside the church door rises! The greater part of Palestine, which is the land of promise, can be seen from here, and all the country of the Jordan, as much at least as can be seen with the naked eye.[154]

To the left we saw all the lands of the Sodomites as well as Segor;[155] but of the five cities, Segor alone stands today.[156] There is indeed a monument there,[157] but nothing else is visible of the other cities except the overturned ruins, just as they were turned to ashes. We were also shown the place, and this place is even mentioned in Scripture, where the pillar of Lot's wife stood.[158] Believe me, reverend ladies, the pillar itself is not visible now, although its location is shown; but the pillar is said to have been covered by the Dead Sea. Indeed we saw the place, but we did not see any pillar, and on this matter I cannot deceive you.[159] The bishop of that place, of Segor, that is,[160] told us that for some years now the pillar has not been visible. The spot where the pillar stood, and which is now totally covered with water, is about six miles from Segor.

Next we approached from the right side of the church, but from the outside, and from there we were shown in the distance two cities. One is Hesebon, which belonged to Sehon, king of the Amorrhites, and which today is called Exebon;[161] the other belonged to King Og of Basan and is now called Safdra.[162] Then from the same place we were shown in the distance Phogor, which was a city of the kingdom of Edom.[163] All the cities which we saw were situated on mountains, but the place beneath, a little farther down, seemed to us somewhat flatter. Then we were told that in the days when the holy man Moses and the children of Israel fought against these cities, they pitched their camps there; in fact signs of the camp were visible there. From that side of the mountain which I said was the left-hand side, and which was above the Dead Sea, we were shown a very sharp mountain which used to be called Agrispecula.[164] It is on this mountain that Balac, son of Beor,[165] put the soothsayer Balaam to curse the children of Israel; but God, as it is written, was unwilling to permit that.[166] And so, after seeing everything which we desired, in the name of God we went back to Jerusalem, returning by way of Jericho and by the route we had come.

CHAPTER 13

Some time afterwards I decided to go next to the land of Ausitis[167] to visit the tomb of the holy man Job in order to pray there.[168] I used to see many holy monks who came from there to Jerusalem to visit the holy places in order to pray there; and as they spoke in detail about that region, they stirred in me a great desire to take upon myself the trouble of going there, if indeed it can be called trouble when a person sees his wishes being fulfilled. I set out from Jerusalem in the company of holy men, who were also going there to pray, and who generously agreed to offer me their company on my journey. This journey from Jerusalem to Carneas requires eight days.[169] The city of Job is now known as Carneas, but it used to be called Dennaba, in the land of Ausitis, on the frontiers of Arabia and Idumea.[170]

On my journey I saw on the banks of the river Jordan a very beautiful and pleasant valley, rich in vines and trees, for water was plentiful there and very good. In this valley there is a large village called Sedima today, situated in the middle of the plain. In the center of the village, there is a small hill that is not very high, with the shape that tombs, large ones, usually have. On the top of it there is a church, and down below, around the small hill, large ancient foundations are visible. In the village there are a number of such mounds today.[171] On seeing such an attractive place, I inquired what this very beautiful place might be, and I was told: "This is the city of King Melchisedech, and it used to be called Salem, from which the present-day village of Sedima takes its name, through a corruption of the word."[172] The structure which you see on top of the hill in the center of the village is a church which is now called in Greek *opu Melchisedech*,[173] for this is the place where Melchisedech offered pure sacrifices of bread and wine to God, as it is written that he did in Scripture.[174]

CHAPTER 14

As soon as I heard this, we dismounted; and there was the saintly bishop of this place, and the clergy as well, graciously coming forth to meet us. After receiving us, they led us immediately up to the church, where, on our arrival, we recited a prayer right away in accord with our custom; then the proper passage from the book of the holy man Moses was read,[175] and a Psalm fitting to the place was sung; and, after reciting a second prayer, we came down. When we had come down, the saintly priest spoke to us. He was an old man, very learned in the Scriptures, and a former monk who was in charge in this place.[176] Many bishops, as we later learned, paid tribute to the life of this priest, and they said of him that he was worthy to be in charge of the place where the holy man Melchisedech first offered pure sacrifice to God, at the time the holy man Abraham came there.[177] When we had come down from the church, as I was saying before, the holy priest said to us: "These foundations which you see around this hill are those of the palace of King Melchisedech. Even today then, if someone wishes to build himself a house right nearby,[178] and if he happens to strike its foundations, he finds now and then a few pieces of silver and bronze. This road here, as you see, runs between the river Jordan and this village. It is the road on which the holy man Abraham travelled as he was returning to Sodom, after slaying Chodorlahomor, king of nations,[179] and on which he was met by the holy man Melchisedech, king of Salem."

CHAPTER 15

Then I remembered that it was written that Saint John had baptized in Ennon near Salim,[180] and I asked him how far away that place was. Whereupon the saintly priest said: "It is two hundred feet from here. If you wish, I can lead you there on foot right away. The large amount of pure water which you see in this village comes from the very spring." I then thanked him and asked him to guide us to that place; and he did so. We went all the way on foot across a very pleasant valley with him, until we came to a very beautiful fruit orchard, in the center of which he showed us a spring of the very purest and best water, which at once gives rise to a real stream. In front of the spring there is a sort of pool where it seems that Saint John the Baptist administered baptism.[181] Then the saintly priest said to us: "To this day this garden is not known by any other name in Greek except *cepos tu agiu Iohanni*, or, as you would say in your tongue, the garden of Saint John."[182]

There are many brothers, holy monks coming from various places, who are drawn here that they may wash in this spring. Once again at this spring, as in every other place, we prayed, read from Scripture, sang a Psalm fitting to the occasion, and did all the other things which it was our custom to do on coming to some holy spot. This also the saintly priest told us, how even today all those who are to be baptized in this village, that is, in the church called the *opu Melchisedech*, are always baptized in this very spring at Easter; and how they return very early by candlelight[183] with the clergy and monks, singing Psalms and antiphons; and how all who have been baptized are led back early from the spring to the church of the holy man Melchisedech. After we had received from the priest gifts out of the orchard of Saint John the Baptist, and also from the holy monks whose cells are in the same orchard, we continued on the way we were going, continually giving thanks to God.

CHAPTER 16

And so we travelled for some time through the valley of the Jordan on the bank above this river, for our route lay along this way for some distance. Suddenly we saw the city of the holy prophet Elias, namely Thesbe, from which he took the name Elias the Thesbite.[184] Even today the cave is there where the holy man sat; and there too is the tomb of the holy man Jephtha, whose name we read in the books of Judges.[185] And giving thanks there to God in accord with our custom, we continued on our journey.

As we moved along on our journey, we saw a very beautiful valley ahead of us on the left. This was a huge valley that sent a great torrent into the Jordan; and there in that same valley we saw the cell of a certain man, now a brother, by which I mean a monk.[186] So, as I am somewhat curious, I asked what was this valley that a holy person, who was now a monk, would build a cell for himself there; for I did not think that it would be without some reason. Whereupon, the holy men who were travelling with us and were therefore acquainted with these places told us: "This is the valley of Corra, where the holy man, Elias the Thesbite, found rest in the days of King Achab, when there was a famine. A crow, at God's command, brought him food, and he drank water from this torrent, for the torrent which can be seen flowing from this valley into the Jordan, this is the Corra."[187] Once again we gave thanks to God who deigned to show us, who were not deserving, all those things which we yearned to see. We then continued our journey as on other days.

We travelled on, day after day. Suddenly, on the left, the side from which we could see in the distance the lands of Phoenecia, there appeared a huge and very high mountain,[188] which was extensive in length. . . .

[*One folio is missing from the manuscript at this point.*][189]

This holy monk, an ascetic man, after having dwelt so many years in the desert, had been obliged to bestir himself and to come down to the city of Carneas to advise the bishop and clergy of that time about what had been revealed to him, namely, that they should excavate the place which had been pointed out to him. And this was done. As they excavated the place shown to them, they found a cave, into which they penetrated about a hundred feet; suddenly, those who were excavating saw a stone. When they had completely uncovered the stone, they found carved on top of it "Job." In honor of Job, at that time and in that place, was built the church which you see, but in such a way that the stone with the body was not moved to another spot, but was placed where the body was found, so that the body would lie beneath the altar.[190] I do not know which tribune built this church, but it has remained unfinished to this day. The next morning we asked the bishop to offer the sacrifice, and this he willingly did. The bishop blessed us, and then we set out. We received Communion there, and, continually giving thanks to God, we returned to Jerusalem by way of each resting station through which we had passed three years before.[191]

CHAPTER 17

Some time later, in the name of God, I decided to return to my homeland, for three full years had now elapsed since my coming to Jerusalem, and I had seen all the holy places to which I had been drawn to pray. Nevertheless, by the will of God, I wished to go to Mesopotamia of Syria,[192] to visit the holy monks who were said to be numerous there and to be of such exemplary life that it can scarcely be described.[193] I also wished to pray at the shrine of Saint Thomas the Apostle, where his uncorrupted body lies, that is, at Edessa.[194] Our Lord Jesus Christ had promised in a letter, which He sent to King Abgar through the messenger Ananias, that Saint Thomas would be sent to Edessa, after His ascension into heaven; and this letter is preserved with great reverence in the city of Edessa, where his shrine is located.[195] I beseech Your Charity to believe me that there is no Christian who has come as far as the holy places of Jerusalem who does not go to Edessa to pray. It is a twenty-five day journey from Jerusalem. Since Antioch[196] is nearer to Mesopotamia, it was very convenient for me, God willing, to go from there to Mesopotamia, on my return to Constantinople, for my route lay through Antioch. And, through God's will, this was done.

CHAPTER 18

In the name of Christ our God, I set out from Antioch to Mesopotamia, travelling through various resting stations and cities of the province of Coele Syria,[197] which is the province of Antioch; and, from there, after crossing the frontier of the province of Augusta Euphratensis, I arrived at the city of Hierapolis, which is the capital of the province of Augusta Euphratensis.[198] As this city is very rich and beautiful, and abounding in all things, I had to make a stop there, since it is not far from the borders of Mesopotamia. After having travelled fifteen miles from Hierapolis, in the name of God, I arrived at the river Euphrates, which Scripture very well described as the *great river Euphrates.*[199] It is large and rather frightening, for it flows with as swift a current as the river Rhone, except that the Euphrates is much larger.[200] Since we had to cross the river by boat, and by very large boats only, I remained there more than half a day. Then, in the name of God, we crossed the river Euphrates and I arrived on the territory of Mesopotamia of Syria.

CHAPTER 19

After making my way through a number of resting stations, I arrived at a city whose name we find in Scripture, namely, Batanis;[201] and this city still stands today. Many shrines of martyrs are located there, as well as a church with a bishop, who is a holy man, a monk, and a confessor.[202] The city is filled with great crowds of men, for an army with its tribune is stationed here.[203]

We then set out from this place and we arrived, in the name of Christ our God, at Edessa; and immediately after our arrival there we hastened to the church and the shrine of Saint Thomas.[204] There, after we had prayed and had done all things that we customarily did at holy places, we then read, in addition, some passages concerning Saint Thomas.[205] The church there is large and very beautiful and of recent design,[206] and very worthy of being a house of God. Since there were many things that I wished to see, I had to make a three-day stop there. I visited in the city many shrines of martyrs and many holy monks, some living near the shrines, others living far from the city in secluded places where they had their cells.[207] The holy bishop of that city, who was truly a religious man, a monk, and a confessor,[208] and who had hospitably received me, said to me: "My daughter, I see that you have taken on yourself, because of your piety, the great task of journeying from very distant lands to these places. Therefore, if you are willing, we will show you whatever places there are here that Christians like to see." Giving thanks first to God then, I freely asked him to do what he had said he would.

Thereupon he took me first to the palace of King Abgar,[209] where he showed me the large statue of the king, a striking likeness, so they said. It is of marble and shines as though it were made of pearls. From the features of this Abgar seen face to face it was clear that he was indeed a very wise and honorable man.[210] The saintly bishop then said to me: "There is King Abgar, who, before seeing the Lord, believed in Him and believed that He was truly the Son of God."[211] Next to this statue was another one, also made of marble, which, he said, was of Abgar's son Magnus;[212] and this statue also had something pleasing in its countenance. We then went into the interior part of the palace, where there were pools full of fish such as I had never seen before, that is, fish of such great size, of such great luster, and of such good taste. The city has no other water within its walls except the water which flows from the palace like a giant stream of silver.[213] Then the holy bishop spoke to me about this water:

"Some time after King Abgar had written to the Lord, and the Lord had responded to Abgar through the messenger Ananias, as it is written in this letter, after a certain time then had elapsed, the Persians came and encircled the city.[214] Abgar, carrying the letter of the Lord, went immediately to pray publicly at the gate with his whole army. There he said: 'Lord Jesus, You promised us that no enemy would enter this city. But look, at this moment the Persians are attacking us.'[215] After the king had spoken, and as he held in his upraised hands the open letter, suddenly there was a great darkness. Now this darkness was outside the city, before the eyes of the Persians, who were approaching so close to the city that they were only three miles away. But soon they were so baffled by the darkness that they were scarcely able to set up their camp and to encircle the city from three miles out. From that time on the Persians were so confused that never afterwards did they see in what way they might penetrate into the city. However, they besieged the city, enclosing it all around from a distance of three miles with soldiers; and their siege lasted for many months.

"Some time afterwards, when they saw that they would be unable to penetrate into the city, they decided to kill those within by cutting off the water supply. My daughter, the hill which you see above the city supplied the city with water at that time. When the Persians saw this, they diverted the water from the city and caused it to flow in the opposite direction to the very place where they had set up their camp. On that day and at the very hour when the Persians diverted the water supply, these springs, which you see here, burst forth immediately, by the command of God. From that day up to the present time these springs have continued to be here through the grace of God. However, the very water which the Persians had diverted dried up in that hour so completely that those who were besieging the city did not have one day's supply of water. And this is equally apparent even to this day; for never since then has any water been seen in this place, even to the present day. So, by the will of God,

who had promised that this would be so, the besiegers had
to return home immediately to Persia. Ever afterwards,
whenever an enemy decided to come to attack this city,
this letter was brought out and read at the gate, and
immediately, by the will of God, all the enemy were
expelled."[216]

Then the holy bishop said this: "The springs burst
forth at a place which had been previously a field within
the city, but lying below the palace of Abgar. This palace
of Abgar had been set on a somewhat elevated place, just
the way it appears today, as you can see. It was the practice at that time that, whenever palaces were built, they
were always constructed on high places. After the springs
had burst forth on this spot, however, then Abgar himself
built the palace which is here for his son Magnus, the one
whose statue you saw placed beside his father's; and in
this way the springs would be included within the
palace."[217]

After the saintly bishop recounted all these things, he
said to me: "Let us go now to the gate, through which
the messenger Ananias entered with the letter which I
have been discussing." On arriving at the gate, the bishop,
remaining standing, said a prayer, read to us the letters,
blessed us, and recited another prayer. This holy man also
told us that, from the day when the messenger Ananias
entered through this gate with the Lord's letter up to the
present day, they take care that no unclean man or any
man in grief should pass through this gate, and further
that no body of a dead man should be borne through this
gate. The saintly bishop then showed us the tomb of
Abgar and his whole family; it was very beautiful, but
built in an older style. He then guided us to the upper

palace, where King Abgar had first lived, and he showed us whatever other places there were.

And this was especially gratifying to me, that I received from the saintly bishop copies of the letters which he had read to us, both Abgar's letter to the Lord and the Lord's letter to Abgar. Although I had copies of them at home, I was clearly very pleased to accept them from him, in case the copy which had reached us at home happened to be incomplete; for the copy which I received was certainly more extensive.[218] If Jesus Christ our Lord wills it and I return home, you, ladies dear to me, will read them.

CHAPTER 20

After spending three days there, I had to go on still farther, as far as Carrhae.[219] This is what it is called now, but in Holy Scripture the place where the holy man Abraham lived was called Haran, just as it is written in Genesis, where the Lord says to Abraham: *Go out of your country, and out of the house of your father, and go into Haran*, and so forth.[220] When I arrived there, in Haran, that is, I went immediately to the church there which is in the city itself. I then saw afterwards the bishop of this place, a very holy man of God, also a monk and a confessor,[221] who then graciously consented to show us all the places there which we desired to visit.

He immediately guided us to the church which is outside the city, on the very spot where the house of Abraham stood, built on the very foundations and with the very stones of the house, so the saintly bishop said. After we had entered the church, a prayer was said, and the proper passage was read from Genesis. A Psalm was sung, another prayer was said, and, after the bishop had blessed us, we went outside. Then he graciously agreed to guide us to the well from which the holy woman Rebecca had drawn water. And the holy bishop said to us: "Here is the well from which the holy woman Rebecca watered the camels of Abraham's servant Eliezer."[222] Then he graciously consented to show us everything.

Ladies, reverend sisters, in the church which, as I mentioned, is outside the city, and where Abraham's house originally stood, there is set up today a shrine of a certain holy monk by the name of Helpidius. It was our good fortune to arrive there on the eve of the martyr's feast day, the feast of this very Saint Helpidius, nine days before the Calends of May.[223] On this day every monk from all over every section of Mesopotamia had to come down to Haran, even the great monks[224] who dwell in the desert and are called ascetics. They come because of the day itself, which is most especially honored here, and on account of the memorial to the holy man Abraham,[225] whose house was where the church now stands and where the body of the holy martyr lies.

It was our very good fortune and quite beyond our expectations that we saw there the truly holy men of God, the Mesopotamian monks, those men whose reputation and way of life is spoken about far from here. I thought that it would be quite impossible for me to see them, not because it would have been impossible for God, who has deigned to grant everything, to grant even this to me, but because I had heard that they do not come down from their cells except on Easter and on this day, for these are the sort of men who do many wondrous things.[226] But, as

I have mentioned, I did not know in what month occurred the feast of the martyr. However, by the will of
God, it so happened that I arrived there for the very day
which I had not expected. We stayed there for two days on
account of the martyr's feast and in order to visit the holy
men who consented very readily to receive me, to ex-
change greetings and to speak, although I was not deserving of this. Immediately after the martyr's feast day, they
are no longer to be seen there; for directly after nightfall
they return to the desert, each man to the cell which he
has there.

In the city, however, except for a few clergy and holy
monks who live there, I found no Christians, for they
are all pagans.[227] Just as we venerate with special reverence
the place where originally stood the house of Abraham, in
memory of him,[228] so the pagans venerate with great
reverence the place where the tombs of Nachor and
Bathuel are located, about a mile from the city.[229] Since
the bishop of this place is very learned in Scripture, I
asked him, saying: "I beg you, my lord, to tell me what
I wish to hear." And he said: "Ask what you wish, daughter, and I will tell you if I can." Then I said to him: "I
know from Holy Scripture that the holy man Abraham
came here with his father, his wife Sarah, and Lot, his
brother's son.[230] However, I have not read when Nachor
and Bathuel came here; I only know this, that afterwards
the servant of Abraham came to Haran to seek in marriage
for Isaac, his master Abraham's son, Rebecca, the daughter of Bathuel, son of Nachor."[231] The saintly bishop then
said to me: "It is indeed written in Genesis, as you say,
daughter, that the holy man Abraham came here with his
family.[232] The canonical Scriptures,[233] however, do not

say when Nachor with his family and Bathuel came here. But it is clear that they also came here afterwards; furthermore, their tombs are here, about a thousand feet from the city. For the Scriptures indeed testify that the servant of the holy man Abraham came here to take away the holy woman Rebecca; and later the holy man Jacob came here when he took the daughters of Laban the Syrian."[234] I then asked him where the well was, where the holy man Jacob had drawn water for the flocks which Rachel, the daughter of Laban the Syrian, was grazing.[235] The bishop then said to me: "Six miles from here there is a place near a village which was at that time the property of Laban the Syrian. Whenever you wish to go there, we will go with you and show it to you, for there are many monks there, very holy ascetics, and there is a holy church there as well."

I then asked the holy bishop where was that place of the Chaldees[236] where Thare originally lived with his family. The holy bishop then said to me: "The place which you seek, my daughter, is a ten-day journey from here, deep into Persia.[237] From here to Nisibis[238] it is a five-day journey, and from there as far as Ur, which was the city of the Chaldees, it is another five days.[239] But now there is no admittance there for Romans, since the Persians hold it all.[240] This area in particular, which lies on the border of the Roman, Persian, and Chaldaean lands, is called the Eastern province."[241]

And he consented to speak about many other matters, just as the other holy bishops and the saintly monks had consented to do, but always about the Divine Scriptures and the acts of holy men, the monks, I mean, either about

the wondrous things they had done, if they were already
dead,[242] or, if they were still living,[243] about what they did
each day, those who are ascetics. For I do not want Your
Charity to think that the conversations of the monks are
about anything except the Divine Scriptures and the
actions of the great monks.[244]

CHAPTER 21

After I had spent two days there, the bishop guided us
to the well where the holy man Jacob had drawn water
for the flocks of the holy woman Rebecca. This well is
about six miles from Carrhae; and in honor of this
particular well, a holy church, very large and beautiful,
has been built beside it. When we had arrived at the
well, the bishop said a prayer, the proper passage from
Genesis was read, and a Psalm fitting to the place was
sung. After a second prayer had been said, the bishop
blessed us. We even saw there, lying beside the well, the
extremely large stone which the holy man Jacob had
moved away from the well, for it is still shown even
today.[245] No one lives around the well except the clergy
of the church which is there and the monks who have
their cells nearby. What the holy bishop told us about
their lives was truly extraordinary. After we had prayed
in the church, I went up with the bishop to the holy
monks in their cells. I gave thanks to God as well as to
those who very readily consented to receive me whenever
I came into their cells, and to speak those words which
properly should come from their mouths. They also
generously bestowed gifts on me and on all those who

were with me, as it is the custom for monks to give to those whom they very readily receive in their cells.

Since this place is in a large field, the bishop pointed out to me, straight ahead, perhaps five hundred feet from the well, a very large village, through which we went. This village, as the bishop said, was formerly the property of Laban the Syrian, and the village is called Fadana.[246] He showed me in the village the tomb of Laban the Syrian, Jacob's father-in-law; and I was also shown the place from which Rachel stole the idols of her father.[247] And so, in the name of God, having seen everything, we said farewell to the holy bishop and the holy monks who had graciously consented to guide us to this place, and we returned by the route and through the resting stations we had taken from Antioch.

CHAPTER 22

After I had returned to Antioch, I remained there for a whole week, until whatever was necessary for our journey had been prepared. I then set out from Antioch and, after journeying for several days, arrived in the province called Cilicia, the capital city of which is Tarsus,[248] the same Tarsus in which I had already been on my trip down to Jerusalem. Since the shrine of Saint Thecla is located a three-day journey from Tarsus, in Isauria,[249] it was a great pleasure for me to go there, particularly since it was so near at hand.

CHAPTER 23

I set out from Tarsus and I came to a certain city by the sea, still in Cilicia, called Pompeiopolis.[250] From there

I crossed over into the regions of Isauria, and I stayed at a city called Corycus.[251] On the third day I arrived at a city called Seleucia of Isauria.[252] On arriving there, I went to the bishop, a very holy man and a former monk. I also saw there in the same city a very beautiful church. Since it is around fifteen hundred feet from the city to the shrine of Saint Thecla,[253] which lies beyond the city on a rather flat hill, I thought it best to go out there to make the overnight stop which I had to make.

At the holy church there is nothing but countless monastic cells for men and women. I met there a very dear friend of mine, and a person to whose way of life everyone in the East bears witness, the holy deaconess Marthana,[254] whom I had met in Jerusalem, where she had come to pray. She governs these monastic cells of *aputactitae*,[255] or virgins. Would I ever be able to describe how great was her joy and mine when she saw me? But to return to the subject: There are many cells all over the hill, and in the middle there is a large wall which encloses the church where the shrine is. It is a very beautiful shrine. The wall is set there to guard the church against the Isaurians,[256] who are evil men, who frequently rob and who might try to do something against the monastery which is established there. Having arrived there in the name of God, a prayer was said at the shrine and the complete Acts of Saint Thecla[257] was read. I then gave unceasing thanks to Christ our God, who granted to me, an unworthy woman and in no way deserving, the fulfillment of my desires in all things. And so, after spending two days there seeing the holy monks and the *aputactitae*, both men and women, who live there, and after praying and receiving Communion, I returned to Tarsus and to my journey.

I made a three-day stop before setting out on my journey from there, in the name of God. On the same day I arrived at the resting station called Mansocrenae,[258] located at the base of Mount Tarsus, and I stopped there. The next day I climbed Mount Tarsus and travelled by a route, already known to me, through several provinces that I had already crossed on my journey down, that is, Cappadocia, Galatia, and Bithynia.[259] Then I arrived at Chalcedon, where I stopped because of the very famous shrine of Saint Euphemia,[260] already known to me from before. On the following day, after crossing the sea, I arrived in Constantinople, giving thanks to Christ our God who deigned to bestow such favor on me, an unworthy and undeserving person. Not only did He deign to fulfill my desire to go there, but He granted also the means of visiting what I desired to see, and of returning again to Constantinople.

After arriving there, I did not cease giving thanks to Jesus our God, who had deigned to bestow His grace upon me, in the various churches, that of the apostles[261] and the numerous shrines that are here. As I send this letter to Your Charity and to you, reverend ladies, it is already my intention to go, in the name of Christ our God, to Asia, that is, to Ephesus,[262] to pray at the shrine of the holy and blessed apostle John. If, after this, I am still living, I will either tell Your Charity in person—if God will deign to grant that—about whatever other places I shall have come to know, or certainly I will write you of it in letters, if there is anything else I have in mind.

You, my sisters, my light, kindly remember me, whether I live or die.[263]

CHAPTER 24

Knowing how pleased Your Charity would be to learn what is the ritual observed day by day in the holy places, I considered it my duty to make known to you the details.[264] Each day before cockcrow, all the doors of the Anastasis are opened;[265] and all the monks and virgins come down—the *monazontes* and the *parthene*[266] as they are called here—and not only they, but laymen as well,[267] men and women who wish to rise very early.[268] From this hour until dawn, hymns are sung, and responses are made to the Psalms, and likewise to the antiphons;[269] and after each hymn a prayer is said.[270] Priests in groups of two or three, and a like number of deacons, take turns on successive days in coming at the same time as the monks, and after each hymn or antiphon they recite prayers. At the time when it begins to grow light, they start singing the morning hymns.[271] Then you see the bishop come in with his clergy. He immediately goes into the grotto,[272] and from within the railings he recites first a prayer for all the people; then he himself mentions the names of those whom he wishes to commemorate,[273] and he blesses the catechumens. Then, after he has said a prayer and blessed the faithful, the bishop comes out from the grotto sanctuary, whereupon all present come forth to kiss his hand,[274] and he blesses each of them in turn as he goes out. And so the dismissal is given,[275] and by now it is daylight.

Once again at the sixth hour,[276] everyone returns a

second time to the Anastasis, where Psalms and antiphons are sung while the bishop is being summoned. When he comes in, he does not sit down but, as before, goes immediately within the railings inside the Anastasis, that is to say, within the grotto where he had been in the early morning. As happened earlier, he first says a prayer and then blesses the faithful. And as he leaves the grotto sanctuary, everyone comes forth once again to kiss his hand. The same thing takes place at the ninth hour as at the sixth hour.[277]

At the tenth hour, which is here called *licinicon*,[278] or, as we say, vespers, a great multitude assemble at the Anastasis. All the torches and candles are lighted, and this makes a tremendous light. The light, however, is not brought in from outside, but is taken from inside the grotto, that is, from within the railings where night and day a lamp always burns. Vesper Psalms and antiphons as well are sung for some time, and then the bishop is called. When he comes in, he sits down, and the priests as well sit in their places. Hymns and antiphons are sung; and, when they have been completed according to the custom, the bishop rises and stands in front of the railings, that is, in front of the grotto, while one of the deacons makes a commemoration of each individual as is the custom. Every time the deacon mentions the name of someone, the many children standing about answer: *Kyrie eleison*, or, as we say: "Lord, have mercy,"[279] and their voices are legion. As soon as the deacon has finished what he has to say, the bishop first says a prayer, and he prays for everyone; and then everyone prays together, both the faithful and the catechumens. Next the deacon cries out that each catechumen, wherever he is standing, must bow

his head, whereupon the bishop, who is standing, pro-
nounces the blessing over the catechumens. A prayer is
said and the deacon raises his voice anew to admonish
each of the faithful present to bow his head; then the
bishop blesses the faithful and the dimissal is given at
the Anastasis; and everyone comes forth in turn to kiss
the bishop's hand.

After this, singing hymns, they lead the bishop from
the Anastasis to the Cross,[280] and all the people go along
also. When they have arrived there, first of all he says a
prayer and blesses the catechumens; then he says a second
prayer and blesses the faithful. Afterwards, both the
bishop and the whole multitude go immediately behind
the Cross,[281] where everything just done before the Cross
is done anew. Just as everyone at the Anastasis and
before the Cross came forward to kiss the bishop's
hand, so they do likewise behind the Cross. Numerous
large glass lamps hang everywhere and there are many
candelabra,[282] not only in front of the Anastasis, but also
before the Cross and even behind the Cross. This is the
ritual that takes place daily on the six weekdays at the
Anastasis and the Cross.[283]

On the seventh day, however, that is, on Sunday, before
the cockcrow, a whole multitude, whatever number can
be accommodated in this place and as many as at Easter,[284]
gather outside in the forecourt adjoining the Anastasis,[285]
where for this reason there are lamps hanging. Fearing
that they will not arrive in time for cockcrow, the people
come beforehand and sit there, singing hymns and
antiphons and reciting prayers after each hymn and
antiphon.[286] Because of the multitude which assembles, there are always priests and deacons ready to hold

the vigil, for, by custom, the holy places are not opened before cockcrow.

As soon as the first cock has crowed, the bishop immediately comes down to the church[287] and goes into the grotto at the Anastasis. All the doors are then opened, and the multitude goes into the Anastasis, where countless lights are already glowing. And as soon as the people have entered, one of the priests sings a Psalm and they all make the response; afterwards, a prayer is said. Next one of the deacons sings a Psalm, and again a prayer is said, whereupon a third Psalm is sung by one of the minor ministers,[288] followed by a third prayer and a commemoration of all. When the three Psalms and prayers have been said,[289] then the censers are brought into the grotto of the Anastasis, with the result that the whole basilica of the Anastasis is filled with odors of incense.[290] Then the bishop stands within the railings, takes up the Gospel, and goes toward the door; there the bishop himself reads the Resurrection of the Lord.[291] As soon as the reading of it has begun, so much moaning and groaning[292] is heard, and there is so much weeping among all the people, that the hardest of men would be moved to tears because the Lord has endured so much on our behalf.

Once the Gospel has been read, the bishop goes out, and singing hymns they lead him to the Cross, and with him go the people. There another Psalm is sung and a prayer said. Then he blesses the faithful, and the dismissal is given. As the bishop leaves, all come forth to kiss his hand. The bishop then withdraws to his house, and from that time on all the monks return to the Anastasis to sing Psalms and antiphons until dawn, and to recite a prayer after each Psalm or antiphon.[293] Each day priests and deacons take turns in holding the vigil at the Anastasis with the people. Among the laity there are men and women who wish to remain there until dawn, while others, not wishing to do so, return to their homes to sleep and to rest.

CHAPTER 25

Since it is Sunday, at dawn they assemble for the liturgy[294] in the major church built by Constantine and located on Golgotha behind the Cross; and whatever is done all over customarily on Sundays is done here.[295] Indeed it is the practice here that as many of the priests who are present and are so inclined may preach; and last of all, the bishop preaches.[296] These sermons are given every Sunday so that the people may be instructed in the Scriptures and the love of God. Because of the sermons that are preached, there is a great delay in giving the dismissal from the church; therefore, the dismissal is not given before the fourth or fifth hour.

However, once the dismissal from the church has been given in the manner which is followed everywhere, then the monks, singing hymns, lead the bishop to the Anastasis. When the bishop, to the accompaniment of hymns, approaches, all the doors of the basilica of the Anastasis are opened, and all the people enter, the faithful, that is, but not the catechumens. Once the people have entered, then the bishop enters and he proceeds immediately to within the railings of the grotto shrine.[297] First, they give thanks to God, and so the sacrifice is offered; and then a prayer is said for everyone.[298] Afterwards, the deacon cries out that all should bow their heads, wherever they are standing, and then the bishop, standing within the inner railings, blesses them; afterwards, he goes out. As he is leaving, all come forth to kiss his hand. And so it is that the dismissal is delayed until as late as the fifth or sixth hour.[299] Later at vespers everything is done exactly according to the daily ritual.

This ritual is observed each day throughout the year, except on solemn feast days—and we shall take note of what is done on those days later. Among all these matters this takes first place, that proper Psalms and antiphons are always sung, so that those sung at night, as well as those sung in the morning, and those sung throughout the day, whether at the sixth hour, the ninth hour, or at vespers, are proper and have a meaning pertinent to what is being celebrated.[300] Although throughout the year on every Sunday they assemble for the liturgy at the major church built by Constantine on Golgotha behind the Cross, yet on one Sunday, that of the feast of the fiftieth day, Pentecost,[301] they assemble for the liturgy at Sion, as you will find described below. So that they may go to Sion before the third hour, the dismissal is first given in the major church. . . .[302]

[*One folio is missing from the manuscript at this point.*]

Blessed is He who comes in the name of the Lord, and whatever else follows.[303] Because of the monks who come on foot, you have to move along at a slow pace. As a result, you reach Jerusalem at that hour when men can begin to recognize one another,[304] that is to say, near daybreak, but before the day has dawned. As soon as they have arrived, the bishop and all who are with him immediately enter the Anastasis, where the lights are already shining brightly. A Psalm is sung, a prayer is said, and first the catechumens and then the faithful are blessed by the bishop, who then retires, while everyone returns to his home to rest. The monks, however, remain there until daybreak, singing hymns.

However, after the people have rested, everyone gathers together again in the major church on Golgotha at the beginning of the second hour. It would be superfluous to describe how the churches—the Anastasis, the Cross, and the church in Bethlehem—are decorated on that day. You see nothing there but gold and gems and silk. If you look at the hangings, they are made of silk with gold stripes; if you look at the curtains, they are also made of silk with gold stripes. Every kind of sacred vessel brought out on that day is of gold inlaid with precious stones.[305] How could the number and weight of the candle holders, the candelabra, the lamps, and the various sacred vessels be in any way estimated and noted down? And what can I say about the decoration of this building which Constantine, with his mother on hand,[306] had embellished with as much gold, mosaics, and marble as the resources of his empire permitted—and not only the major church, but the Anastasis as well, and the Cross and the other holy places in Jerusalem?

Let us return to the subject, however. On the first day, then, the service takes place in the major church on Golgotha.[307] Whatever sermons are preached, whatever passages from Scripture are read, whatever hymns are sung, everything is appropriate to the day. Afterwards, when the dismissal has been given from the church, everyone goes from there to the Anastasis singing hymns according to the custom; and the dismissal is given around the sixth hour. At vespers on that day everything is done according to the daily ritual. On the next day one assembles again for the liturgy in the church on Golgotha; and likewise on the third day. For three days then, all the solemn liturgy is celebrated[308] up to the sixth hour in the church built by Constantine. Everything is celebrated in exactly the same manner and identically embellished on the fourth day at the Eleona,[309] which is the very beautiful church on the Mount of Olives; on the fifth day, at the Lazarium,[310] which is about a mile and a half from Jerusalem; on the sixth day, at Sion;[311] on the seventh day, at the Anastasis; and on the eighth day, at the Cross.[312] And so for eight days all the solemn liturgy is celebrated with great pomp in all the holy places which I have named above.

In Bethlehem, however, on every day throughout the eight-day period, this solemn liturgy is celebrated with pomp by the priests, by all the clergy of that place, and by all the monks who are assigned to this place. From the hour when all return by night to Jerusalem with the bishop, whichever monks there are of that place keep watch until dawn in the church at Bethlehem,[313] chanting hymns and antiphons. The bishop, however, must always celebrate these feast days in Jerusalem. Because of the solemnity and ritual of this feast, an enormous crowd gathers together in Jerusalem, composed not only of monks, but also of the laity, both men and women.

CHAPTER 26

The fortieth day after Epiphany[314] is indeed celebrated here with the greatest solemnity. On that day there is a procession into the Anastasis, and all assemble there for the liturgy;[315] and everything is performed in the prescribed manner with the greatest solemnity,[316] just as on Easter Sunday. All the priests give sermons, and the bishop, too; and all preach on the Gospel text describing how on the fortieth day Joseph and Mary took the Lord to the temple, and how Simeon and Anna the prophetess, the daughter of Phanuel, saw Him, and what words they spoke on seeing the Lord, and of the offering which His parents brought.[317] Afterwards, when all ceremonies have been performed in the prescribed manner, the Eucharist is then celebrated[318] and the dismissal is given.

CHAPTER 27

When the season of Lent[319] is at hand, it is observed in the following manner. Now whereas with us the forty days[320] preceding Easter are observed, here they observe the eight weeks before Easter.[321] This is the reason why they observe eight weeks: On Sundays and Saturdays they do not fast, except on the one Saturday which is the vigil of Easter, when it is necessary to fast. Except on that day, there is absolutely no fasting here on Saturdays at any time during the year.[322] And so, when eight Sundays and seven Saturdays have been deducted from the eight weeks—for it is necessary, as I have just said, to fast on one Saturday—there remain forty-one days which are spent in fasting, which are called here *eortae*, that is to say, Lent.[323]

On each day of each week this is what is done. On Sunday, at the first cockcrow, the bishop inside the Anastasis reads from the Gospel the passage of the Resurrection of the Lord, as is done on every Sunday throughout the year; and all the same ceremonies are performed until daybreak at the Anastasis and at the Cross as are performed on every other Sunday during the year. Afterwards, in the morning, as always happens on Sunday, everyone assembles for the liturgy in the major church called the Martyrium, on Golgotha behind the Cross, where the rites customarily performed on Sunday are accomplished. When the dismissal has been given from the church, everyone chanting hymns goes to the Anastasis, as is always done on Sundays. By the time these ceremonies are completed, the fifth hour is at hand. The usual vespers service takes place at its regular hour at the Anastasis and the Cross, just as it does in all holy places. On Sundays there is no service at the ninth hour.[324]

On Monday[325] one also goes to the Anastasis at cockcrow, where everything is done just as it always is until morning. Once again at the third hour everyone returns to the Anastasis, where the ritual customarily observed at the sixth hour throughout the year is now celebrated, for during Lent a service has been added, so that they go at the third hour as well.[326] At the sixth hour and at the ninth hour and at vespers those services take place which customarily are celebrated throughout the year in these holy places. The same ritual is celebrated in exactly the same manner on Tuesday as on Monday.

On Wednesday, while it is still night, they go to the Anastasis, where the usual ritual is observed until morning; and the third and sixth hours are observed as usual. But as it is always the custom at the ninth hour throughout the year on Wednesdays and Fridays to assemble for the liturgy in the Church of Sion at this hour—for in these parts on Wednesdays and Fridays they always fast,[327] even the catechumens, unless the day happens to be the feast of a martyr—they consequently assemble for the liturgy at Sion at the ninth hour. If by chance during Lent the feast day of a martyr occurs on a Wednesday or a Friday, they do not assemble for the liturgy at Sion at the ninth hour.[328] During Lent, as I have already said, on Wednesday everyone assembles for the liturgy at Sion at the ninth hour as is customary throughout the year, and whatever ritual is customarily observed at that time takes place, except for the offering of the sacrifice.[329] So that the people will know the law, the bishop and a priest preach assiduously. When the dismissal has been given, the people, chanting hymns, lead the bishop from there to the Anastasis. They come from there in such a way that it is already the hour of vespers when they enter the Anastasis. Hymns and antiphons are sung, prayers are said, and the vespers service takes place at the Anastasis and the Cross. The vespers service[330] during Lent is always held later than it is on other days throughout the year.

On Thursday everything is done just as on Monday and Tuesday. On Friday everything is done as on Wednesday; and so everyone goes to Sion at the ninth hour, and the bishop is likewise led back from there to the Anastasis to the accompaniment of hymns. But on Friday they celebrate the vigil in the Anastasis from the hour when they have returned from Sion singing hymns until morning, that is, from the hour of vespers until the beginning of morning on the following day, which is Saturday.[331] The sacrifice is offered early in the Anastasis so that the dismissal may be given before sunrise. All during the night Psalms with responses and antiphons are sung alternately; there are readings from Scripture; and all this continues until morning. The divine service which takes place on Saturdays at the Anastasis—I mean, of course, the offering of the sacrifice—is celebrated before sunrise, so that at the hour when the sun begins to rise, the divine service has taken place at the Anastasis.[332] This is how the ritual is celebrated every week during Lent.

As I have said, the service is held earlier on Saturdays, that is, before sunrise, and this is done so that those whom they call here *hebdomadarii*[333] may be more quickly released from their fast.[334] Such is the practice of fasting here during Lent that those who are called *hebdomadarii*, by which I mean those who fast the whole week, eat on Sunday, after the dismissal is given at the fifth hour. Once they have eaten on Sunday morning, they do not eat again until the following Saturday morning, immediately after they have received Communion at the Anastasis. For their sake, that they may be more quickly released from their fasting, the divine service takes place before sunrise in the Anastasis on Saturday. If I have stated that the divine service takes place early on their account, it is not that they alone receive Communion, but all who wish to receive Communion on that day do so.

CHAPTER 28

This is a summary of the fasting practices here during Lent.[335] There are some who, having eaten on Sunday after the dismissal,[336] that is, at the fifth or the sixth hour, do not eat again for the whole week until Saturday, following the dismissal from the Anastasis. These are the ones who observe the full week's fast. Having eaten once in the morning on Saturday, they do not eat again in the evening, but only on the following day, on Sunday, that is, do they eat after the dismissal from the church at the fifth hour or later. Afterwards, they do not eat again until the following Saturday, as I have already said.

It is the practice here that all who are, as they call them here, *aputactitae*,[337] including both men and women, eat, when they do eat, only once a day, and this is not only in Lent, but throughout the year. If there are some among the *aputactitae* who are not able to observe the full week of fasting throughout Lent, such as I have described above, they take food in the middle of the week on Thursday; and those who cannot do that, fast two full days at a time during Lent; and those who cannot do that, eat every evening.[338] No one requires that anyone fast a certain number of days, but each man does as he is able; and no one is praised for doing more, nor is anyone blamed for doing less.[339] For this is the custom here. Such is their fare during the Lenten season that they take no leavened bread (for this cannot be eaten at all), no olive oil, nothing which comes from trees, but only water and a little flour soup.[340] And this is what is done throughout Lent, as we have said.[341]

CHAPTER 29

As the week comes to a close,[342] the vigil is held on Friday in the Anastasis from the hour of vespers, when they return from Sion to the accompaniment of hymns, until Saturday morning, when the sacrifice is offered in the Anastasis. The same ritual is observed during the second, third, fourth, fifth, and sixth weeks as during the first week of Lent. When the seventh week has come and there remain two weeks, including this one, before Easter, everything continues to be done daily as during the other weeks which have preceded, but with this difference, that the vigils which were held on Friday in the Anastasis during the first six weeks are held on the Friday of the seventh week in Sion, but exactly as they were held in the Anastasis during the preceding six weeks. At each hour Psalms and antiphons are sung which are appropriate both to the day and the place.

When it is getting to be dawn, at the first light on Saturday, the bishop officiates and offers the sacrifice[343] at dawn on Saturday. Just as the dismissal is to be given, the archdeacon[344] raises his voice and says: "Let us all make ready to be this day at the Lazarium at the seventh hour."[345] And so, as it gets to be the seventh hour, everyone comes to the Lazarium, which is at Bethany, approximately two miles from the city.[346] On the way from Jerusalem to the Lazarium, at about a half mile from that place, there is a church along the road at the very place where Mary, the sister of Lazarus, came forth to meet the Lord.[347] When the bishop reaches this place, all the monks come forth to meet him, and the people go into the church, where a hymn and an antiphon are sung and the proper passage from the Gospel is read, describing how Lazarus' sister met the Lord.[348]

When a prayer has been said and a blessing given to all, everyone continues on to the Lazarium, chanting hymns; and by the time they have come to the Lazarium, such a multitude has gathered that not only the place itself, but all the surrounding fields are filled with people. Hymns are sung as well as antiphons appropriate to the day and the place; various scriptural readings, also fitting to the day, are read. Just before the dismissal is given, the Pasch is proclaimed, that is to say, a priest mounts to an elevated spot and reads the passage from Scripture where it is written: *When Jesus came into Bethany six days before the Pasch.*[349] When this has been read and the Pasch has been proclaimed, the dismissal is given. Because it is written in Scripture that six days before the Pasch this was done in Bethany, therefore on this day this ceremony takes place.[350] There are six days from Saturday to the following Thursday, when, after supper, the Lord was arrested in the night. Everyone then returns directly to the city and to the Anastasis, where vespers is celebrated as customary.

CHAPTER 30

The following day, Sunday, marks the beginning of Holy Week,[351] which they call here the Great Week.[352] On this Sunday morning, at the completion of those rites which are customarily celebrated at the Anastasis or the Cross from the first cockcrow until dawn, everyone assembles for the liturgy according to custom in the major church, called the Martyrium. It is called the Martyrium because it is on Golgotha, behind the Cross, where the Lord suffered His Passion, and is therefore a shrine of martyrdom.[353] As soon as everything has been celebrated in the major church as usual, but before the dismissal is given, the archdeacon raises his voice and first says: "Throughout this whole week, beginning tomorrow at the ninth hour, let us all gather in the Martyrium, in the major church." Then he raises his voice a second time, saying: "Today let us all be ready to assemble at the seventh hour at the Eleona." When the dismissal has been given in the Martyrium or major church, the bishop is led to the accompaniment of hymns to the Anastasis, and there all ceremonies are accomplished which customarily take place every Sunday at the Anastasis following the dismissal from the Martyrium. Then everyone retires to his home to eat hastily, so that at the beginning of the seventh hour everyone will be ready to assemble in the church on the Eleona, by which I mean the Mount of Olives, where the grotto in which the Lord taught is located.[354]

CHAPTER 31

At the seventh hour all the people go up to the church on the Mount of Olives, that is, to the Eleona. The bishop sits down, hymns and antiphons appropriate to the day and place are sung, and there are likewise readings from the Scriptures.[355] As the ninth hour approaches, they move up, chanting hymns, to the Imbomon, that is, to the place from which the Lord ascended into heaven;[356] and everyone sits down there. When the bishop is present, the people are always commanded to be seated, so that only the deacons remain standing. And there hymns and antiphons proper to the day and place are sung, interspersed with appropriate readings from the Scriptures and prayers.

As the eleventh hour draws near, that particular passage from Scripture is read in which the children bearing palms and branches came forth to meet the Lord, saying: *Blessed is He who comes in the name of the Lord.*[357] The bishop and all the people rise immediately, and then everyone walks down from the top of the Mount of Olives, with the people preceding the bishop and responding continually with *Blessed is He who comes in the name of the Lord* to the hymns and antiphons. All the children who are present here, including those who are not yet able to walk because they are too young and therefore are carried on their parents' shoulders,[358] all of them bear branches, some carrying palms, others, olive branches. And the bishop is led in the same manner as the Lord once was led.[359] From the top of the mountain as far as the city, and from there through the entire city as far as the Anastasis, everyone accompanies the bishop the whole way on foot, and this includes distinguished ladies and men of consequence,[360] reciting the responses all the while; and they move very slowly so that the people will not tire. By the time they arrive at the Anastasis, it is already evening. Once they have arrived there, even though it is evening, vespers is celebrated; then a prayer is said at the Cross and the people are dismissed.

CHAPTER 32

On Monday, the following day, they carry out in the Anastasis whatever ceremonies are customarily performed from the first cockcrow until dawn, as well as whatever is done at the third and sixth hours throughout Lent. However, at the ninth hour everyone comes together in the major church or Martyrium, and until the first hour of the night they continually sing hymns and antiphons, and read passages from the Scriptures fitting to the day and the place, always interrupting them with prayers.[361] Vespers is celebrated in the Martyrium, when the hour for it is at hand. The result is that it is already night when the dismissal is given at the Martyrium.[362] As soon as the dismissal has been given, the bishop is led from there to the Anastasis to the accompaniment of hymns. When he has entered the Anastasis, a hymn is sung, a prayer is said, first the catechumens and then the faithful are blessed, and finally the dismissal is given.

Chapter 33

On Tuesday they do everything in the same way as on Monday. Only this is added on Tuesday: late at night, after the dismissal has been given in the Martyrium and they have gone to the Anastasis, and a second dismissal has been given at the Anastasis, they all go at that hour in the night to the church which is located on Mount Eleona.[363] As soon as they have arrived in this church, the bishop goes into the grotto where the Lord used to teach His disciples.[364] There the bishop takes up the book of the Gospels and, while standing, reads the words of the Lord which are written in the Gospel according to Matthew at the place where He said: *Take heed that no man seduce you.*[365] Then the bishop reads the Lord's entire discourse. When he has finished reading it, he says a prayer and blesses the catechumens and then the faithful. The dismissal is given, and they return from the mountain, and everyone goes to his own home, for it is now very late at night.

CHAPTER 34

On Wednesday everything is done throughout the day
from the first cockcrow just as on Monday and Tuesday.
However, following the dismissal at night at the Martyrium, the bishop is led to the accompaniment of hymns
to the Anastasis. He goes immediately into the grotto
within the Anastasis, and he stands within the railings. A
priest, however, standing in front of the railings, takes up
the Gospel and reads that passage where Judas Iscariot
went to the Jews to set the price they would pay him to
betray the Lord.[366] While this passage is being read, there
is such moaning and groaning from among the people that
no one can help being moved to tears in that moment.
Afterwards, a prayer is said, first the catechumens and
then the faithful are blessed, and finally the dismissal is
given.

CHAPTER 35

On Thursday whatever is customarily done from the
first cockcrow until morning and what is done at the
third and sixth hours takes place at the Anastasis. At the
eighth hour all the people gather as usual at the Martyrium,[367] earlier, however, than on other days, because the
dismissal must be given more quickly. When all the people have assembled, the prescribed rites are celebrated. On
that day the sacrifice is offered at the Martyrium, and the
dismissal from there is given around the tenth hour. Before the dismissal is given, however, the archdeacon raises
his voice, saying: "At the first hour of the night let us
assemble at the church which is on the Eleona, for much

toil lies ahead of us on this day's night." Following the
dismissal from the Martyrium, everyone proceeds behind
the Cross, where, after a hymn is sung and a prayer is
said, the bishop offers the sacrifice and everyone receives
Communion. Except on this one day, throughout the year
the sacrifice is never offered behind the Cross save on
this day alone.[368] The dismissal is given there, and everyone goes to the Anastasis, where a prayer is said, the catechumens as well as the faithful are blessed, as is customary,
and the dismissal is given.[369]

Everyone then hurries home to eat, because, immediately after having eaten, everyone goes to the Eleona, to
the church where the grotto in which the Lord gathered
with His disciples on that day is located. And there, until
around the fifth hour of the night, they continually sing
hymns and antiphons and read the scriptural passages
proper to the place and to the day. Between these, prayers
are said. Moreover, they read those passages from the
Gospels in which the Lord spoke to His disciples on that
day while sitting in the same grotto which lies within this
church.[370] And from here, around the sixth hour of the
night, everyone goes up to the Imbomon, singing hymns.
That is the place from which the Lord ascended into
heaven. There also they sing hymns and antiphons and read
scriptural passages proper to the day; and whatever
prayers are said, whatever prayers the bishop recites, they
will always be proper to the day and to the place.

CHAPTER 36

As soon as it begins to be the hour of cockcrow, everyone
comes down from the Imbomon singing hymns and pro-

ceeds toward the very place where the Lord prayed, as it is written in the Gospel: *And He went as far as a stone's throw and He prayed*, and so forth.[371] On that spot stands a tasteful church.[372] The bishop and all the people enter there, where a prayer fitting to the day and the place is said, followed by an appropriate hymn, and a reading of that passage from the Gospel where He said to His disciples: *Watch, that you enter not into temptation.*[373] The whole of this passage is read there, and a second prayer is then said. Next, everyone, including the smallest children, walk down from there to Gethsemani, accompanying the bishop with hymns. Singing hymns, they come to Gethsemani[374] very slowly on account of the great multitude of people, who are fatigued by vigils and exhausted by the daily fasts, and because of the rather high mountain they have to descend. Over two hundred church candles are ready to provide light for all the people.[375]

On arriving in Gethsemani a suitable prayer is first said, followed by a hymn, and then the passage from the Gospel describing the arrest of the Lord is read.[376] During the reading of this passage there is such moaning and groaning with weeping from all the people that their moaning can be heard practically as far as the city. And from that hour everyone goes back on foot to the city singing hymns, and they arrive at the gate[377] at the hour when men can begin to recognize one another. From there, throughout the center of the city, all without exception are ready at hand, the old and the young, the rich and the poor, everyone; and on this day especially no one withdraws from the vigil before early morning. It is in this fashion that the bishop is led from Gethsemani to the gate, and from there through the whole city to the Cross.[378]

When they finally arrive before the Cross, it is already beginning to be broad daylight. There then is read the passage from the Gospel where the Lord is led before Pilate, and whatsoever words are written that Pilate spoke to the Lord or to the Jews, all this is read.[379] Afterwards, the bishop addresses the people, comforting them, since they have labored the whole night and since they are to labor again on this day, admonishing them not to grow weary, but to have hope in God who will bestow great graces on them for their efforts. And comforting them as he can, he addresses them saying: "Go, for the time being, each of you, to your homes; sit there awhile, and around the second hour of the day let everyone be on hand here so that from that hour until the sixth hour you may see the holy wood of the cross, and thus believe that it was offered for the salvation of each and every one of us. From the sixth hour on we will have to assemble here, before the Cross, so that we may devote ourselves to prayers and scriptural readings until nightfall."

Chapter 37

After this, following the dismissal from the Cross, which occurs before sunrise, everyone now stirred up goes immediately to Sion to pray at the pillar where the Lord was whipped.[380] Returning from there then, everyone rests for a short time in his own house, and soon all are ready. A throne is set up for the bishop on Golgotha behind the Cross, which now stands there.[381] The bishop sits on his throne, a table covered with a linen cloth is set before him, and the deacons stand around the table. The gilded silver casket containing the sacred wood of the cross is brought in and opened.[382] Both the wood of the cross and the inscription[383] are taken out and placed on the table. As soon as they have been placed on the table, the bishop, remaining seated, grips the ends of the sacred wood with his hands, while the deacons, who are standing about, keep watch over it. There is a reason why it is guarded in this manner. It is the practice here for all the people to come forth one by one, the faithful as well as the catechumens, to bow down before the table, kiss the holy wood, and then move on. It is said that someone (I do not know when) took a bite and stole a piece of the holy cross. Therefore, it is now guarded by the deacons standing around, lest there be anyone who would dare come and do that again.[384]

All the people pass through one by one; all of them bow down, touching the cross and the inscription, first with their foreheads, then with their eyes; and, after kissing the cross, they move on. No one, however, puts out his hand to touch the cross. As soon as they have kissed the cross and passed on through, a deacon, who is standing, holds out the ring of Solomon and the phial with which the kings were anointed.[385] They kiss the phial and venerate the ring from more or less the second hour; and thus[386] until the sixth hour all the people pass through, entering through one door, exiting through another. All this occurs in the place where the day before, on Thursday, the sacrifice was offered.[387]

When the sixth hour is at hand, everyone goes before the Cross, regardless of whether it is raining or whether it is hot. This place has no roof, for it is a sort of very large and beautiful courtyard lying between the Cross and the Anastasis.[388] The people are so clustered together there that it is impossible for anything to be opened. A chair is placed for the bishop before the Cross, and from the sixth to the ninth hours nothing else is done except the reading of passages from Scripture.[389]

First, whichever Psalms speak of the Passion are read. Next, there are readings from the apostles, either from the Epistles of the apostles or the Acts, wherever they speak of the Passion of the Lord. Next, the texts of the Passion from the Gospels are read. Then there are readings from the prophets, where they said that the Lord would suffer; and then they read from the Gospels, where He foretells the Passion. And so, from the sixth to the ninth hour, passages from Scripture are continuously read and hymns are sung, to show the people that whatever the prophets had said would come to pass concerning the Passion of the Lord can be shown, both through the Gospels and the writings of the apostles, to have taken place. And so, during those three hours, all the people are taught that nothing happened which was not first prophesied, and that nothing was prophesied which was not completely fulfilled. Prayers are continually interspersed, and the prayers themselves are proper to the day. At each reading and at every prayer, it is astonishing how much emotion and groaning there is from all the people. There is no one, young or old, who on this day does not sob more than can be imagined for the whole three hours, because the Lord suffered all this for us. After this, when the ninth hour is at hand, the passage is read from the Gospel according to Saint John where Christ gave up His spirit.[390] After this reading, a prayer is said and the dismissal is given.

As soon as the dismissal has been given from before the Cross, everyone gathers together in the major church, the Martyrium,[391] and there everything which they have been doing regularly throughout this week from the ninth hour when they came together at the Martyrium, until evening, is then done. After the dismissal from the Martyrium, everyone comes to the Anastasis, and, after they have arrived there, the passage from the Gospel is read where Joseph seeks from Pilate the body of the Lord and places it in a new tomb.[392] After this reading a prayer is said, the catechumens are blessed, and the faithful as well; then the dismissal is given.[393]

On this day no one raises his voice to say the vigil will be continued at the Anastasis, because it is known that the people are tired. However, it is the custom that the vigil be held there. And so, those among the people who wish, or rather those who are able, to keep the vigil, do so until dawn; whereas those who are not able to do so, do not keep watch there. But those of the clergy who are either strong enough or young enough, keep watch there, and hymns and antiphons are sung there all through the night until morning. The greater part of the people keep watch, some from evening on, others from midnight, each one doing what he can.[394]

CHAPTER 38

On the following day, which is Saturday, there is as usual a service at the third hour and again at the sixth hour. There is no service, however, at the ninth hour on Saturday, for preparation is being made for the Easter vigil in the major church, the Martyrium. The Easter vigil is observed here exactly as we observe it at home.[395] Only one thing is done more elaborately here. After the neophytes[396] have been baptized and dressed as soon as they came forth from the baptismal font,[397] they are led first of all to the Anastasis with the bishop. The bishop goes within the railings of the Anastasis, a hymn is sung, and he prays for them.[398] Then he returns with them to the major church, where all the people are holding the vigil as is customary.[399]

Everything is done which is customarily done at home with us, and after the sacrifice has been offered, the dismissal is given. After the vigil service has been celebrated[400] in the major church, everyone comes to the Anastasis singing hymns. There, once again, the text of the Gospel of the Resurrection is read, a prayer is said, and once again the bishop offers the sacrifice. However, for the sake of the people, everything is done rapidly, lest they be delayed too long. And so the people are dismissed. On this day the dismissal from the vigil takes place at the same hour as at home with us.

CHAPTER 39

The eight days of Easter are observed[401] just as at home with us. The liturgy[402] is celebrated in the prescribed manner throughout the eight days of Easter just as it is celebrated everywhere from Easter Sunday to its octave.[403] There is the same decoration, and the same arrangement for these eight days of Easter, as for the Epiphany,[404] both in the major church and in the Anastasis, in the Cross as well as the Eleona, in Bethlehem, and in the Lazarium, too, and indeed everywhere, for this is Easter time.[405]

On that first Sunday, Easter Day, everyone assembles for the liturgy in the major church, in the Martyrium, and on Monday and Tuesday also. But it always happens that, once the dismissal has been given from the Martyrium, everyone comes to the Anastasis singing hymns. On Wednesday everyone assembles for the liturgy in the Eleona; on Thursday, in the Anastasis; on Friday, at Sion; and on Saturday, before the Cross. On Sunday, however, on the octave that is, they go once again to the major church, to the Martyrium.[406] During the eight days of Easter, everyday after lunch,[407] in the company of all the clergy and the neophytes[408]—I mean those who have just been baptized—and of all the *aputactitae*, both men and women, and of as many of the people as wish to come, the bishop goes up to the Eleona. Hymns are sung and prayers are said, both in the church which is on the Eleona and where the grotto in which Jesus taught His disciples is located, and at the Imbomon, the place, that is, from which the Lord ascended into heaven. After Psalms have been sung and a prayer has been said, everyone comes down from there, singing hymns, and goes to the Anastasis at the hour for vespers. This is done throughout the eight days.[409]

On Easter Sunday, after the dismissal from vespers at the Anastasis,[410] all the people singing hymns conduct the bishop to Sion. When they have arrived there, hymns proper to the day and the place are sung, and a prayer is said. Then is read the passage from the Gospel describing how on this day and in this very place where there is now this same Church of Sion, the Lord came to His disciples, although the doors were closed, at the time when one of the disciples, namely, Thomas, was not there.[411] When he returned, he said to the other apostles, who had told him that they had seen the Lord: *I will not believe, unless I see.*[412] After this passage has been read, a prayer is again said, the catechumens and then the faithful are blessed, and everyone returns to his home late, around the second hour of the night.

CHAPTER 40

Then on Sunday, on the octave of Easter, immediately after the sixth hour[413] all the people go up to the Eleona with the bishop. First of all everyone sits down for a time in the church which is there; hymns are sung as well as antiphons proper to the day and to the place, and prayers also that are proper to the day and the place. Then, everyone, singing hymns, goes from there up to the Imbomon above; and what was done in the Eleona[414] is done in like manner again here. When it is time, all the people and all the *aputactitae*, singing hymns, lead the bishop to the Anastasis. They arrive at the Anastasis at the hour when vespers is customarily celebrated, and the vespers service is held both at the Anastasis and at the Cross.

From there, all the people without exception, singing hymns, lead the bishop as far as Sion. When they have arrived there, hymns proper to the place and to the day are sung as usual. Then they read the passage from the Gospel where, on the octave of Easter,[415] the Lord came into where the disciples were, and He reproved Thomas because he had not believed.[416] The whole passage from Scripture is then read. After a prayer has been said and the catechumens and the faithful have been blessed according to custom, then everyone returns to his home at the second hour of the night, just as on Easter Sunday.

CHAPTER 41

From Easter to the fiftieth day, that is, to Pentecost,[417] absolutely no one fasts here, not even the *aputactitae*.[418] During the period the customary services are held at the Anastasis from the first cockcrow until morning, as is done throughout the year, and likewise at the sixth hour and at vespers.[419] On Sundays they assemble as always for the liturgy in the Martyrium, the major church, according to custom; then, from there, singing hymns, they go to the Anastasis. On Wednesdays and Fridays, since absolutely no one fasts here on these days, they assemble for the liturgy at Sion, but in the morning.[420] The divine service is celebrated in the prescribed manner.[421]

CHAPTER 42

On the fortieth day after Easter[422]—this is a Thursday—everyone goes to Bethlehem after the sixth hour of the day before, that is, on Wednesday, to celebrate the vigil.[423] The vigil is held in the church in Bethlehem, the church where the grotto in which the Lord was born is located.[424] On the following day, that is, on Thursday, the feast of the fortieth day,[425] the divine service is celebrated in the prescribed manner,[426] and as a result the priests and the bishop preach, delivering sermons appropriate to the day and the place. And afterwards everyone returns in the evening to Jerusalem.

CHAPTER 43

On the feast of Pentecost,[427] which falls on Sunday, the day on which there is the greatest strain on the people, everything is done exactly according to custom from the first cockcrow. The vigil is held in the Anastasis, so that the bishop may read the passage from the Gospel which is always read on Sundays, that of the Resurrection of the Lord. Afterwards, the customary ritual is carried out in the Anastasis, just as it is throughout the year. As soon as it is morning, all the people assemble for the liturgy in the major church,[428] in the Martyrium, where everything customarily done is accomplished. The priests preach and afterwards the bishop. All the prescribed rites[429] are accomplished, that is, the sacrifice is offered in the manner in which it is customarily done on Sundays. On this one day, however, the dismissal is moved up in the Martyrium, so that it is given before the third hour.[430]

As soon as the dismissal has been given in the Martyrium, all the people without exception, singing hymns, lead the bishop to Sion, but in such a manner that they are in Sion at precisely the third hour.[431] When they arrive, there is read from the Acts of the Apostles[432] that passage in which the Holy Spirit came down so that all tongues might be heard and all might understand what was being said.[433] Afterwards the divine service is celebrated in the prescribed manner.[434] Now the priests read there from the Acts of the Apostles that passage which is

read because this is the place on Sion—the church now is
something else—where at an earlier time, after the Passion
of the Lord, the multitude was gathered with the apostles,
and where that which we mentioned above was done.[435]
Afterwards, the divine service is celebrated in the prescribed manner, and the sacrifice is offered.[436] Then, just
before the people are dismissed, the archdeacon raises his
voice to say: "Today, immediately after the sixth hour, let
us all be ready at the Imbomon on the Eleona."[437] All the
people then return home, each one to rest in his own
house.

Immediately after lunch, everyone, insofar as is possible,
goes up to the Mount of Olives, that is to the Eleona,
with the result that not a single Christian remains in the
city, for they have all gone.[438] As soon as they have
climbed the Mount of Olives, the Eleona, that is, they go
first of all to the Imbomon, that is, to the place from
which the Lord ascended into heaven[439] The bishop
sits down there, and the priests and all the people,
too. Passages from Scripture are read, hymns are interspersed and sung, and also antiphons proper to the day
itself and the place are sung. The prayers which are interspersed are said in such a manner[440] that they fit both the
day and the place. Then the passage from the Gospel is
read which speaks of the Ascension of the Lord;[441] then
there is the reading from the Acts of the Apostles which
speaks of the Ascension of the Lord into Heaven after the
Resurrection.[442] When this has been done, the catechumens are blessed and then the faithful. Then at the
ninth hour everyone comes down from there and goes,
singing hymns, to the church which is also on the Eleona,
that is to say, in that grotto where the Lord sat teaching the

apostles. By the time they arrive there it is already past the tenth hour. Vespers is held there, a prayer is said, the catechumens and then the faithful are blessed.

Then all the people without exception come down from there singing hymns, everyone together with the bishop singing hymns and antiphons proper to the day itself. And in this fashion they make their way slowly and easily[443] to the Martyrium. When they reach the city gate, it is already night, and around two hundred church candles are brought out[444] for the people. Since it is quite far from the city gate to the major church or Martyrium, it is definitely around the second hour of the night when they arrive, because they move slowly and easily all the way so that the people will not be tired out from walking. And when the great doors which are on the market street side[445] are opened, then all the people, singing hymns, enter the Martyrium with the bishop.

After they have entered the church, hymns are sung, a prayer is said, and the catechumens and then the faithful are blessed. From there, everyone, singing hymns, then goes to the Anastasis. When they have arrived at the Anastasis, in like manner hymns and antiphons are sung, a prayer is said, and the catechumens and then the faithful are blessed. And the same thing is done at the Cross.[446]

Then all the Christian people without exception, singing hymns, lead the bishop to Sion. When they get there, appropriate passages from Scripture are read, Psalms and antiphons as well are sung, and a prayer is said. The catechumens are blessed and then the faithful, and the dismissal is given. Once the dismissal has been given, everyone comes forth to kiss the bishop's hand. Everyone then returns to his own home around midnight.

And so a great deal of toil is borne on this day, for the vigil at the Anastasis starts with the first cockcrow, and from then on throughout the whole day there is no stopping. Everything that is celebrated is drawn out to the point that only at midnight, after the dismissal has been given at Sion, does everyone return to his home.

CHAPTER 44

Starting with the day after Pentecost,[447] everyone again observes the fast that prevails throughout the year, each according to his ability, fasting every day except Saturdays and Sundays, on which days there is never any fast in these areas.[448] In like manner, during the subsequent days everything is done just as it is throughout the whole year, that is to say, the vigil is always held at the Anastasis starting with the first cockcrow. However, if it is Sunday, at the first cockcrow the bishop reads, as is customary, within the Anastasis, the Gospel passage of the Resurrection of the Lord, which is always read on Sunday. Afterwards, hymns and antiphons are sung in the Anastasis until daybreak.

If it is not a Sunday, however, only hymns and antiphons[449] are sung from the first cockcrow until dawn in the Anastasis. All the *aputactitae* come; those of the people who are able to come, do so; and the clergy take turns coming each day at cockcrow.[450] The bishop, however, always comes at dawn with all the clergy so that the morning service may be held,[451] except on Sundays when it is necessary for him to come with all his clergy at the first cockcrow to read the Gospel in the Anastasis. Then whatever is customary is done at the sixth and the ninth hours; at vespers, whatever is supposed to be done throughout the year is likewise done according to custom in the Anastasis. However, on Wednesdays and Fridays there is always a service at the ninth hour according to custom at Sion.[452]

CHAPTER 45

I must also describe how those who are baptized at Easter are instructed.[453] Whoever gives his name does so the day before Lent,[454] and the priest notes down all their names;[455] and this is before those eight weeks during which, as I have said, Lent is observed here. When the priest has noted down everyone's name, then on the following day, the first day of Lent, on which the eight weeks begin, a throne is set up for the bishop[456] in the center of the major church, the Martyrium. The priests sit on stools on both sides, and all the clergy stand around. One by one the candidates[457] are led forward, in such a way that the men come with their godfathers and the women with their godmothers.[458]

Then the bishop questions individually the neighbors of the one who has come up, inquiring: "Does he lead a good life? Does he obey his parents? Is he a drunkard or a liar?" And he seeks out in the man other vices which are more serious.[459] If the person proves to be guiltless in all these matters concerning which the bishop has questioned the witnesses who are present, he notes down the man's name with his own hand.[460] If, however, he is accused of anything, the bishop orders him to go out and says: "Let him amend his life, and when he has done so, let him then approach the baptismal font." He makes the same inquiry of both men and women. If, however, someone is a stranger, he cannot easily receive baptism, unless he has witnesses who know him.[461]

CHAPTER 46

Ladies, my sisters, I must describe this, lest you think that it is done without explanation.[462] It is the custom here, throughout the forty days on which there is fasting, for those who are preparing for baptism to be exorcised by the clergy[463] early in the morning, as soon as the dismissal from the morning service has been given at the Anastasis.[464] Immediately a throne is placed for the bishop in the major church, the Martyrium. All those who are to be baptized, both men and women, sit closely around the bishop, while the godmothers and godfathers stand there; and indeed all of the people who wish to listen may enter and sit down, provided they are of the faithful. A catechumen,[465] however, may not enter at the time when the bishop is teaching them the law. He does so in this way: beginning with Genesis he goes through the whole of Scripture during these forty days, expounding first its literal meaning and then explaining the spiritual meaning.[466] In the course of these days everything is taught not only about the Resurrection but concerning the body of faith. This is called catechetics.[467]

When five weeks of instruction have been completed, they then receive the Creed.[468] He explains the meaning of each of the phrases of the Creed in the same way he explained Holy Scripture, expounding first the literal and then the spiritual sense. In this fashion the Creed is taught.[469]

And thus it is that in these places all the faithful are able to follow the Scriptures when they are read in the churches, because all are taught through those forty days, that is, from the first to the third hours, for during the three hours instruction is given.[470] God knows, ladies, my sisters, that the voices of the faithful who have come to catechetics to hear instruction[471] on those things being said or explained by the bishop are louder than when the bishop sits down in church to preach about each of those matters which are explained in this fashion. The dismissal from catechetics is given at the third hour, and immediately, singing hymns, they lead the bishop to the Anastasis, and the office of the third hour takes place.[472] And thus they are taught for three hours a day for seven weeks. During the eighth week, the one which is called the Great Week, there remains no more time for them to be taught, because what has been mentioned above must be carried out.

Now when seven weeks have gone by and there remains only Holy Week, which is here called the Great Week, then the bishop comes in the morning to the major church, the Martyrium. To the rear, at the apse behind the altar, a throne is placed for the bishop, and one by one they come forth, the men with their godfathers, the women with their godmothers. And each one recites the Creed back to the bishop.[473] After the Creed has been recited back to the bishop, he delivers a homily to them all,[474] and says: "During these seven weeks you have been instructed in the whole law of the Scriptures, and you have heard about the faith. You have also heard of the resurrection of the flesh. But as for the whole explanation of the Creed, you have heard only that which you are able to know while you are still catechumens.[475] Because you are still catechumens, you are not able to know those things which belong to a still higher mystery, that of baptism. But that you may not think that anything would be done without explanation, once you have been baptized in the name of God, you will hear of them during the eight days of Easter in the Anastasis following the dismissal from church. Because you are still catechumens, the most secret of the divine mysteries cannot be told to you."[476]

CHAPTER 47

When it is Easter week, during the eight days from Easter Sunday to its octave, as soon as the dismissal has been given from the church,[477] everyone, singing hymns, goes to the Anastasis. Soon a prayer is said, the faithful are blessed, and the bishop stands up.[478] Leaning on the inner railing, which is in the grotto of the Anastasis, he explains everything which is accomplished in baptism.[479] At this hour no catechumen goes into the Anastasis; only the neophytes and the faithful who wish to hear the mysteries enter the Anastasis.[480] Indeed, the doors are closed, lest any catechumen come that way. While the bishop is discussing and explaining each point, so loud are the voices of praise that they can be heard outside the church.[481] And he explains all these mysteries[482] in such a manner that there is no one who would not be drawn to them, when he heard them thus explained.

A portion of the population in this province knows both Greek and Syriac; another segment knows only Greek; and still another, only Syriac. Even though the bishop may know Syriac, he always speaks Greek and never Syriac; and, therefore, there is always present a priest who, while the bishop speaks in Greek, translates into Syriac so that all may understand what is being explained.[483] Since whatever scriptural texts are read must be read in Greek, there is always someone present who can translate the readings into Syriac for the people, so that they will always understand. So that those here who are Latins, those consequently knowing neither Greek nor Syriac, will not be bored, everything is explained to them, for there are other brothers and sisters who are bilingual in Greek and Latin[484] and who explain everything to them in Latin. But this above all is very pleasing and very admirable here, that whatever hymns and antiphons are sung, whatever readings and prayers are recited by the bishop, they are said in such a manner as to be proper and fitting to the feast which is being observed and to the place where the service is being held.

CHAPTER 48

Also, Feast of the Dedications is the name they use[485] for the day when the Martyrium, the holy church on Golgotha, was consecrated to God. Moreover, the holy church which is at the Anastasis, at the place, that is, where the Lord rose after His Passion, was also consecrated to God on the same day.[486] The dedication of these churches is observed with the most solemn liturgy,[487] since the cross of the Lord was found on that day also.[488] This is why it was decreed that when the above-mentioned holy churches were first consecrated the consecrations would be on the same day as that on which the cross of the Lord was found, so that these events might be celebrated at the same time, on the same day and with full liturgy. It was also discovered from the Scriptures that this Feast of the Dedications would be on the day when the holy ruler Solomon stood and prayed before the altar of God in the newly completed house of God which he had built, as it is written in the books of Paralipomenon.[489]

CHAPTER 49

When this Feast of the Dedications is at hand, it is observed for a period of eight days.[490] Many days beforehand a crowd of monks and *aputactitae* begin gathering together from various provinces, not only from Mesopotamia and Syria, from Egypt and the Thebaid, where the monks are numerous, but also from all other places and provinces.[491] In fact, there is no one who would not go to Jerusalem on this day for such solemn liturgy and for such a splendid feast. Lay people, both men and women, also gather together in Jerusalem on these days from all provinces in the spirit of faith and on account of the feast day. Though fewer in number, there are still more than forty or fifty bishops in Jerusalem during these days, and with them come many of their clergy. What can I add? Everyone considers that he has fallen into great sin if he is not present on days of such solemnity, unless there be conflicting obligations, such as would keep a man from fulfilling a good intention. During the Feast of the Dedications, the decoration of all the churches is similar to that at Easter and at Epiphany,[492] and on each day they assemble for the liturgy in various holy places, just as at Easter and at Epiphany. On the first and second days, everyone goes to the major church, called the

Martyrium; then on the third day to the Eleona, the church situated on the mountain from which the Lord ascended into heaven after His Passion. Within the church there is a grotto, in which the Lord taught the apostles on the Mount of Olives. Then on the fourth day. . . .[493]

NOTES

LIST OF ABBREVIATIONS

AASS	Acta sanctorum, ed. by the Bollandists (Antwerp and Brussels 1643–)
AB	Analecta Bollandiana (Brussels 1882–)
ACW	Ancient Christian Writers (Westminster, Md. - London - New York, N.Y. - Paramus, N.J. 1946–)
ALL	Archiv für lateinische Lexikographie und Grammatik (Leipzig 1884–1908)
ALMA	Archivum latinitatis medii aevi (Bulletin Du Cange, Brussels-Paris 1924–)
Anglade	J. Anglade, *De latinitate libelli qui inscriptus est Peregrinatio ad loca sancta* (Paris 1905)
BASOR	Bulletin of the American Schools of Oriental Research (Baltimore 1919–)
Bastiaensen	A. A. R. Bastiaensen, *Observations sur le vocabulaire liturgique dans l'Itinéraire d'Egérie* (Latinitas christianorum primaeva 17, Nijmegen 1962)
Bechtel	E. A. Bechtel, *Sanctae Silviae Peregrinatio. The Text and a Study of the Latinity* (Studies in Classical Philology 4, Chicago 1902)
Blaise	A. Blaise, *Dictionnaire latin-français des auteurs chrétiens* (Strasbourg 1954)
Bludau	A. Bludau, *Die Pilgerreise der Aetheria* (Studien zur Geschichte und Kultur des Altertums 15, Paderborn 1927)
Cabrol	F. Cabrol, *Étude sur la Peregrinatio Silviae. Les églises de Jérusalem, la discipline et la liturgie au IVᵉ siècle* (Paris-Poitiers 1895)
CCL	Corpus christianorum, series latina (Turnhout-Paris 1953–)
CSEL	Corpus scriptorum ecclesiasticorum latinorum (Vienna 1866–)

DACL	Dictionnaire d'archéologie chrétienne et de la liturgie (Paris 1907–53)
DB	Dictionnaire de la Bible (Paris 1895–1912; Suppl. 1926 ff.)
DHGE	Dictionnaire d'histoire et de géographie ecclésiastique (Paris 1912–)
Dict. Spir.	Dictionnaire de spiritualité (Paris 1932 ff.)
DTC	Dictionnaire de théologie catholique (Paris 1903–50)
Du Cange	Du Cange, *Glossarium ad scriptores mediae et infimae latinitatis* (ed. L. Fabre, 10 vols., Niort 1883–88)
EL	Ephemerides liturgicae (Rome 1887–)
Erkell	H. Erkell, "Zur sog. *Peregrinatio Aetheriae*," *Eranos* 56 (1958) 41–58
Ernout	A. Ernout, "Les mots grecs dans la *Peregrinatio Aetheriae*," *Emerita* 20 (1952) 289–307
Férotin	M. Férotin, "Le véritable auteur de la *Peregrinatio Silviae*: la vierge espagnole Ethérie," *Revue des questions historiques* 74 (1903) 369–97
Franceschini-Weber	*Itinerarium Egeriae*, ed. E. Franceschini and R. Weber, in CCL 175 (1965) 27–90
Geyer	*S. Silviae, quae fertur, peregrinatio ad loca sancta*, ed. P. Geyer, in CSEL 39 (1898) 35–101
Lewis-Short	C. Lewis and C. Short, *A Latin Dictionary* (Oxford 1955)
Löfstedt	E. Löfstedt, *Philologischer Kommentar zur Peregrinatio Aetheriae* (Untersuchungen zur Geschichte der lateinischen Sprache, Uppsala 1911; 2nd ed. 1936)
LTK	Lexikon für Theologie und Kirche (2nd ed. Freiburg 1957–67)
Meister	K. Meister, "De itinerario Aetheriae abbatissae perperam nomini s. Silviae ad-

	dicto," *Rheinisches Museum für Philologie* N.S. 64 (1909) 337–92
Meistermann	P. B. Meistermann, *Guide du Nil au Jourdain par le Sinaï et Petra sur les traces d'Israël* (Paris 1909)
MG	Patrologia graeca, ed. J. P. Migne (Paris 1844–55)
ML	Patrologia latina, ed. J. P. Migne (Paris 1857–66)
NCE	New Catholic Encyclopedia (New York 1967)
ODC	*The Oxford Dictionary of the Christian Church*, ed. F. L. Cross (Oxford 1961)
Pétré *Journal*	H. Pétré, *Ethérie: Journal de voyage. Texte latin, introduction et traduction* (Sources chrétiennes 21, Paris 1948)
Quasten *Patr.*	J. Quasten, *Patrology*. 3 vols. thus far (Westminster, Md.-Utrecht-Antwerp): 1 (1950) *The Beginnings of Patristic Literature;* 2 (1953) *The Ante-Nicene Literature after Irenaeus;* 3 (1960) *The Golden Age of Greek Patristic Literature from the Council of Nicaea to the Council of Chalcedon*
RB	Revue bénédictine (Maredsous 1884–)
RBibl	Revue biblique (Paris 1892–)
RE	A. Pauly-G. Wissowa-W. Kroll, *Realencyclopädie der klassischen Altertumswissenschaft* (Stuttgart 1893–)
RPh	Revue de philologie, de littérature et d'histoire anciennes (Paris 1877)
RSR	Recherches de science religieuse (Paris 1910–)
SE	Sacris erudiri (Bruges 1948–)
Souter	A. Souter, *A Glossary of Later Latin to 600 A.D.* (Oxford 1949)
Spitzer	L. Spitzer, "The Epic Style of the Pilgrim Aetheria," *Comparative Literature* 1 (1949) 225–58

Thibaut	J. B. Thibaut, *Ordre des offices de la semaine sainte à Jérusalem du IVe au Xe siècle* (Paris 1926)
TLL	Thesaurus linguae latinae (Leipzig 1900–)
Van Oorde	W. Van Oorde, *Lexicon Aetherianum* (Amsterdam 1930)
VC	Vigiliae christianae (Amsterdam 1947–)
Wistrand	E. Wistrand, "Textkritisches zur *Peregrinatio Aetheriae*," Göteborgs Kungl. Vetenskaps och Vetterhets Samhälles Handlingar F. 6, Ser. A, Bd. 6, no. 1 (Göteborg 1955) 3–25
Ziegler *Onomastikon*	J. Ziegler, "Die *Peregrinatio Aetheriae* und das *Onomastikon* des Eusebius," *Biblica* 12 (1931) 70–84
Ziegler *Schrift*	J. Ziegler, "Die *Peregrinatio Aetheriae* und die hl. Schrift," *Biblica* 12 (1931) 162–98

BIBLIOGRAPHY

1. EDITIONS (*in order of publication*)

J. F. Gamurrini, S. *Hilarii tractatus de mysteriis et hymni et S. Silviae Aquitanae peregrinatio ad loca sancta* (Biblioteca dell' Accademia storico-giuridica 4, Rome 1887)

J. F. Gamurrini, S. *Silviae Aquitanae peregrinatio ad loca sancta*, in Studii e documenti di storia e diritto 9 (1888) 97–174

J. Pomialowsky, *Peregrinatio ad loca sancta saeculi IV* (Scripta Societatis Rossicae Palaestinensis, Petrograd 1889)

L. Duchesne, *Origines du culte chrétien* (Paris 1889; 5th ed. Paris 1925) appendix 5 (= chs. 24–49 of the text)

J. H. Bernard, *The Pilgrimage of S. Silvia of Aquitania to the Holy Places circa 385 A.D.* (Palestine Pilgrim's Text Society, London 1891)

P. Geyer, S. *Silviae, quae fertur, peregrinatio ad loca sancta*, in CSEL 39 (1898) 35–101

E. A. Bechtel, S. *Silviae Peregrinatio. The Text and a Study of the Latinity* (Studies in Classical Philology 4, Chicago 1902)

W. Heraeus, *Silviae vel potius Aetheriae peregrinatio ad loca sancta* (Sammlung vulgärlateinischer Texte 1, Heidelberg 1908; 2nd ed. 1921; 3rd ed. 1929; 4th ed. 1938)

E. Franceschini, *Aetheriae Peregrinatio ad loca sancta* (Testi e documenti di storia e di letteratura latina medioevale 2, Padua 1940)

H. Pétré, *Éthérie: Journal de voyage. Texte latin, introduction et traduction* (Sources chrétiennes 21, Paris 1948)

K. Vretska, *Die Pilgerreise der Aetheriae* (*Peregrinatio Aetheriae*), eingeleitet und erklärt von H. Pétré (Klosterneuberg 1958)

A. Hamman, *Itinerarium Egeriae* (Patrologiae latinae supplementum 1, Paris 1958)

O. Prinz, *Itinerarium Egeriae* (*Peregrinatio Aetheriae*) (Sammlung vulgärlateinischer Texte 5, Heidelberg 1960)

E. Franceschini and R. Weber, *Itinerarium Egeriae*, in CCL 175 (1965) 27–90

2. ADDITIONAL FRAGMENTS OF THE TEXT

D. de Bruyne, "Nouveaux fragments de l'*Itinerarium Eucheriae*," RB 26 (1909) 481–4

3. TRANSLATIONS

a. *English*

J. H. Bernard, *The Pilgrimage of S. Silvia of Aquitania to the Holy Places circa 385 A.D.* (Palestine Pilgrim's Text Society, London 1891)

M. L. McClure and C. L. Feltoe, *The Pilgrimage of Etheria* (Translations of Christian Literature, Series 3: Liturgical Texts, London 1919)

b. *French*

H. Pétré, *Ethérie: Journal de voyage. Texte latin, introduction et traduction* (Sources chrétiennes 21, Paris 1948)

c. *German*

H. Richter, *Pilgerreise der Aetheria* (*oder Silvia*) *von Aquitanien nach Jerusalem und den heiligen Stätten, ins Deutsche übersetzt* (Essen 1919)

H. Dausend, *Pilgerbericht der Nonne Aetheria* (Religiose Quellenschriften 85, Düsseldorf 1933)

K. Vretska, *Die Pilgerreise der Aetheriae* (*Peregrinatio Aetheriae*), eingeleitet und erklärt von H. Pétré (Klosterneuberg 1958)

d. *Greek*

K. Koikulides, 'Οδοιπορικὸν τῆς ἁγίας Σίλβιας τῆς 'Ακυτάνιας εἰς τοὺς ἁγίους τόπους, in Νέα Σίων 7 (1908) 109–21, 209–32, 533–47

e. *Italian*

G. Marinoni, *Il pellegrinagio di s. Silvia Aquitana* (Milan 1890)

f. *Spanish*

P. Galindo Romeo, *Eteria. Itinerario a los santos lugares, traducido, completado, anotado* (Saragossa 1924)

B. Avila, *Un diario de viaje del siglo IV. Egeria, la peregrina española* (Biblioteca Pax, Madrid 1935)

J. Monteverde, *Eteria, Itinerario* (Buenos Aires 1955)

4. BIBLIOGRAPHIES

C. Baraut, "Bibliografía Egeriana," *Hispania sacra* 7 (1954)
203–15
Note: Select bibliographies also accompany the various editions
and translations of the text.

5. STUDIES ON LANGUAGE AND SYNTAX

a. Books and monographs

J. Anglade, *De latinitate libelli qui inscriptus est Peregrinatio ad loca sancta* (Paris 1905)

A. A. R. Bastiaensen, *Observations sur le vocabulaire liturgique dans l'Itinéraire d'Egérie* (Latinitas christianorum primaeva 17, Nijmegen 1962)

E. A. Bechtel, *S. Silviae Peregrinatio. The Text and a Study of the Latinity* (Studies in Classical Philology 4, Chicago 1902)

P. Geyer, *Kritische Bemerkungen zu S. Silviae Aquitanae Peregrinatio ad loca sancta* (Programm des Gymnasiums Augsburg, Augsburg 1890)

R. Haida, *Die Wortstellung in der Peregrinatio ad loca sancta* (Breslau 1928)

E. Löfstedt, *Philologischer Kommentar zur Peregrinatio Aetheriae* (Untersuchungen zur Geschichte der lateinischen Sprache, Uppsala 1911; 2nd ed. 1936)

W. Van Oorde, *Lexicon Aetherianum* (Amsterdam 1930)

G. F. M. Vermeer, *Observations sur le vocabulaire de pèlerinage chez Egérie et chez Antoine de Plaisance* (Nijmegen 1965)

b. Articles

R. Ambrosini, "Il tipo sintagmatico *in eo loco* e questioni di principio nello studio della *Peregrinatio Aetheriae*," *Annali della Scuola Normale Superiore di Pisa*, Serie 2, 24 (1955) 97–109

L. B. Ellis, "The Relative Construction *Qui locus* in the *Peregrinatio ad loca sancta*," *Three Studies in Philology* (University of Oregon Monographs: Studies in Literature and Philology 1, Eugene 1961) 5–6

H. Erkell, "Zur sog. *Peregrinatio Aetheriae*," *Eranos* 56 (1958) 41–58

A. Ernout, "Les mots grecs dans la *Peregrinatio Aetheriae*," *Emerita* 20 (1952) 289-307

P. Geyer, "Zur *Peregrinatio ad loca sancta*," ALL 4 (1887) 611-15

H. W. Klein, "Zur Latinität des *Itinerarium Egeriae* (früher *Peregrinatio Aetheriae*). Stand der Forschungen und neue Erkenntnismöglichkeiten," *Romanica: Festschrift Gerhard Rohlfs* (1958) 243-58

F. Pfester, "Zum Sprachgebrauch der Silvia," *Wochenschrift für klassische Philologie* (1912) 196-8

J. G. Preaux, "*Panis qui delibari non potest*," VC 15 (1961) 105-15

O. Prinz, "Philologische Bemerkungen zu einer Neuausgabe des *Itinerarium Egeriae*," ALMA 30 (1960) 143-53

L. Spitzer, "The Epic Style of the Pilgrim Aetheria," *Comparative Literature* 1 (1949) 225-58

J. Svennung, "In *Peregrinatio Aetheriae* annotatiuncula," *Eranos* 32 (1934) 93-7

F. Thomas, "Sur une manière d'exprimer la répétition et l'antériorité en latin tardif," RPh 16 (1942) 22-30

R. Weber, "Note sur le texte de la *Peregrinatio Aetheriae*," VC 6 (1952) 178-82

R. Weber, "Note sur *Itinerarium Egeriae* XXVIII," VC 12 (1958) 93-7

E. Wistrand, "Textkritisches zur *Peregrinatio Aetheriae*," Göteborgs Kungl. Vetenskaps och Vetterhets Samhälles Handlingar F. 6, Ser. A, Bd. 6, no. 1 (Göteborg 1955) 3-25

E. Wölfflin, "Über die Latinität der *Peregrinatio ad loca sancta*," ALL 4 (1887) 259-76

6. STUDIES ON AUTHORSHIP AND DATING AND ON HISTORICAL, TOPOLOGICAL, AND LITURGICAL DATA IN THE TEXT

a. Books and monographs

F.-M. Abel and H. Leclercq, "Jérusalem," DACL 7.2304-92

D. Baldi, *La liturgia della chiesa di Gerusalemme dal IV al IX secolo* (La Terra Santa. Studio Biblico Francescano, Jerusalem 1939) 1-131

A. Baumstark, *Abendländische Palästinapilger des ersten Jahrtausends und ihre Berichte* (Cologne 1906)

A. Baumstark, *Nocturna Laus. Typen frühchristlicher Vigi-*

lienfeier und ihr Fortleben vor allem im römischen und monastischen Ritus (Liturgiegeschichtliche Quellen und Forschungen 32, Münster 1957)

A. Bludau, *Die Pilgerreise der Aetheria* (Studien zur Geschichte und Kultur des Altertums 15, Paderborn 1927)

D. Brooke, *Pilgrims Were They All. Studies in Religious Adventures in the 4th Century of Our Era* (London 1937)

F. Cabrol, *Étude sur la Peregrinatio Silviae. Les églises de Jérusalem, la discipline et la liturgie au IVᵉ siècle* (Paris-Poitiers 1895)

L. Duchesne, *Origines du culte chrétien* (Paris 1889; 5th ed. Paris 1925)

M. Férotin and H. Leclercq, "Ethérie," DACL 5.552–84

D. Gorce, "Egérie," DHGE 15.1–5

D. Gorce, *Les voyages, l'hospitalité et le port des lettres dans le monde chrétien des IVᵉ et Vᵉ siècles* (Paris 1925)

D. Gorce, "Pèlerins et résidents du Sinaï des premiers siècles de l'ère chrétienne," in *Le Sinaï hier . . . aujourd'hui. Étude topographique, biblique, historique et archéologique* (Paris 1937) 127–82

J. A. Jungmann, *Pastoral Liturgy* (New York 1962)

B. Kötting, *Peregrinatio religiosa. Wallfahrten in der Antike und das Pilgerwesen in der alten Kirche* (Forschungen zur Volkskunde 33–5, Münster 1950)

H. Leclercq, "Pèlerinages aux lieux saints," DACL 14.65–176, esp. 92–110

J. Mateos, *Lelya-Sapra. Essai d'interprétation des matines chaldéennes* (Orientalia christiana analecta 156, Rome 1959)

P. B. Meistermann, *Guide du Nil au Jourdain par le Sinaï et Petra sur les traces d'Israël* (Paris 1909)

A. Pagliaro, "Da *Missa est* a *Missa Messa*," *Rendiconti della classe di scienze morali, storiche et filologiche dell'Accademia Nazionale dei Lincei*, Ser. 8, 10 (1955) 104–35

H. Pétré, "Ethérie," Dict. Spir. 4.1448–53

H. Pétré, *Ethérie: Journal de voyage. Texte latin, introduction et traduction* (Sources chrétiennes 21, Paris 1948) 7–95

J. B. Thibaut, *Ordre des offices de la semaine sainte à Jérusalem du IVᵉ au Xᵉ siècle* (Paris 1926)

A. Vaccari, "Egeria," *Encyclopedia cattolica* 5.133–6

F. Wotke, "*Peregrinatio ad loca sancta*," RE Suppl. 7.875–85

R. Zerfass, *Die Schriftlesung im Kathedraloffizium Jerusalems* (Liturgiegeschichtliche Quellen und Forschungen 48, Münster 1968)

b. Articles

F.-M. Abel, "L'exploration du sud-est de la vallée du Jourdain," RBibl 40 (1931) 214–26, 374–400

A. Baumstark, "Das Alter der *Peregrinatio Aetheriae*," *Oriens christianus* N.S. 1 (1911) 32–76

A. Bludau, "Der Katechumenat in Jerusalem im 4. Jahrhundert," *Theologie und Glaube* 16 (1924) 225–42

C. Bourdon, "La route de l'Exode, de la terre de Gesse à Mara," RBibl 41 (1932) 370–92, 538–49

C. A. Bouman, "Een pelgrimage in het jaar 400. De Heilige Week in Jeruzalem," *De Nieuwe Mens* 1 (1949) 10 ff.

E. Bouvy, "Le Pèlerinage d'Eucheria," *Revue augustinienne* 1 (1903) 514–22, and "Eucheria et Silvia," *Revue augustinienne* 2 (1904) 80–83

F. Cavallera, "Notes et critiques: *Galla non gente sed nomine*," *Bulletin de littérature ecclésiastique* 38 (1937) 186–90, and "Egeria," *Bulletin de littérature ecclésiastique* 39 (1938) 93–4

A. Coppo, "Una nuova ipotesi sull'origine di *Missa*," EL 71 (1957) 225–67

J. Crehan, "The Assumption and the Jerusalem Liturgy," *Theological Studies* 30 (1969) 312–25

J. G. Davies, "The *Peregrinatio Egeriae* and the Ascension," VC 8 (1954) 93–100

J. Deconinck, "Karl Meister: *De Itinerario Aetheriae abbatissae perperam nomini s. Silviae addicto*," RBibl N.S. 7 (1910) 432–45

E. Dekkers, "De datum der *Peregrinatio Egeriae* en het feest van Ons Heer Hemelvaart," SE 1 (1948) 181–205

P. Devos, "La date du voyage d'Egérie," AB 85 (1967) 165–94 and 86 (1968) 87–108

P. Devos, "Egérie à Edesse. S. Thomas l'Apôtre. Le Roi Abgar," AB 85 (1967) 381–400

E. Dhorme, "Le pays de Job," RBibl N.S. 8 (1911) 102–7

F. J. Dölger, "Zu den Zeremonien der Messliturgie: *Ite, missa est* in kultur- und sprachgeschichtlicher Beleuchtung," *Antike und Christentum* 6 (1940) 81–132

M. Férotin, "Le véritable auteur de la *Peregrinatio Silviae*: la vierge espagnole Ethérie," *Revue des questions historiques* 74 (1903) 367–97

Z. García-Villada, "La lettre de Valerius aux moines de Vierzo sur la bienheureuse Aetheria," AB 29 (1910) 377–99

Z. García-Villada, "Egeria ou Aetheria?" AB 30 (1911) 444–7

Z. García-Villada, "La virgin Eteria y su peregrinacion a Tierra Santa," *Hist. eccl. de España* 1.2 (1929) 268–96

P. Geyer, "Die wirkliche Verfasserin der *Peregrinatio Silviae*," ALL 15 (1908) 233–52

W. Heraeus, "Zur sogenannten *Peregrinatio Aetheriae*," ALL 15 (1908) 549–59

C. Iarecki, "*Silvaniae itinerarium* appelé *Peregrinatio ad loca sancta*," *Eos. Commentarii societatis philol. polonorum* 31 (1928) 453–73, 32 (1929) 43–70, 33 (1930) 241–88

C. Kohler, "Note sur un manuscript de la Bibliothèque d'Arezzo," *Bibl. de l'école des Chartres* 45 (1884) 141–51

G. Kretschmar, "Himmelfahrt und Pfingsten," *Zeitschrift für Kirchengeschichte* 66 (1954–55) 209 ff.

A. Lambert, "Egeria. Notes critiques sur la tradition de son nom et celle de l'*Itinerarium*," *Revue Mabillon* 26 (1936) 71–94

A. Lambert, "Egeria, soeur de Galla," *Revue Mabillon* 27 (1937) 1–42

A. Lambert, "L'*Itinerarium Egeriae* vers 414–416," *Revue Mabillon* 28 (1938) 49–69

C. Lambot, "Un *ieiunium quinquagesimae* en Afrique au IV* siècle et date de quelques sermons de s. Augustin," RB 47 (1935) 114–24

M. Le Cour Grandmaison and B. Billet, "Le pèlerinage au fumier de Job et la date de la *Peregrinatio Aetheriae*," RSR 48 (1960) 460–5

A. Mader, "Peregrinatio (Aetheriae) ad loca sancta," LTK 8.80

K. Meister, "De itinerario Aetheriae abbatissae perperam nomini s. Silviae addicto," *Rheinisches Museum für Philologie* N.S. 64 (1909) 337–92

U. Monneret de Villard, "La fiera di Batnae e la translazione di s. Tomaso a Edessa," *Rendiconti della classe di scienzi morali, storiche e filologiche dell'Accademia Nazionale dei Lincei,* Ser. 8, 6 (1951) 77–104

C. Mohrmann, "Missa," VC 12 (1958) 67–92

C. Mohrmann, review of H. Pétré's *Ethérie: Journal de voyage. Texte latin, introduction et traduction,* VC 4 (1950) 119–23

G. Morin, "Un passage énigmatique de s. Jérôme contre la pèlerine espagnole Eucheria?" RB 30 (1913) 174–86

J. F. Mountford, "Silvia, Aetheria or Egeria?" *Classical Quarterly* 17, (1923) 40–41

L. Saint-Aignon, "Le pèlerinage de s. Silvia aux lieux saints en 385," Académie de Sainte-Croix d'Orléans Lettres et mémoires 6 (1891) 213–33

A. Servin, "La tradition judéo-chrétienne da l'Exode," *Bulletin de l'Institut d'Egypte* 31 (1948–49) 315–55

J. B. Thibaut, "Solennité du dimanche des palmes," *Echos d'Orient* 24 (1921) 68–78, 155–67

A. Vaccari, "Itinerarium Egeriae," *Biblica* 24 (1943) 388–97

E. Wiegand, "Zur Datierung der Peregrinatio Aetheriae," *Byzantinische Zeitschrift* 20 (1911) 1–26

A. Wilmart, "L'Itinerarium Eucheriae," RB 25 (1908) 458–67

A. Wilmart, "Egeria," RB 28 (1911) 68–75

A. Wilmart, "Encore Egeria," RB 29 (1912) 91–6

H. Windisch, "Die ältesten christlichen Palästinapilger," *Zeitschrift des deutschen Palestinavereins* 48 (1925) 145–57

J. Ziegler, "Die *Peregrinatio Aetheriae* und das *Onomastikon* des Eusebius," and "Die *Peregrinatio Aetheriae* und die hl. Schrift," *Biblica* 12 (1931) 70–84 and 162–98

INTRODUCTION

[1] Cf. G. F. Gamurrini, "I misteri e gl' imni di s. Ilario vescovo di Poitiers ed una peregrinazione ai luoghi santi nel quarto secolo," *Studii e documenti di storia e diritto* 5 (1884) 81 ff., and "Della inedita peregrinazione ai luoghi santi," *Studii e documenti di storia e diritto* 6 (1885) 145 ff.

[2] Cabrol 169 ff. gives a brief history of the manuscript. It was mentioned in a catalogue of Monte Cassino in 1532, but not in a subsequent inventory of 1650; it may have been brought to Arezzo by Ambrogio Rostrellini, abbot of Monte Cassino who in 1610 became abbot of the convent of Sts. Flora and Lucille, where the manuscript was known to be in 1788. When that latter convent was suppressed by Napoleon in 1810, some of its manuscripts were given to the Pia Fraternità dei Laici. The Fraternità is popularly referred to as the Brotherhood of St. Mary. In 1891, Gamurrini, himself a native of Arezzo, became director of the Fraternità's museum and library.

[3] Cf. Dom de Bruyne, "Nouveaux fragments de l'*Itinerarium Eucheriae*," RB 26 (1909) 481–4. The Benedictine scholar had found eleven short excerpts from the *Diary*, most of them variants of the *Codex Aretinus*, in a 9th-century manuscript from Toledo in the Biblioteca Nacional at Madrid.

[4] Cf. J. F. Gamurrini, *S. Hilarii tractatus de mysteriis et hymni et s. Silviae Aquitanae peregrinatio ad loca sancta. Accedit Petri Diaconi liber de locis sanctis* (Biblioteca dell' Accademia storico-giuridica 4, Rome 1887).

[5] Cf. Palladius, *Hist. Laus.* 55.1 (= ACW 34.136).

[6] Bludau 191–5 reviews the evidence for Silvia as author. Cf. also Bludau's studies on the identity of Silvia in *Der Katholik* 30 (1904) 61–74, 81–98, and 167–89. Cabrol 177 cites a study on Silvia by L. Couture, in *Revue d'Aquitaine* 1 (1856). F. L. Cross in ODC 1256 still described Silvia as either the sister or sister-in-law of Rufinus.

[7] C. Butler, *The Lausiac History of Palladius* (Texts and

143

Studies: Contributions to Biblical Patristic Literature 6, 2 vols., Cambridge 1898–1904) 2.229 f.

[8] Cf. C. Iarecki, "Silvaniae itinerarium appelé Peregrinatio ad loca sancta," Eos. Commentarii societatis philol. polonorum 31 (1928) 453–73, 32 (1929) 43–70, and 33 (1930) 241–88.

[9] Cf. C. Kohler, "Note sur un manuscript de la Bibliothèque d'Arezzo," Bibliothèque de l'École des Chartres 45 (1884) 141–51.

[10] Cf. H. Goussen, Liturgie und Kunst 4 (1923) 1 ff.

[11] Cf. Férotin 367–97.

[12] For the biography, personality, and works of Valerius, cf. Férotin 371 ff. and Bludau 197–201. On the ecclesiastical history of Bierzo, cf. the article of A. Lambert in DHGE 8.1440–5. Bierzo is located in the province of Leon, diocese of Astorga, at the foot of the Cantabrian mountains.

[13] The Valerius letter says that the sanctimonialis Aetheria was extremo occidui maris Oceani litore exorta. The text of the letter is reproduced by Z. García-Villada, "La lettre de Valerius aux moines de Vierzo sur la bienheureuse Aetheria," AB 29 (1910) 393–6. First published by Florez in España sagrada 16 (Madrid 1762) 366 ff., and later by Migne in ML 87.421–6, the letter appears in French translation in Pétré Journal 268–74.

[14] On the word sanctimonialis here, cf. Bastiaensen 23.

[15] Cf. Férotin 378.

[16] The original Toledo manuscript is no longer extant, but a copy of it is preserved in Madrid. Florez based his edition on this copy. The two 18th-century editions were those of Manuel de la Huerta (1736) and Cifuentes (1793).

[17] Cf. Férotin 378 f. This is, of course, an oversimplification. In the Toledo version the name appears once as Heteria, and there is considerable doubt as to the correct original reading of the Carracedo manuscript, which is now lost.

[18] Cf. Férotin 378 f.: "On rencontre en Espagne le nom Etheria sous sa forme masculine; c'est celui que portait au 8ᵉ siècle un évêque d'Osma, saint Etherius, l'ami de Béatus de Liebana et l'adversaire d'Elipand de Tolède. La liturgie wisigothique faisait grand usage de l'épithète etherea."

[19] Cf. Bludau 191–214, where the evidence in favor of the title Peregrinatio Aetheriae is summarized. See the Bibliography on pp. 135–142 above for the imposing list of critics and editors who, after 1903, adopted this title.

[20] Cf. Férotin 397.

[21] Cf. E. Bouvy, "Le pèlerinage d'Eucheria," *Revue augustinienne* 1 (1903) 514–22, and "Eucheria et Silvia," *Revue augustinienne* 2 (1904) 80–3.

[22] Cf. E. Bouvy, "Le pèlerinage d'Eucheria," *Revue augustinienne* 1 (1903) 522.

[23] Cf. A. Wilmart, "L'Itinerarium Eucheriae," RB 25 (1908) 458–67.

[24] Cf. A. Wilmart, "Egeria." RB 28 (1911) 68–75, and "Encore Egeria," RB 29 (1912) 91–6.

[25] Cf. esp. the first article cited in the preceding note for the outline of the argument.

[26] The first to reject Wilmart's arguments was Z. García-Villada; cf. his "Egeria ou Aetheria?" AB 30 (1911) 444–7. The second article of Wilmart cited in n. 24 above is essentially a reply to García-Villada's arguments.

[27] Cf. J. F. Mountford, "Silvia, Aetheria, or Egeria?" *Classical Quarterly* 17 (1923) 40 f.

[28] The text speaks about the garden of St. John. It is first given in transliterated Greek, then in Latin. For the context of the quotation, see ch. 15 of the *Diary*.

[29] J. F. Mountford, *art. cit.* 41.

[30] Cf. A. Lambert, "Egeria. Notes critiques sur la tradition de son nom et celle de l'*Itinerarium*," *Revue Mabillon* 26 (1936) 71–94.

[31] *Ibid.* 91 ff. In evidence, Lambert cites numerous parallel phonological changes in Spanish.

[32] F. Cavallera, "Le *De fide* de Bachiarius, Egeria, le symbole de Toletum 1," *Bulletin de littérature ecclésiastique* 39 (1938) 88–97, esp. 93 f.

[33] A. Vaccari, "Itinerarium Egeriae," *Biblica* 24 (1943) 388–97.

[34] H. Pétré, *Ethérie: Journal de voyage. Texte latin, introduction et traduction* (Sources chrétiennes 21, Paris 1948).

[35] E. Franceschini and R. Weber, *Itinerarium Egeriae* (CCL 175.37–90).

[35] O. Prinz, *Itinerarium Egeriae (Peregrinatio Aetheriae)* (Sammlung vulgärlateinischer Texte 5, Heildelberg 1960).

[37] This is the translation of the title given by O. B. Hardison, Jr., *Christian Rite and Christian Drama in the Middle Ages* (Baltimore 1965) 112.

[38] Our choice was in part influenced by the title of Pétré's

edition and translation and by that of B. Avila, *Un diario de viaje del siglo IV. Egeria, la peregrina española* (Madrid 1935). It is interesting to note that a year before Lambert's influential study the Spanish translator had adopted the form Egeria.

[39] Valerius refers to her as "the blessed nun Egeria," who is now "in the midst of the choir of holy virgins." The first reference to her as abbess is in the catalogue of Limoges. The other, in the 1532 catalogue of Monte Cassino, is less certain.

[40] Meister 341.

[41] Cf. A. Lambert, *art. cit.* 82 ff.

[42] Cf. D. Brooke, *Pilgrims Were They All* (London 1938) 104: ". . . written to friends or relatives whom she left behind at home, and whom she calls, in the manner of her day, ladies, reverend sisters, light of my eyes, your affection, and by other flattering titles."

[43] On travel in antiquity, cf. D. Gorce, *Les voyages, l'hospitalité et le port des lettres dans le monde chrétien des IVe et Ve siècles* (Paris 1925) esp. 3–124.

[44] Cf. Férotin 396.

[45] Cf. G. Morin, "Un passage énigmatique de s. Jérôme contre la pèlerine espagnole Eucheria?" RB 30 (1913) 174–86. The passage in question, to be found in Jerome's *Ep.* 54.13, reads: *Vidimus nuper ignominiosum per totum Orientem volitasse; et aetas et cultus et habitus et incessus, indiscreta societas, exquisitae epulae, regius apparatus Neronis et Sardanapalli nuptias loquebantur.*

In a long note on this passage, J. Labourt, *Saint Jérôme: Lettres* 3 (1953) 237–9, added some interesting speculation regarding names: "Quant à son nom de Silvania (Silvia?), ne pouvait-elle le conjoindre avec un autre? Nous en connaissons plusieurs cas: par example, celui de la fille de sainte Paule, qui s'appelait Julia Eustochium; pourquoi n'y aurait-il pas eu une Eucheria (Aetheria) Silvania (Silvia)?"

[46] Cf. A. Lambert, "Egeria, soeur de Galla," *Revue Mabillon* 27 (1937) 1–42.

[47] Jerome, *Ep.* 133.4. Lambert mentions that both Le Nain de Tillemont and P. Alès had dealt with the passage. The latter identified the heresy as Arianism and understood the passage to mean that Priscillian had been joined by a woman of Gaul named Euchrotia who had a sister named Galla, whom he identified with the second wife of the emperor Theodosius the Great.

[48] An identical argument was sketched by F. Cavallera, "Notes et critiques: *Galla non gente sed nomine*," *Bulletin de littérature ecclésiastique* 38 (1937) 186–90.

[49] Cf. A. Lambert, "Egeria, soeur de Galla," *Revue Mabillon* 27 (1937) 41 f.

[50] Cf. Meister 363–8, the section titled "De Aetheriae patria."

[51] Cf. Meister 367 f. The passage considered to be based on the lost pages of the *Diary* is found in Peter the Deacon's *Liber de locis sanctis*, the text of which may be conveniently found either in Geyer's edition in CSEL 39.105–21 or in the Franceschini-Weber edition in CCL 175.93–103.

[52] Cf. Meister 368.

[53] Férotin 390 f. n. 1 listed certain hispanisms. J. Anglade studied the question throughout his *De latinitate libelli qui inscriptus est Peregrinatio ad loca sancta* (Paris 1905). Cf. also García-Villada, "La lettre de Valerius aux moines de Vierzo sur la bienheureuse Aetheria," AB 29 (1910) 386–92, and, for a review of the whole question, Bludau 237–43.

[54] Cf. Löfstedt 6 ff.

[55] Cf. n. 13 above.

[56] Two such authors may be cited: Idatius, who states of Galicia: *extrema universi orbis Gallaecia*, and Isidore of Seville, who use language similar to that of Valerius: *in ista ultimae extremitatis occiduae partis*.

[57] Bludau 215–32 discusses the "personality" of the pilgrim as it emerges from the *Diary*.

[58] J. G. Davies, "The *Peregrinatio Egeriae* and the Ascension," VC 8 (1954) 93–100.

[59] Cf. J. Deconinck, "Karl Meister, *De Itinerario Aetheriae abbatissae perperam nomine s. Silviae addicto*," RBibl N.S. 7 (1910) 432–45, esp. 432. This article is an extensive review of Meister's study, and Deconinck concentrated exclusively on the question of timing.

[60] Bludau 245 summarizes their conclusions: Gamurrini, 381–385; Geyer, 378–388; Heisenberg, 383; Usener, the early 380s. For a new defense of a date late in the 4th century, see P. Devos, "La date du voyage d'Egérie," AB 85 (1967) 165–94. Cf. also below, n. 216 to the text.

[61] Cf. Meister 341–63, the section titled "*De aetate Aetheriae.*"

[62] It should be noted that Meister had been preceded in his views by R. Duval, *Journal asiatique* 18 (1891) 244 ff.; Chabet,

De s. Isaaci Ninivitae vita (Louvain 1892); and C. Clermont-Ganneau, *Recueil d'archéologie orientale* 6 (1905) 128 ff.
[63] Cf. J. Deconinck, *art. cit.*; A. Baumstark, "Das Alter der *Peregrinatio Aetheriae*," *Oriens christianus* N.S. 1 (1911) 32–76; and E. Wiegand, "Zur Datierung der *Peregrinatio Aetheriae*," *Byzantinische Zeitschrift* 20 (1911) 1–26. Cf. Bludau 245–86 for a summary of the arguments generally alleged against Meister's dating. Bludau himself preferred a date around 394.
[64] Cf. n. 45 above.
[65] Cf. J. Ziegler's conclusion to his study "Die *Peregrinatio Aetheriae* und das *Onomastikon* des Eusebius," *Biblica* 12 (1931) 70–84.
[66] This information is contained in the Chronicle of Edessa, which refers to the transfer as having taken place on the "27th Ab of the year 705 of the Seleucid era." Critics favoring an earlier date argued that Egeria visited the relics in a separate shrine, not in the basilica. Cf. below, n. 204 to the text.
[67] For the legend of the correspondence, cf. Quasten *Patr.* 1.140–3; on the date of Rufinus' translation of Eusebius, cf. Quasten *Patr.* 3.315.
[68] Cf. the conclusions of J. Ziegler to his study "Die *Peregrinatio Aetheriae* und die hl. Schrift," *Biblica* 12 (1931) 162–98.
[69] Cf. A. Lambert, "L'*Itinerarium Egeriae* vers 414–416," *Revue Mabillon* 28 (1938) 49–69.
[70] Cf. E. Dekkers, "De datum de *Peregrinatio Egeriae* in het feest van Ons Heer hemelvaart," SE 1 (1948) 181–205.
[71] Cf. E. Dekkers, *art. cit.* 205.
[72] For Davies' objections, cf. the article in n. 58 above. F. L. Cross, *St. Cyril of Jerusalem's Lectures on the Christian Sacraments* (Oxford 1951) xviii n. 1, emphasized that Dekkers was basing his evidence for the dedication of the church at Bethlehem on a late Georgian calendar, not the earlier *Rituale armenorum*.
[73] Basil of Seleucia, *De vita ac miraculis s. Theclae virginis martyris iconiensis* (MG 85.477–618).
[74] This view is reflected by Pétré *Journal* 16.
[75] Pages are missing from chs. 16 and 25 of the text as we have it today.
[76] While this is the commonly held view, Lambert believed

that Valerius was the first editor of the text and that he was acquainted with a text approximately the same as that we have today.

[77] Regarding the text of the Valerius letter, cf. n. 13 above.

[78] Cf. Bludau 7.

[79] Cf. n. 51 above.

[80] For the description of Clysma in Peter the Deacon's work, cf. CCL 175.100 ff.

[81] Cf. CCL 175.102 and Num. 33.8; also Exod. 15.

[82] Cf. CCL 175.102 and Num. 33.9; also Exod. 16.

[83] Cf. CCL 175.102 f. and Num. 33.14; also Exod. 16 ff.

[84] An excellent critical summary of the contents of the text is given in Pétré *Journal* 26–88. Summaries will also be found in H. Leclercq, "Pèlerinages aux lieux saints," DACL 14.92–110; Férotin-Leclercq, "Ethérie," DACL 5.552–84; F. Wotke, "Peregrinatio ad loca sancta," RE Suppl. 7.875–85.

[85] On the vogue of pilgrimages in the 4th century, cf. H. Leclercq, "Pèlerinages aux lieux saints," DACL 14.65–176, and C. Kopp, "Pèlerinages aux lieux saints," DB Suppl. fss. 38.589–605.

[86] On this point, cf. H. Pétré, "Ethérie," Dict. Spir. 4.1448–53.

[87] Egeria's desire to visit with the monks is evidenced by her going out of her way to meet with them. Cf. chs. 7, 21, and 23 of the *Diary*.

[88] The text of the *Itinerarium Burdigalense* is given in CCL 175.1–26.

[89] Cf. ch. 16: *ego, ut sum satis curiosa.*

[90] She frequently uses the phrase *valde pulcher* to describe such diverse places as the region around the Sinai peninsula, the valley of the Jordan, the various churches she visited.

[91] Cf. p. 13 of this Introduction and the articles by Ziegler cited in nn. 65 and 68 above.

[92] On the various sites proposed for the location of Mount Sinai, cf. L. Vincent, "Un nouveau Sinaï biblique," RBibl 39 (1930) 73–83.

[93] On the early Christian history of the Sinai penisula, cf. R. Devreesse, "Le christianisme dans la péninsule sinaïtique, des origines à l'arrivée des musulmans," RBibl 49 (1940) 205–23.

[94] Cf. esp. ch. 6 of the *Diary*.

[95] Cf. Num. 33.1.

[96] Cf. E. Naville, *The Store-City of Pithom and the Route of*

the Exodus (London 1885) and *The Shrine of Saft el-Henneh* (London 1888).

[97] Cf. C. Bourdon, "La route de l'Exode, de la terre de Gesse à Mara," RBibl 41 (1932) 370–92 and 538–49; A. Servin, "La tradition judéo-chrétienne de l'Exode," *Bulletin de l'Institut d'Egypte* 31 (1948–49) 315–55.

[98] The reference to Peter the Iberian is taken from F.-M. Abel, "L'exploration du sud-est de la vallée du Jourdain," RBibl 40 (1931) 214–26, 375–400.

[99] Cf. E. Power, "The Site of the Pentapolis," *Biblica* 11 (1930) 23–62, 149–82.

[100] Cf. ch. 13 of the *Diary* and nn. 170 and 172 thereto.

[101] Cf. John 3.23.

[102] Cf. ch. 16 of the *Diary*. Cf. also R. Aigrain, "Arabie," DHGE 3.1159–78.

[103] Each of the three bishops, of Batanis, Edessa, and Carrhae, is called *monachus et confessor*. Cf. below, n. 202 to the text.

[104] On the *Acts of St. Paul and St. Thecla*, cf. Quasten *Patr.* 1.130–3.

[105] Cf. the Bibliography on pp. 135–142 above. The principal liturgical commentaries are those of F. Cabrol, *Étude sur la Peregrinatio Silviae. Les églises de Jérusalem, la discipline et la liturgie au IV*ᵉ *siècle* (Paris-Poitiers 1895); A. Bludau, *Die Pilgerreise der Aetheria* (Studien zur Geschichte und Kultur des Altertums 15, Paderborn 1927); and J. B. Thibaut, *Ordre des offices de la semaine sainte à Jérusalem du IV*ᵉ *au X*ᵉ *siècle* (Paris 1926). This last is a comparative study of the evolution of the Jerusalem liturgy for Holy Week based on the *Itinerarium Egeriae* and three later documents: an Armenian Lectionary, dated 460/4, modeled on the Jerusalem Ordo and published by F. C. Conybeare, *Rituale armenorum* (Oxford 1905) 516–27; the Georgian Canonarion of the Jerusalem liturgy, dated *ca.* 631/8, published by C. Kekelidze *Jerusalimskij Kanonar VII veka* (Tiflis 1912); and the Typicon of Jerusalem for Holy Week, dating from the 9th or 10th century, published by A. Papadopoulous-Kerameus in 1894.

[106] Cf. Cabrol ch. 1 and Pétré *Journal* 57–64.

[107] Cf. Cabrol 33 f.

[108] Our summary on the churches of Jerusalem is drawn from Cabrol, Pétré, and F.-M. Abel and H. Leclercq, "Jérusalem,"

DACL 7.2304–92. See also the monumental work of H. Vincent and F.-M. Abel, *Jérusalem. Recherches de topographie, d'archéologie et d'histoire* (2 vols., Paris 1912–26).

[109] Ch. 42.

[110] Cf. ch. 29 of the *Diary*.

[111] For a description of the Anastasis, cf. Vincent-Abel, *op. cit.* 2.181–5. St. Jerome remarks (*Ep.* 58.3) that for about 180 years between the reigns of Hadrian and Constantine, a figure of Jupiter occupied the site of the Resurrection and a statue of Venus was on the place of the Crucifixion. A floor plan of Constantine's Basilica of the Holy Sepulchre is given in Vincent-Abel, *op. cit.* 2.155; Abel-Leclercq, *art cit.*; E. Lussier, "Holy Sepulchre," NCE 13.99.

[112] Cf. ch. 37 of the *Diary* for a description of this courtyard. Generally, the meaning of the term Ante Crucem and all references to it in the *Diary* are clear. Two unusual references may be noted, however. In ch. 24, in describing a vigil preceding the opening of the doors of the Anastasis, Egeria speaks of the faithful gathering in the forecourt of the Anastasis (*in basilica, quae est loco juxta Anastasim*), by which we understand her to be referring to a section of the Ante Crucem (cf. below, n. 285 to the text). In ch. 39 the term *ante Cruce* appears in an ambiguous context. In a listing of stational churches for the celebration of the liturgy during the Easter octave, Egeria refers to a service *sabbato ante Cruce*. The standard phrase to designate a liturgical service at the Cross is *ad Crucem*, while the phrase *ante Crucem* is employed either to refer to the whole area of the courtyard or to contrast the area in front of the Cross with the area and/or structures behind the Cross (cf. below, n. 114). In ch. 25, for example, in her list of stational churches during the Epiphany octave, Egeria refers to a service *octava die ad Crucem*. Also, in several places she says the conclusion of daily vespers and of the Sunday vigil was held *ad Crucem*. It is unlikely that she intended to differentiate the site of a celebration of the liturgy *ad Crucem*, such as that during the Epiphany octave, from the site of the service *ante Cruce* on the Saturday of Easter week. The phrase *ante Cruce* in ch. 39 probably can be attributed to a lapse on the author's part, or possibly to her use of the phrase as a vague synonym for *ad Crucem*.

[113] Egeria uses the phrase *ad Crucem* once as a substantive; cf. ch. 25: *Constantinus . . . honoravit auro, musivo et marmore*

pretioso, tam ecclesiam maiorem quam Anastasim vel ad Crucem vel cetera loca sancta in Ierusolima. As is clear from the context, she distinguishes the three major churches of the Holy Sepulchre. In the same chapter she specifically ranks the Ad Crucem among the churches of Jerusalem and vicinity when she describes how elaborately decorated they were for the Epiphany: *ornatus . . . ecclesiae vel Anastasis aut Crucis aut in Bethleem.* For further details on the Ad Crucem, cf. Vincent-Abel, *op. cit.* 2.185–9.

[114] Cf. chs. 35 and 37 of the *Diary* for the use of *post Crucem* to designate the chapel directly behind the Cross. Cf. also nn. 368, 381, and 387 to the text. However, the author frequently employs the expression *post Crucem* in referring to the Martyrium, for that structure was also situated behind the Cross; cf., e.g., ch. 30: *Propterea autem Martyrium appellatur, quia in Golgotha est, id est post Crucem, ubi Dominus passus est, et ideo Martyrio.* Occasionally, however, Egeria cryptically states that a ceremony took place *post Crucem,* such as one part of the rites of dismissal from vespers; cf., e.g., ch. 24: *Et post hoc denuo tam episcopus quam omnis turba vadent denuo post Crucem et ibi denuo similiter fit sicuti et ante Crucem. Et similiter ad manum episcopus acceditur sicut ad Anastasim, ita et ante Crucem, ita et post Crucem.* In such cases it is impossible to tell precisely what *post Crucem* means, whether the reference is to the small chapel of the *post Crucem,* the *Martyrium* itself, or to a general area behind the Cross.

[115] Cf. Vincent-Abel, *op. cit.* 2.189–94.

[116] *Quintana pars* is variously translated by "exonarthex," meaning a porch opening on to a street, or by "market." Bludau 165 states that the expression used by Egeria confirms the statement of Eusebius that the *propylaeum* or colonnade of the Martyrium was in the middle of the market street. Cf. also below, n. 445 to the text.

[117] Cf. Vincent-Abel, *op. cit.* 2.441–81.

[118] The name Imbomon (or Inbomon), which Egeria glosses with "the place from which the Lord ascended to heaven," refers to the church commemorating the Ascension which was built by a Roman matron named Poemenia before 378. Commentators (F. L. Cross, ODC 982; Bludau 122 f.; Abel-Leclercq, *art. cit;* etc.) have for the most part adopted the hypothesis that the name Imbomon derives from ἐν βωμῷ, "on the altar." Vincent-Abel, *op. cit.* 2.384, have suggested other possible

etymologies. The name may have at its root either of two Greek verbs, ἐμβαίνειν or ἀναβαίνειν (both here understood in the sense of "to enter heaven"). However, Vincent-Abel consider that the name is more likely the result of hellenization of the semitic word *bâmah*, which signifies a summit, a high place, or an altar. They suggest, therefore, that Imbomon probably means "l'église du monticule, *in monticulo*, ou l'église du haut sommet."

¹¹⁹ For a detailed study of the Eleona, with many plates and floor plans, cf. H. Vincent, "L'église de l'Eléona," RBibl 8 (1911) 219–65. Cf. also Vincent-Abel, *op. cit.* 2.337–60, 374–92. In referring to this church Egeria uses the indeclinable form *Eleona* and invariably in a construction with the preposition *in*. At times by *Eleona* she clearly means the church itself (cf., e.g., ch. 25: *in Eleona, id est in ecclesia quae est in monte Oliveti*); more frequently she appears to be designating the Mount of Olives, on which the church stood (cf. ch. 30: *in ecclesia . . . , quae est in Eleona, id est in monte Oliveti*). In a few places (e.g., in ch. 33) she refers to the church located *in monte Eleona*.

¹²⁰ A phrase or sentence such as *antiphonae, hymni, lectiones, orationes, psalmi Hierosolymis semper dicuntur apti diei et loco* will recur throughout the text.

¹²¹ Cf., e.g., ch. 24, where the Psalms, prayers, and readings for the daily services are left unspecified.

¹²² Cf. ch. 24.

¹²³ Cf. chs. 24 f.

¹²⁴ Cf. ch. 43.

¹²⁵ Cf. Bastiaensen 94.

¹²⁶ The *Didache* 8 (= ACW 6.19) calls for prayer three times a day. Tertullian, *De oratione* 25 (CSEL 20.197) speaks of the third, sixth, and ninth hours as hours of prayer, and in his *De ieiunio* 10 (CSEL 20.287) he calls them the Apostolic Hours, because certain events in Scripture were associated with them: the descent of the Holy Spirit, Peter's prayer, and the entry of the two Apostles into the temple were set at the third, sixth, and ninth hours.

¹²⁷ Cf. *Apostolic Constitutions* 8.

¹²⁸ There are several passages in Jerome designating these hours of prayer. The passage quoted here is from his *Ep.* 108.20 (CSEL 55.335). Cf. also his *Ep.* 107.9 (CSEL 55.300).

¹²⁹ Cf. Cassian, *De institutis coenobiorum* 3.

¹³⁰ That is, *de pullo primo vigiletur, ad pullorum cantu,* and *ad vigilias.*

¹³¹ Cf. J. A. Jungmann, *Pastoral Liturgy* (New York 1961) 123.

¹³² That is, *ad lucem, ad mane, ubi coeperi luscere.*

¹³³ On the origin of these terms, cf. F. Massai, "Les noms des heures et les textes de Cassien intéressant l'histoire de prime," ALMA 19 (1945) 23–37.

¹³⁴ On the origins of matins or the night office, cf. Jungmann, *op. cit.* 105–22; J. M. Hanssens, *Nature et genèse de l'office des matines* (Rome 1952); P. Salmon, "Aux origines du Bréviaire Romain," *La Maison Dieu* 27 (1951) 114–36; and A. Baumstark, *Nocturna Laus. Typen frühchristlicher Vigilienfeier und ihr Fortleben vor allem im römischen und monastischen Ritus* (Liturgiegeschichtliche Quellen und Forschungen 32, Münster 1957).

¹³⁵ On vespers, cf. Cross, "Vespers," ODC 1414, and Dom G. M. (Morin?), "Vêpres," DACL 15.2939–49. Bludau 55–8 mentions that there is evidence of an *officium vespertinum* in the third century, and he cites the *Apostolic Constitutions* 8.34 and 13.31. Vespers was originally called *lucernarium* (λυχνικόν) because candles were lit at its celebration. In structure vespers consists of five Psalms, their antiphons, a lesson, a hymn, the Magnificat, and the *preces feriales.*

¹³⁶ Cf. L. Duchesne, *Origines du culte chrétien* (Paris 1903) 229 and 435; Cabrol 51.

¹³⁷ Cf. J. Mateos, *Lelya-Sapra. Essai d'interprétation des matines chaldéennes* (Orientalia christiana analecta 156, Rome 1959) 429 f.

¹³⁸ On the reading of the *Resurrectio Domini* on Sundays, cf. A. Baumstark, *Liturgie comparée* (3rd ed., rev. by B. Botte, Chevetogne 1952) 44 ff.

¹³⁹ Cf. Cabrol 53 and 58; Bludau 60 ff.; Hanssens, *op. cit.* 72.

¹⁴⁰ Cf. Mateos, *op. cit.* 430 f., in particular the analytical table there presented contrasting Egeria's description of the structure of the service with the Chaldean *Qale d-sahra.*

¹⁴¹ Cf. Cabrol 54; Bludau 62; Mateos, *op. cit.* 431.

¹⁴² Cf. H. Leclercq, "Bréviaire," DACL 2.1268.

¹⁴³ Cf. Bludau 65 f.

¹⁴⁴ Cf. ch. 25 of the *Diary.*

¹⁴⁵ Cf. ch. 43 of the *Diary.*

¹⁴⁶ Cf. Wistrand 13–21 and also below, n. 298 to the text.

[147] Cf. ch. 38 of the *Diary*.

[148] Cf. Wistrand 8 ff. and also below, n. 302 to the text. For the celebration of the Eucharist on Wednesdays and Fridays outside of Lent, cf. below, n. 329 to the text.

[149] For a discussion of this concept of Sunday, cf. J. Gaillard, "Dimanche," Dict. Spir. 3.948–82.

[150] Cf. Ambrose, *Ep.* 23.13: *triduum illud sacrum . . . intra quod et passus est et quievit et resurrexit.*

[151] In this presentation I have drawn heavily on Jungmann, *op. cit.* 387–407.

[152] Cf. Baumstark, *Liturgie comparée* 173. Cf. also Jungmann, *op. cit.* 396: "The great liturgies of the East, like the Roman liturgy, follow the line we have described, preferring to dwell on the full depth of the redemptive significance of the events celebrated. . . ."

[153] Jungmann, *op. cit.* 396. Cf. also Baumstark, *Liturgie comparée* 173: "C'est en Palestine qu'elles se sont liées de plus en plus intimement avec l'histoire néotestamentaire, parce que, vers la fin du IV⁰ siècle, le souvenir de la vie terrestre de Jésus y était encore très vivant."

[154] Hardison, *op. cit.* 86.

[155] Hardison, *op. cit.* 87.

[156] For a discussion of the history and interpretation of the feast of the Epiphany, cf. Bludau 68–89; Baumstark, *Liturgie comparée* 168–81; E. Norden, *Die Geburt des Kindes. Geschichte einer religiösen Idee* (Leipzig-Berlin 1924); B. Botte, *Les origines de Noël et de l'Epiphanie* (Louvain 1932).

[157] Cf. ch. 25 of the *Diary*. The celebration of an all-night vigil service is mentioned also in ch. 9.

[158] Cf. Baumstark, *Liturgie comparée* 170–3.

[159] For the identify of these stational churches, cf. above, pp. 24 ff.

[160] Cf. ch. 26. On the origins and early history of the feast of the Presentation, cf. Baumstark, *Liturgie comparée* 166 f.; Bludau 89–93.

[161] Cf. ch. 27. On the nature of the Lenten fast in 5th-century Jerusalem and for the order of services during the Lenten season, cf. also ch. 28 and nn. 321–340.

[162] Cf. Chrysostom, *Expositio 2 in ps.* 145 (MG 55.520). The Holy Week liturgy is amply commented by Bludau 119–48 and by Thibaut. According to Cabrol 83–7, the commemoration of

the resurrection of Lazarus occupied an important position in the ancient church, and in the Byzantine rite churches the Saturday of Passion Week is still called Lazarus Saturday. In the Latin church the Gospel account of Lazarus' resurrection (John 11.1–45) is read on the Friday of the fourth week in Lent. In the Coptic church Lazarus Saturday is observed in the seventh week of Lent, and a Syriac *codex evangeliorum* refers to this Saturday before Palm Sunday as *sabbato resuscitationis Lazari*, while Rabulas' Syriac compilation of Gospel texts prescribes John 11.55–7 and 12.1–4 as readings *in matutinis septimanae suscitationis Lazari*. A Sunday *de Lazaro* is mentioned in the Mozarabic and Gallican liturgies, but in the Ambrosian *Ordo* the Saturday of the fourth week of Lent is called Lazarus Saturday. On the festive nature of Lazarus Saturday in the Byzantine rite churches, cf. Baumstark, *Liturgie comparée* 217 f.

[163] Cf. ch. 29: *Propterea autem ea die hoc agitur, quoniam sicut in evangelio scriptum est, ante sex dies paschae factum hoc fuisset in Bethania.* . . .

[164] Cf. John 11 and 12.1–11.

[165] Cf. John 11.20–32.

[166] The proclamation of the Pasch marked the inauguration of the Holy Week ritual. By the 6th century the ceremony at Bethany had been transferred to Sunday (cf. Theodosius in CCL 175.123).

[167] On the extension of the Palm Sunday procession to other churches, cf. Bludau 119 ff. and Baumstark, *Liturgie comparée* 163–6. In the early 6th century this procession had been introduced into the Nestorian church of Persia and into Edessa; it was known in the Spain of Isidore of Seville, and by the 8th century was observed in various parts of Western Europe (cf. Aldhelm, *De laudibus virginitatis* [ML 89.122 f.]). The role of the Palm Sunday procession in 9th-century Carolingian liturgy is well known through the writings of such liturgists as Amalarius of Metz (cf. his *Liber officialis* [ML 105.1008]), and legend states that Theodolphus of Orleans' hymn, *Gloria, laus et honor*, was sung on Palm Sunday in Angers. There is no evidence, however, for the Palm Sunday procession in the Roman *ordines* before the accession of the German emperors. For a general treatment of Palm Sunday, cf. Leclercq, "Dimanche des rameaux," DACL 15.1154 ff.

[168] Ch. 31. Baumstark, *loc. cit.*, states that in Egypt Christ was represented by a cross borne through the countryside.

[169] The reading probably consisted of Matt. 21.1–9 (perhaps 21.1–16). The verse that constitutes the refrain sung by the people is given in Matt. 21.9.

[170] Cf. Leclercq, "Dimanche des rameaux," DACL 15.1154 ff.

[171] These services are described in chs. 32 ff. of the *Diary*.

[172] The scriptural justification for such a tradition is in Matt. 26.1 f.: *And it came to pass, when Jesus had ended all these words, He said to His disciples: You know that after two days shall be the Pasch; and the Son of Man shall be delivered up to be crucified.* On the tradition that the Eleona was built over the grotto where Christ preached His eschatological discourse, cf. Thibaut 28 ff. and also below, n. 364 to the text.

[173] For Judas' betrayal, cf. Matt. 26.14 ff.; Mark 14.10 f.; Luke 22.3–6. In the liturgy of the 9th century, Wednesday in Holy Week had much of the character of Good Friday; cf. Amalarius of Metz, *Liber officialis* (ML 105.1027), who explains the similarity by the fact that on Wednesday Christ's death was plotted and on Friday was carried out.

[174] Cf. ch. 34 of the *Diary*. At several points Egeria refers to the loud wailing of the people; cf., e.g., ch. 24: *tantus rugitus et mugitus fit omnium hominum et tantae lacrimae. . . .* Cf. also chs. 36 and 37.

[175] Cf. Thibaut 42 f. and also below, n. 369 to the text.

[176] Cf. Thibaut 47–50.

[177] For the tradition that Christ and His disciples assembled at the grotto of the church of the Eleona on Holy Thursday, cf. Thibaut 31.

[178] Cf. n. 174 above.

[179] A summary of the Holy Thursday night offices according to the Georgian Canonarion will be found in Thibaut 63–72.

[180] On the extension to other churches of the *adoratio crucis* rite, which had its origin in the Jerusalem liturgy, cf. Bludau 139 ff. and Baumstark, *Liturgie comparée* 157–60. The ceremony is no longer observed in the Byzantine rite churches, and by the middle of the 7th century it had already been discontinued in Jerusalem, according to the Georgian Canonarion. Its greatest development occurred in the West, at Rome and in the Carolingian empire. For the ritual of the *adoratio crucis*, cf. L.

A. Molien, *La prière de l'église* (Paris 1924) 392–8; H. Leclercq, "Vendredi saint," DACL 15.1167–75.

[181] A list of scriptural readings for the three-hour service according to the Armenian Lectionary is given in Thibaut 93–7.

[182] Cf. ch. 37: *et ibi cum ventum fuerit, legitur ille locus de evangelio ubi petit corpus Domini Joseph a Pilato, ponet illud in sepulchro novo.* It should be noted that there was no Mass of the Pre-Sanctified celebrated in Jerusalem either according to Egeria's *Diary* or according to the nearly contemporary Armenian Lectionary. The Georgian Canonarion indicates that there was such a rite in the 7th century; cf. Thibaut 105.

[183] Unfortunately, the *Diary* gives us very little detail on this vigil service, and that terse account must be supplemented by other sources. Cf. Bludau 145–50; Thibaut 114–20; J. Quasten, "Die Ostervigil in *Testamentum Domini*," in *Paschatis sollemnia. Studien zur Osterfeier und Osterfrömmigkeit* (Freiburg 1959) 87–96; P. T. Weller, *The Easter Sermons of St. Augustine* (Catholic University of America Studies in Sacred Theology, 2nd ser., 87, Washington 1955); Leclercq, "Samedi saint," DACL 15.1175–85.

[184] For the details of the preparation for baptism, cf. chs. 45 ff. of the *Diary* and the notes to those chapters.

[185] Augustine, *De fide et op.* 6.9, says candidates *catechizantur, exorcizantur,* and *scrutantur.* On instruction for baptism, cf. in this series ACW 31 (1963), *St. John Chrysostom: Baptismal Instructions,* tr. and annot. by P. W. Harkins.

[186] Bludau 178 indicates that the day for this ceremony varied considerably. In North Africa it may have occurred either on the Saturday before Laetare Sunday or on the Saturday before Passion Sunday. Weller, *op. cit.* 37, suggests the latter day. He conjectures that the catechumens were doubtless already familiar with the substance of the faith, but that the formula probably was given to them for the first time on this occasion. The ceremony probably consisted of two parts, the so-called *apertio aurium* and then the actual oral transmission of the Creed. On the history of the Creed, cf. J. N. D. Kelly, *Early Christian Creeds* (London 1950); F. J. Badcock, *The History of the Creeds* (London 1930); H. J. Carpenter, "Creeds and Baptismal Rites in the First Four Centuries," *Journal of Theological Studies* 43 (1942) 1–11; Quasten *Patr.* 1.23–9, where additional literature is cited.

[187] The day of the *redditio symboli* varied between localities. In North Africa, for example, according to Weller, *op. cit.* 37 f., the *redditio symboli* took place either on the eve of Palm Sunday or on Palm Sunday itself, and on the day of the *redditio symboli* occurred also the *traditio orationis dominicae*, the formal transmission of the Lord's Prayer to the prospective candidates for baptism. On this occasion sermons were delivered to impress the catechumens with the importance of the Lord's Prayer, the significance of its verses, and the honor of the candidate to be able shortly to address God as Father. We have no precise information on the time of the *traditio orationis dominicae* in Jerusalem.

[188] According to the Gelasian Sacramentary (ML 74.1105 f.), the last scrutiny was held on Holy Saturday morning, and at that time there was a formal *redditio* of the Creed and the Lord's Prayer.

[189] Cf. Thibaut 115 f.

[190] For the list of scriptural readings, cf. Thibaut 117 ff.

[191] Cf. the comments and discussion of J. Quasten in *Monumenta eucharistica et liturgica vetustissima* 2 (Bonn 1935) 72–79. Cf. also R. Zerfass, *Die Schriftlesung im Kathedraloffizium Jerusalems* (Liturgiegeschichtliche Quellen und Forschungen, Heft 48, Münster 1968).

[192] Cf. Quasten, "Die Ostervigil im *Testamentum Domini*" 94 f., and Weller, *op. cit.* 60–73. Several of Augustine's Easter sermons refer to the reception of the Eucharist; cf., e.g., his *Sermo* 227 (ML 38.1099): *Promiseram enim vobis, qui baptizati estis, sermonem quo exponerem mensae dominicae sacramentum, quod modo etiam videtis, et cuius nocte praeterita participes facti estis. . . . Panis ille quem videtis in altari, sanctificatus per verbum Dei, corpus est Christi. Calix ille, imo quod habet calix, sanctificatum per verbum Dei, sanguis est Christi.*

[193] This instruction forms the substance of the *Catecheses mystagogicae* attributed to Cyril of Jerusalem.

[194] Cf. John 20.19–29.

[195] The *Diary* refers to the feast only as the fortieth day after Easter: *die autem quadragesimarum post pascha.* On Egeria's terminology for the Ascension, cf. Bastiaensen 132–51 and below, n. 422 to the text. For Egeria's account of the feast and its celebration, see her ch. 42.

[196] Cf. ch. 42 of the *Diary: in qua ecclesia spelunca est ubi natus est Dominus.*

[197] Cf. Cabrol 121 ff.

[198] Cf. Bludau 154–62 and the article of Davies cited in n. 58 above. Davies emphasizes that the Fathers generally speak about the Ascension in terms of the Incarnation, for the Ascension "consummates the work of redemption" begun with the Incarnation, and signifies the "taking into heaven of the humanity which the Son had assumed at the moment of the Incarnation." Celebration of the Ascension in Bethlehem would have been in accord with this. Cf. further below, n. 423 to the text.

[199] Cf. the article of E. Dekkers cited above in n. 70. It should be emphasized that Dekkers' explanation rests upon the coincidence of an annual feast with a special dedication ceremony. Egeria, however, describes the event in the present tense, a fact which strengthens the view that the observance of the feast in Bethlehem was a regular occurrence, not an isolated instance.

[200] Cf. ch. 43 of the *Diary* and the notes thereto for an interpretation of various stages of the Pentecost ritual.

[201] Cf. Baumstark, *Liturgie comparée* 176 f.

[202] For the feast of the Dedication of the Basilica of the Holy Sepulchre, cf. chs. 48 f. of the *Diary* and the notes thereto.

[203] Cf. Bechtel 154–7 and Meister 368–71. Both authors treat of Egeria's use of Scripture and biblical language.

[204] Cf. the articles cited in nn. 65 and 68 above.

[205] Cf. the Bibliography on pp. 135–142 above.

[206] Cf. Bechtel 133–6.

[207] Cf. his *Observations sur le vocabulaire liturgique dans l'Itinéraire d'Egérie* (Latinitas christianorum primaeva 17, Nijmegen 1962).

[208] On the use of Greek in the text, cf. Ernout 289–307.

[209] In *Comparative Literature* 1 (1949) 225–58.

[210] Spitzer 226.

[211] Cf. Spitzer 239.

[212] Cf. Spitzer 249 ff.

[213] These texts may all be found in CSEL 39 or CCL 175.

TEXT

[1] *ostendebantur iuxta scripturas.* On the lost pages of the *Diary,* and in particular on the probable contents of the missing

initial pages, see above, Intro. pp. 15 ff. According to Peter the Deacon's account of the stages of the journey from Clysma to Sinai, Egeria, at the point where our copy of her text begins, would have just left a place which her guides mistakenly identified as the biblical Haseroth (cf. Num. 11.34; also n. 5 below). Peter the Deacon (CCL 175.103) tells us that the traveller would have seen three elevated stone thrones reserved for Moses, Aaron, and Jethro, and the cell where Mary, sister of Moses, lived in isolation after being stricken with leprosy. In fact, the incident of Mary and her leprosy, narrated in Num. 12.10–15, occurred far from the environs of Mount Sinai, but the locale had been transposed by the guides.

² The approach to the valley is through the Nagb Hawa, the "Pass of the Wind." C. W. Wilson (see his "Appendix: The Topography of the Pilgrimage of S. Silvia," in J. H. Bernard, *The Pilgrimage of S. Silvia of Aquitania to the Holy Places circa 385 A.D.* [Palestine Pilgrim's Text Society, London 1891] 137) describes it as "a fine pass through the wall of granite cliffs that, in the eyes of the Bedawín, seem to guard the inner recesses of the 'Mountains of Our Lord Moses.' It is from 200 to 300 yards wide, and on either side granite peaks and precipices tower to a height of 2000 feet above the path."

³ Egeria describes the valley, the Wadi er Rahah, or "Plain of Rest," as *infinitam, ingens, planissima et valde pulchram*. Bechtel 140 suggests that *infinitus* and *ingens* are used by Egeria as synonyms for *magnus* and that the original superlative force of the words was lost in late Latin—"in consequence of the weakening of *grandis, infinitus* and *ingens, magnus* is almost driven out." Löfstedt 35 interprets *ingens* here not as an adjective but as a neuter particle intensifying *planissima*. I have given each of Egeria's words here the force that seems warranted to reflect fully her impression of the valley. At other places in the first five chapters of her *Diary* Egeria emphasizes the vastness of the valley.—Unless otherwise indicated, all quotations in these Notes from the Latin text of the *Diary* are taken from the edition of E. Franceschini and R. Weber in CCL 175. The Arezzo manuscript shows frequent departures from classical Latin in syntax and orthography, and in general the Franceschini-Weber edition reproduces these departures.

⁴ Wilson, *op. cit.* 138, states that a visitor would have his first glimpse of the cliffs of the Sinai mountain range some four miles

from the entrance to the valley. However, as he goes on to state, "the spot at which she really stopped to pray was two miles further on, at the highest point of the pass, where the traveller is face to face with the *Ras Sufsafeh*, less than two miles distant, and obtains a full view of the entire plain of Er Rahah." For the reaction of another traveller to the first view of Mount Sinai, cf. M. J. Lagrange, "De Suez à Jérusalem par le Sinaï," RBibl 5 (1896) 641: "Puis les montagnes s'ouvrent, bornant une longue plaine jusqu'au pied d'un triple sommet qui termine l'horizon, c'est lui, ce Sinaï!. . . Je constate, on en conclura ce qu'on voudra, qu'à ce moment les doutes s'évanouissent, une terreur religieuse s'abat sur les sens à l'aspect de cette montagne triple et une. Cette plaine, isolée dans le chaos des montagnes, paraît disposée comme un rendez-vous avec Dieu sur les hauteurs."—The Sinai mountain range runs from southeast to northwest and is about two miles long and a mile wide. It consists of two great mountains, the Ras Safsafeh, a triple-peaked mass at the northwestern end, which has a height of around 6,700 feet above sea level, and the Djebel Musa, at the southeastern end, which rises to a height of around 7,500 feet above sea level. On the identification of the Djebel Musa with the biblical Sinai, cf. M. J. Lagrange, "Le Sinaï biblique," RBibl 8 (1899) 362–92. Cf. also L. Vincent, "Un nouveau Sinaï biblique," RBibl 39 (1930) 73–83; A. Legendre, "Sinaï," DB 5.1751–83; D. Nielson, "The Site of the Biblical Mount Sinai," *Journal of the Palestine Oriental Society* 7 (1927) 187–208; H. Haag, "Sinai," LTK 9.782 f.

5 On the Graves of Lust, cf. Num. 11.34. Situating the Graves of Lust here is another example of the transposition of locales to the neighborhood of Sinai mentioned in n. 1 above. Meistermann 184–7 states that Haseroth, where the Hebrews camped after the events narrated in Num. 11.34, was far to the northeast of Mount Sinai and in the opposite direction from which Egeria's party was coming. The Graves of Lust lay along the route to Haseroth, perhaps in the vicinity of *Eroueis Ebeirig*. Guides such as those which escorted Egeria were able, however, to point out to pilgrims before their arrival at Sinai large stone structures called *nawamis*, which may have served as bedouin tombs and which were identified with the Graves of Lust (cf. Meistermann 95 ff.; also A. Legendre, "Sépulchres de concupiscence," DB 5.1665 f., where a photograph of *nawamis* may be seen). Peter the Deacon states that the whole valley was full of tomb-like

structures: *Ab Aseroth autem usque ad montem sanctum Syna inter montes ad dexteram et sinistram totum per vallem ipsam monumentis plenum est* (CCL 175.103).—Egeria's term for "Graves of Lust" is *Memoriae concupiscentiae*, which is a more literal translation of the LXX than is the *sepulchra concupiscentiae* of the Vulgate. On Egeria's use of the *Vetus Latina*, cf. Ziegler *Schrift* 162–98.

⁶ "the holy men who were guiding us" = *deductores sancti illi, qui nobiscum erant*. *Sanctus*, "holy," is employed frequently by Egeria (Ernout 305 finds 186 examples), particularly as an epithet applied to figures of the Old and New Testament. Meister 389 f. counted sixty examples of usage such as *sanctus Abraam, sanctus Melchisedech, sanctus Thomas, sancta Thecla*. Löfstedt 110 found *sanctus* used by Egeria 20 times in references to bishops and 19 times in references to monks. It is very probable that by *deductores sancti illi* Egeria means that the guides were monks, for, as Bechtel 136 asserts, "*illi sancti* is almost a synonym for *monachi*." Bastiaensen 24 f. remarks that when Egeria uses *sanctus* as a substantive in reference to the living, she restricts this usage to references to monks and priests. The word *sanctus* is further used in such phrases as *sancta ecclesia, loca sancta, scriptura sancta*. On the use of *sanctus* in the early Church, cf. H. Delahaye, "Le mot *Sanctus* dans la langue chrétienne," AB 28 (1909) 161–86, and the same author's "De martyrologii romani origine fontibus fide historica" in *Propylaeum ad Acta Sanctorum Decembris* (Brussels 1940) xvii: *in libris antiquis homines sive moribus sive etiam dignitate venerandi sancti appellantur, qui proprie sancti non sunt*. In attempting to demonstrate that Egeria reflects Priscillian tenets, Dom Lambert, "Egérie, soeur de Galla" 30, cites her devotion to the figures of the Old Testament and particularly her calling of them "saints." In translating the *Diary* I have consistently rendered *sanctus*, when applied to an Old Testament figure, by "the holy man," reserving the epithet "saint" for those expressly so designated in the Church.

⁷ The Latin text here shows particularly loose sentence construction: *In eo ergo loco cum venitur, ut tamen commonuerunt deductores sancti illi, qui nobiscum erant, dicentes: "Consuetudo est, ut fiat hic oratio ab his qui veniunt, quando de eo loco primitus videtur mons Dei": sicut et nos fecimus*. On the anacoluthon, which is characteristic of Egeria's free style, cf. Löfstedt 43 and Bechtel 151 ff.

[8] These are, of course, Roman miles. The Roman mile measured about 5,000 feet.

CHAPTER 2

[9] *iacens subter latus montis Dei.* Wilson, *op. cit.* 138, remarks that "to the north of the *Ras Sufsafeh* and sloping uniformly down to its very base, lies the plain, or Wady er Rahah." My translation here has been influenced by Wilson's description. The valley measures about 400 acres.

[10] This description exaggerates the size of the valley. Measured from the base of the Ras Safsafeh, the Wadi er Rahah proper is about two and a half miles long, and it is a little over half a mile wide at its widest point. From subsequent remarks (cf. n. 14 below) it is clear that Egeria considered the Wadi ed Deir, running along the eastern slope of the mountain, to be an extension of the valley. Along the western slope of Mount Sinai is the ravine known as the Wadi el Leja. Running parallel to this valley but already within the mountain mass is the Wadi Schreich. For a convenient sketch of the route, cf. Wilson, *op. cit.* 41; for a map of the area, cf. Meistermann 112 f.

[11] *montem ingredi.* I have followed Bechtel 140 and Van Oorde 107 in interpreting *ingredi* in this passage as synonymous with *ascendere.*

[12] This reference to Moses' sojourn on Mount Sinai is a paraphrase of Exod. 24.18. As Ziegler *Onomastikon* 70–84 indicates, Egeria's scriptural quotations or references almost always differ from the language of the Vulgate. These Notes will cite only those variations from the Vulgate which are in themselves significant or which affect the translation of the text.

[13] On the building of the golden calf, cf. Exod. 32. Meistermann 114 mentions a hill called the Djebel Haroun, the Mount of Aaron, at the eastern end of the valley and to the left of the Ras Safsafeh, with a Moslem chapel where once a year the bedouins offer sacrifice to Aaron. According to tradition, Aaron built the golden calf on this site.

[14] Cf. Exod. 3.1 f. For the expression *caput vallis,* "head of the valley," Van Oorde 35 gives *extrema pars vallis,* "far end of the valley," which would mean the opposite end from which Egeria entered. M. J. Lagrange, "Chronique II: Le Sinaï," RBibl 6 (1897) 125, translates the phrase by "le dessus de la vallée." The

phrase appears seven times in the first five chapters of the *Diary* and usually designates specifically the site of the Burning Bush, which tradition places not in the Wadi er Rahah itself, but at the end of the Wadi ed Deir, or Valley of the Cloister, which probably took its name from the fortress-like monastery of St. Catherine founded by Justinian. According to Meistermann 115, the bedouins called the valley Wadi Choaïb (the Koran's name for Jethro).

[15] The Latin text here has frequently been emended. The manuscript reads: *montem Dei ascenderemus, qui hinc paret, unde veniebamus melior ascensus erat.* Most editors have followed Geyer, who inserted a *quia* between *paret* and *unde.* Erkell 54 ff., developing a suggestion of Cholodniak, changed *qui hinc paret* to *quia hac parte* (the word *pars* here would be equal to *latus,* a meaning it has elsewhere in the text). I have translated the passage as emended by Erkell.

[16] Pharan is both the name of a desert region of the north-central Sinai peninsula and the name of a city located in the Wadi Feiran, about 31 miles from Mount Sinai. Egeria refers to the desert and the city in chs. 5 and 6. Here she obviously means the city of Pharan, which became an episcopal see around 400 A.D. and attracted numerous monks and anchorites. It has been identified with the biblical Raphidim (cf. A. Molini, "Raphidim," DB 5.980–86; also Peter the Deacon in CCL 175.103). It may seem surprising that Egeria confines herself here to a mere mentioning of the city's name, but it is supposed that she wrote more extensively of it earlier in the missing pages of the *Diary.* In support of this view we might cite the first of the fragments discovered by Dom de Bruyne, *op. cit.* 481: *Tanta inter se cum cordia vibunt sicut veri monachi, nihil similantes amalacites, nam sic exacrant nomina amalacitarum, ut pro iuramentum dicant: sic non corpus meun iaceat inter amalcites.* The sojourn of the Israelites at Raphidim (cf. Exod. 17.8–16) is associated with the battle against Amalec, and it may be conjectured that Egeria learned of the monks' oath while at Pharan. Two 6th-century travel memoirs—the *De situ terrae sanctae* of Theodosius (CCL 175.123) and the *Itinerarium* of Anthony of Piacenza (CCL 175.149 f.)—confirm the tradition.

[17] *et sic plecaremus nos ad montem Dei.* For *plicare* Van Oorde 151 gives *appropinquare,* a meaning I have adopted in preference to the "to turn" given in Bechtel 141. From this description of

the approach to the mountain, it is not too clear from what side she intended to make the climb. Wilson, *op. cit.* 139 ff., indicates that she went down the Wadi el Leja on the west side of the mountain.

[18] *per giro*, a vulgar Latin adverbial phrase meaning "around." This phrase (or the variants *per girum* and *in giro*) appears 17 times in the text. Ernout 293 sees it as a biblicism introduced by the translators of the *Itala*. Cf. also Souter 167 and TLL 6.2385–8.

[19] *ubi descendit maiestas Dei*. This clause, in the same or nearly same wording, appears three more times in this and the following chapter. Cf. Exod. 19.18 (*descendisset Dominus super eum* [i.e., *montem Sinai*]), 20 (*Descenditque Dominus super montem Sinai*), and Exod. 24.16 (*habitavit gloria Domini super Sinai*). As Ziegler *Schrift* 168 notes, the *Vetus Latina* used a variety of words to translate δόξα–*gloria, maiestas, claritas, honos*.

[20] *et de contra illum vides*. For the meaning here I have followed Erkell 41 f., who suggests that the late Latin adverbial phrase *de contra* and the cognate form *e contra* are used by Egeria for *procul*, "far," "at a distance." Anglade 77 sees these phrases as biblicisms, as does Erkell 46–9; they are translations of the LXX ἀπέναντι or ἐξ ἀπέναντι, and they usually mean "facing," "opposite." Cf. Souter 89 and 116. The precise meaning of *de contra* and *e contra* will decisively influence the meaning of the text in several passages. Wilson, *op. cit.* 139, commenting on Bernard's translation ("you see it from the other side"), says that our writer "is also correct in stating that the peak of J. Musa cannot be seen by anyone ascending, as she did, from the west, until he comes to its very foot, and that it is visible from *Wady ed Deir* on the east side."

[21] By *fratribus*, which Bechtel 134 translates as "brethren," Egeria most probably means the monks who were guiding her, as Van Oorde 84 indicates. In three places Egeria explicitly glosses *frater (fratres)* with *monachus (monachi)*; cf. chs. 10 (*fratribus aliquantis, id est monachis*), 15 (*multi fratres sancti monachi*), and 16 (*fratris nunc, id est monachi*). In ch. 47 (cf. n. 484 below), *fratres* would appear to have the more general meaning of "brothers in Christ," "brothers in the faith"; for this sense of *fratres*, cf. H. Pétré, *Caritas: Étude sur le vocabulaire latin de la charité chrétienne* (Specilegium sacrum lovaniense. Études et documents 22, Louvain 1948) 104–40, and C. Mohrmann, "La

langue de saint Benoît" in *Études sur le latin des chrétiens. II. Latin chrétien et médiéval* (Rome 1961) 325–45.

[22] For the first and last days of the week Egeria uses the Christian terms *dies dominica* and *sabbatum*. For clarity I have rendered these as "Sunday" and "Saturday," not with the more literal "Lord's day" and "Sabbath."

[23] *ad monasteria quaedam*. Bechtel 131 translates *monasterium* as "monastery," but Van Oorde 131 gives *cellula*. Bastiaensen 19 n. 4 cites J. Van Den Bosch, *Cappa Basilica Monasterium et le culte de saint Martin de Tours* (Nijmegen 1959) 108, who prefers the meaning of monk's cell or group of cells, thus giving the word its basic meaning, a hermit's quarters where a solitary monk (*monachus*) would live. Egeria never uses *laura*, the technical term to describe an anchorite's dwelling in Palestine in the 5th century. Bludau 263 refers to Nilus' *Narrationes* in equating the *monasteria* to the καλύβαι, the huts in which, according to Nilus, the solitaries of Sinai dwelt.

[24] *susceperunt nos ibi satis humane monachi, qui ibi commorabantur, prebentes nobis omnem humanitatem*. Egeria uses *humane* and *humanitas* to render the notion of hospitality. The terms had become specialized among Christians to describe those acts of charity relating to the reception of pilgrims, a practice recommended by the Councils and the Fathers. Cf. Augustine, *Sermo* 355.2: *vide necesse habere episcopum exhibere humanitatem assiduam quibusque venientibus sive transeuntibus: quod si non fecisset episcopus, inhumanus diceretur;* also John Chrysostom, *In Acta Apostolorum hom.* 4.5, where the Christian's home is compared to an inn of Christ. According to D. Gorce, *Les voyages, l'hospitalité et le port des lettres dans le monde chrétien des IV* et V* siècles* (Paris 1925) 137–89, who describes in detail the practices of Christian hospitality in late antiquity, Egeria was lodged in a *xenodochium*, a hospice maintained by bishops, laymen, and especially monks for the reception of pilgrims, the poor, and the sick. The full ritual of hospitality consisted of the sending of a delegation to meet the pilgrim, an examination of his credentials (the *litterae communicatoriae* or *formatae* attesting to his orthodoxy), the kiss of peace, the washing and anointing of feet, the offer of refreshments, especially fruit, the provision for

material needs, and an invitation to participate in the prayers and liturgy of the community. Some of these practices will be noted in the various receptions given Egeria on her journeys.
[25] Bludau 10 f. suggests that this church was probably located on the site of the later Monastery of the Forty, in honor of the monks massacred by Saracens in the 4th century (cf. Ammonius, *Relatio de sanctis patribus barbarorum incursione in monte Sina et Raithu peremptis*, in Combefis, *Illustrium Christi martyrum lecti triumphi* [Paris 1660] 88–192). If that is correct, the church would have been midway down the Wadi el Leya. Another possibility cited by Bludau is the location of the present-day cloister of *el-Bustan*, at the foot of the Ras Safsafeh and at the entrance of a narrow valley running parallel to the Wadi el Leya, the Wadi Schreich.

[26] "in a spiral path" = *in coclea*. The original manuscript reading is *in cocleas*, but the change to *in coclea* was proposed by Löfstedt 85 and adopted by Franceschini-Weber. Löfstedt accepted Bernard's interpretation of "by a spiral path" and rejected Wölfflin's suggestion of "slow as a snail." *Coclea* (*cochlea*) has as its primary meaning "snail," but also the figurative meaning of "spiral," an extension first attested in Celsus 8. Cf. also 3 Kings 6.8 in the Vulgate: *per cochleam* (Douay: "by winding stairs") *ascendebant in medium cenaculum.* . . . Cf. also Lewis-Short 357.

[27] *iubente Christo Deo nostro* (literally, "Christ our God commanding"). Ziegler *Schrift* 163 cites this phrase as an example of the religiously impregnated speech patterns present in the text, one which has become a stylized formula. This and similar phrases I have most frequently translated with such wordings as "by the will of God," "God willing." This phrase is one of those cited by Dom Lambert, "Egeria, soeur de Galla" 30, as a possible echo of Priscillian tendencies.

[28] *in sella ascendi*, with the *sella* here to be interpreted as "saddle," not "litter." Cf. Van Oorde 184 (where *sella* is glossed with *ephippium*) and Bechtel 142. It is clear that Egeria means that it was impossible to climb Sinai riding on an animal, i.e., most likely, a donkey (cf. ch. 11: *sedendo in asellis*). Cf. also Souter 371.

[29] This is another striking example of anacoluthon (cf. n. 7 above). This sentence and the two preceding ones are a single sentence in the Latin text: *Hac sic ergo iubente Christo Deo*

nostro, adiuta orationibus sanctorum, qui comitabantur, et sic cum grandi labore, quia pedibus me ascendere necesse erat, quia prorsus nec in sella ascendi poterat, tamen ipse labor non sentiebatur—ex ea parte autem non sentiebatur labor, quia desiderium, quod habebam, iubente Deo videbam compleri:—hora ergo quarta pervenimus in summitatem illam montis Dei sancti Syna, ubi data est lex in eo, id est locum, ubi descendit maiestas Domini in ea die, qua mons fumigabat.

[30] Cf. Exod. 19.18, 20. Cf. also above, n. 19.

[31] This is the second church Egeria visited at Sinai. According to Theodoret, *Hist. eccl.* 2 (MG 82.1315), Julian Sabas from Osroene was credited with having been the founder of the church. According to Meistermann 149–52, it had three aisles and a polygonal apse and was considerably larger than the modest chapel visited by Anthony of Piacenza (cf. CCL 175.148: *inde ascendimus milia continuo tria in summum cacumen montis, In quo est oratorium modicum, plus minus pedes sex in latitudine et in longitudine*). For a floor plan, cf. Lagrange, "Chronique II. Le Sinaï" 119.

[32] *ascitis.* Egeria uses this term six times to describe certain monks. Bastiaensen 19 f. cites her reference to the monks around Charrae (Haran) in Mesopotamia (ch. 20: "the great monks who dwell in the desert and are called ascetics") as a clue to the type of monk she considered to be an ascetic. Du Cange 1.148 describes the *ascetae: monachi qui virtutem, continentiam, ac vitam angelicam excelunt. Non tam monachi, praesertim in primis Christianismi saeculis, quam quivis Christiani strictioris vitae, ac sacris pietatis officiis vocantes, quique in iis sedulo se exercebant, ut olim athletae in arena, quos et ASKETAS Attici vocabant.* J. M. Besse, *Les moines d'Orient antérieures au Concile de Chalcédoine (451)* (Paris 1900) 21 ff., speaks of the ascetics as the veterans of the monastic movement, those who during the first three centuries of Christianity practiced to a high degree the evangelical counsels of renunciation. They lived lives of celibacy, abstinence, and penance, and generally they wore a special garment. Frequently the clergy was selected from among them, Origen being the best-known example of this. Löfstedt 95 cites the essentially phonological spelling used by Egeria as evidence that she may never have seen the word for ascetic in writing but only heard it in the East.

[33] Cf. Exod. 33.22.

[34] The Latin text here reads: *facta oblatione ordine suo*. *Facere oblationem* is the technical liturgical term most frequently used by Egeria to designate the offering of the sacrifice of the Mass. On *facere* as a verb for liturgical action and on *oblatio*, cf. Bastiaensen 39–51 and 81 f. Bastiaensen distinguishes between Egeria's use of *oblatio* (*offerre*) and her use of *processio* (*procedere*). Egeria generally uses the former to refer to a service in which only the eucharistic sacrifice takes place, reserving the latter for the larger liturgical offices of Jerusalem, of which *oblatio* was a part. For further discussion, cf. n. 294 below.— *Ordine suo* appears seven times in the text; in each case the phrase is associated with a service and there is suggestion or indication that Mass was celebrated. Cf. Bastiaensen 161 ff.

[35] *iam ut exiremus de aecclesia*. On the sense here, cf. Erkell 47–50 and F. Thomas, "Sur une manière d'exprimer la répétition et l'antériorité en latin tardif," RPh (1942) 22–30. In the manuscript this sentence and the preceding one constitute a single sentence: *Lecto ergo, ipso loco, omnia de libro Moysi et facta oblatione ordine suo, hac sic communicantibus nobis, iam ut exiremus de aecclesia, dederunt nobis presbyteri loci ipsius eulogias, id est de pomis, quae in ipso monte nascuntur.* For the first words of the sentence I have followed the emendation of Geyer (CSEL 39.40): *Lecto ergo ipso loco omni. . . .* On *ipse locus* as a standard phrase in the *Diary* in designating a reading from Scripture, cf. n. 52 below.

[36] *eulogias*, a Greek word in origin. A. Souter, *Lexicon to the Greek New Testament* (Oxford 1916) 101, says εὐλογίαι has the meaning of "blessing" in the New Testament and corresponds to *benedictio*. Bechtel 131 gives "elegant speech" as the original meaning, but "alms" as the New Testament sense. In the primitive Church the word had acquired the precise sense of blessed bread. Cf. J. P. Migne, *Onomasticon rerum et verborum difficiliorum* (ML 74.443): *Vocantur . . . eulogiae cibaria benedictionis gratia transmissa. Post missas alicui eas dare vel transmittere erat signum communionis et caritatis.* As the word came to have the wider meaning of food bestowed out of the spirit of brotherhood, particularly to pilgrims (cf. Gorce, *op. cit.* 176 f.), it was superseded in its more sacred sense by *eucharistia*. In the present passage I have translated *eulogias* as "gifts."

[37] *id est de pomis*. On the partitive construction, cf. Löfstedt 106–9. Löfstedt cites Schmalz, *Lateinische Syntax und Stylistik*

(Munich 1910) 407, for the translation "some apples." Gorce, *op. cit.* 176 f., translates a similar passage in ch. 15 of the *Diary* (*eulogias, id est de pomario sancti Iohannis*) with "an apple from the apple orchard of St. John." The word *pomum*, however, had the general meaning of a fruit with a pip or kernel. In view of the locale, it is more likely that the fruit given here consisted of dates or figs.

³⁸ The Arezzo manuscript reads: *tamen deorsum prope radicem montium ipsorum . . . modica nerrola est.* Gamurrini accepted the reading *nerrola* and connected it with the Arabian *nahr* or the Greek νάω. Bechtel 141 cites Du Cange for *nero* meaning *rivulus* and accepts *nerrola* as "a small stream." Franceschini-Weber accept Cholodniak's substitution of *terrola* for *nerrola*, and it is likely that *terrola* is the correct word here. It is *terrola* that I have translated.

³⁹ *et pomariola instituunt vel arationes*, Franceschini-Weber adopt Löfstedt's emendation of the Arezzo manuscript here, replacing the manuscript's *orationes* (in the sense of "places of prayer"), which was accepted by Geyer, Anglade, and Bechtel, with *arationes*. The word *aratio*, "farming," very early acquired the added meaning of "plowed field." *Oratio*, "prayer," did not as readily acquire the meaning of "place of prayer," "oratory."

⁴⁰ *illi sancti dignati sint.* The verb *dignare* (*dignari*) is used by Egeria frequently in referring to services rendered her by bishops, clergy, and monks, and in statements that God "has deigned" to fulfill her will (cf. chs. 10 and 23). The usage illustrates the penetration of the language of prayer into the everyday vocabulary of a Christian pilgrim; cf. Ziegler *Schrift* 164 and Bastiaensen 182 f. Bastiaensen cites the frequent combination of *dignare* and *praestare*, particularly with God as the subject, as an echo of prayer formulas often heard; Löfstedt 204 ff., on the other hand, considers the combination a reflection of the author's attempt to rise above the level of her colloquial language.

⁴¹ Cf. Exod. 33.22.

⁴² Cf. Exod. 34 and 32.19.

⁴³ *dominae venerabiles sorores.* This is one of several phrases used by Egeria for her addressees. Others are *dominae animae meae* (ch. 19), *domnae lumen meum* (ch. 23), and *dominae sorores* (ch. 46). On *domina* as a title of honor, cf. Blaise 290. *Sorores*, "sisters," has three possible meanings here—(a) blood

relatives; (b) sisters in the faith, i.e., fellow Christians; and (c) fellow religious. It is in the last sense that the word has usually been understood in the present instance. However, P. J. Corbett, *The Latin of the Regula Magistri* (Louvain 1958) 133, states that "there are objections to the notion that Egeria is a nun; her prolonged absence from home, the deference with which she is treated even by bishops, the use of the term *dominae*, which is applied in the religious life only to abbesses, all these make against the uncritical acceptance of her and the recipients of her correspondence as nuns."

⁴⁴ *mare illut Parthenicum.* The term *mare Parthenicum* is used twice by Ammianus Marcellinus to describe the easternmost half of the Mediterranean Sea, between Egypt and Cyprus, and refers specifically to the Gulf of Issus. Gamurrini, *S. Silviae Aquitanae peregrinatio ad loca sancta* (Rome 1888) 9 f., n. 7, suggests that it describes the narrow stretch of the Mediterranean between Pelusium and Alexandria; Pétré *Journal* 108 n. 1 cites D. Gorce, *Le Sinaï hier . . . aujourd'hui* (Paris 1937) 145, for the same interpretation.

⁴⁵ The Greeks and Romans had given the name of Saracens to the nomad Arabs of the Syro-Arabian desert who harassed the frontiers of the empire and who were responsible for the depredations at Sinai (cf. n. 25 above); cf. Moritz, "Saraka," RÉ² 1.2387–90.

CHAPTER 4

⁴⁶ *qui locus appellatur in Choreb.* The expression *in Choreb* is probably a transliteration from the LXX reading for Exod. 17.6.—As W. F. Albright, *From the Stone Age to Christianity* (New York 1957) 262, shows, the early Israelites made little effort to establish the exact locations of Pentateuchal sites, and in Egeria's day the tradition reflected in the *Onomasticon* 173 seemed to place Horeb next to Sinai: *Choreb, mons Dei . . . iuxta montem Sinai.* Although Exod. 17.6 would indicate that Horeb was in the vicinity of Raphidim (cf. n. 16 above), the "Horeb" in that verse is regarded by modern critics as a gloss. Legendre, *op. cit.* 1774, suggested that Egeria's Horeb is the Djebel Aribeh on the other side of the Wadi ed Deir, and Anthony of Piacenza as well speaks of a valley between Horeb and Sinai (CCL 175.149: *Inter Sina et Choreb est vallis . . .*). However, it is

apparent from the *Diary* text (note the reference to the chapel of Elias; also n. 47 below) that Egeria is referring not to the Djebel Aribeh but to another summit in the same range as the Djebel Musa.

[47] On this third church mentioned by Egeria at Sinai, cf. Meistermann 146 ff. The grotto where Elias hid is within the small chapel that today is dedicated to Elias. Its dimensions are minute—approximately three feet high, four feet wide, and eight feet deep.

[48] *qua fugit a facie Achab regis.* The flight of Elias is described in 3 Kings 19. Meister 370 cites the phrase *fugit a facie Achab* as a biblicism; cf. 3 Kings 12.2 (*profugus a facie regis Salomonis*), 1 Par. 11.13 (*fugeratque populus a facie Philisthinorum*), Ps. 3.1 (*cum fugeret a facie Absalom*).

[49] 3 Kings 19.9. Egeria's wording here (*Quid tu hic Helias?*) is a literal translation of the LXX. The Vulgate reads: *Quid hic agis, Elia?*

[50] Cf. 3 Kings 19.9. Cf. also n. 47 above.

[51] In 3 Kings 19 there is no mention of an altar of sacrifice on Horeb. Perhaps the monks alluded to the altar mentioned in 3 Kings 18, where the sacrifice of Elias and that of the priests of Baal are described. Cf. esp. 3 Kings 18.32: "And he built with the stones an altar to the name of the Lord. . . ."

[52] The Arezzo manuscript reads here: *id enim nobis vel maxime ea desideraveram semper, ut ubicumque venissemus, semper ipse locus de libro legeretur.* Franceschini-Weber retain the manuscript reading, except for the *ea* after *maxime*. In translating the passage, however, I have followed the change proposed by Geyer (CSEL 39.41): *id enim nobis vel maxime consuetudinis erat semper, ut ubicumque ad ea loca, quae desideraveram, venissemus, semper ipse locus de libro legeretur.* Geyer suspected that there was a lacuna in the text, and his attempt at reconstruction was influenced by a somewhat similar passage in ch. 10 of the *Diary*.— Egeria frequently refers to the practice of reading the "proper passage" from Scripture (cf. chs. 11, 14, 15, etc.). Bechtel 145 remarks that *ipse locus* means the appropriate or proper passage.

[53] Cf. Exod. 24.9–14. Meistermann 145 states that this place is in the center of a large, relatively fertile natural amphitheater on the slopes of the Sinai massif. It is still known today as the Rock of the Seventy Elders of Israel.

[54] The manuscript reading here, *licet et tectum non sit,* has

been accepted by most editors. Heraeus conjectured that *tectum* should be *lectum*. J. Svennung, "In *Peregrinationem Aetheriae* annotatiunculae," *Eranos* 32 (1934) 93–97, rejected the suggestion, principally because of the presence of a *lectus est* in the following sentence. Erkell 55 f., however, justifies the Heraeus proposal on the grounds that in the passage read from Exod. 24.9 there is indeed no mention of a huge, flat rock on which Aaron and the seventy elders stood. I have adopted the proposed change and translated accordingly.

⁵⁵ Possibly a reflection of Exod. 24.4: "And Moses . . . built an altar at the foot of the mount. . . ."

⁵⁶ Anthony of Piacenza (CCL 175.148) states that the cave of Elias was located three miles from the Monastery of St. Catherine, the site of the Burning Bush. He does not, however, refer to a church adjoining the cave.

⁵⁷ This would be in the Wadi ed Deir; cf. n. 10 above. Egeria indicates that she began the descent around the eighth hour (i.e., *ca.* 2:00 p.m.) and had reached the site of the Burning Bush around the tenth hour. Bludau 14 believes that she probably came down by the path called the *Sikket Saïd Sidna Mousa,* and he estimates the descent would normally take an hour and three quarters.

⁵⁸ Eutychius, patriarch of Alexandria, *Annales* (MG 111.1071), states that prior to the construction of the Monastery of St. Catherine there existed at the site of the Burning Bush a tower enclosing a church dedicated to the Mother of God (Θεότοκος). That was probably the church visited by Egeria here. In the present-day Basilica of St. Catherine, a chapel also dedicated to the Mother of God and commemorating the Burning Bush may be found behind the apse.

⁵⁹ Anthony of Piacenza (CCL 175.148) mentions a spring at the foot of the mountain where Moses watered the flocks of sheep and saw the "sign of the Burning Bush" (*signum rubi ardentis*). By the time of Anthony of Piacenza's visit the spring had been enclosed within the walls of the Monastery of St. Catherine.

⁶⁰ Exod. 3.5. Cf. below, n. 62.

⁶¹ *ac sic ergo fecimus ibi mansionem.* The phrase *facere mansionem* is probably a biblicism; cf. John 14.23: *et mansionem apud eum faciemus* ("and will make our abode with Him"). In

ch. 3 the verb *manere* is used absolutely: *ibi ergo mansimus in ea nocte*. Both here and in ch. 3 the construction is equivalent to *pernoctavimus*. Cf. Löfstedt 76.—The noun *mansio*, from which is derived the French "maison," is an important term in this text. In addition to its classical sense of "dwelling place" or "inn," it had developed the meaning of "station" or "resting place," and had become the technical term to describe a certain type of posting house. Gorce, *op. cit.* 56 f., distinguishes the *stationes* and *mutationes*, which were simple relay stations, from the *mansiones*, regular inns equipped with stores, stables, and lodging facilities. Since the *mansio* was an overnight stopping place, the word also acquired in time the meaning of "a day's journey" (i.e., from one *mansio* to the next), and it is used in this sense several times in the *Diary*, notably in chs. 7 (to describe the distance from Clysma to Arabia), 13 (for the distance between Jerusalem and Carneas), and 21 (for the length of the journey from Antioch to Tarsus). Cf. Kubitschek, "Mansio," RE $14^1.1231-51$.

CHAPTER 5

[62] Exod. 3.5. *Solve corrigiam calceamenti tui* is Egeria's wording for where the Vulgate has *solve calceamentum de pedibus tuis*, "put off the shoes from thy feet." Ziegler *Schrift* 169 f. rejected Meister's and Bludau's contention that Egeria's phrasing here is a reminiscence of Mark 1.7 (*non sum dignus procumbens solvere corrigiam calceamentorum eius*), Luke 3.16 (*non sum dignus solvere corrigiam calceamentorum eius*), and John 1.27 (*non sum dignus ut solvam eius corrigiam calceamenti*). Ziegler cites a wording similar to Egeria's in Rufinus' translation of the *Homilies* of Origen as evidence that Egeria was quoting from a version of the *Vetus Latina*.

[63] In this section there is a succession of sentences introduced by *monstraverunt* or *ostenderunt*. Bechtel 152 notes the passage as "an excellent illustration of sentence after sentence formed in exactly the same way; [where] the writer has apparently made no attempt to secure variety of expression." Spitzer, *op. cit.* 249, taking a different slant, considers the usage here to be a style feature peculiar to the pilgrimage genre, in which the repetition serves to reinforce the author's conviction about the reality of what was seen. Cf. Intro. pp. 44 ff.

[64] Cf. above, n. 13.

[65] "at a distance" = *de contra*. Cf. above, n. 20. Erkell contends that Egeria is emphasizing that now, as she comes down the middle of the Wadi ed Deir, she can see the east side of Mount Sinai, whereas earlier, when she was preparing to ascend the mountain, the west side was blocked from view by the adjoining mountains.

[66] Cf. Exod. 32.19.

[67] *cum Iesu filio Naue* (*Nave*). The use of *Iesus Nave* or *Iesus filius Nave* (this appears twice in ch. 10 of the *Diary*) for "Josue, the son of Nun" (cf., e.g., Jos. 1.1) apparently dated from the time of Origen, who translated the Hebrew for "son of Nun" by υἱὸς Ναυῆ. The form Ναυῆ appears in the earliest LXX manuscripts. The name *Iesu Nave* could be seen by many of the Fathers as typifying Jesus, the Ship (*navis*) in which the world is saved.—On Josue's presence with Moses during the descent from Sinai, cf. Exod. 32.17.

[68] Cf. Exod. 32.19, where, however, there is no specific reference to a rock. The desire of pilgrims to see concrete evidence of the events in Scripture created the need for such tangible signs. Cf. Intro. p. 18.

[69] Cf. Exod. 32.27.

[70] Cf. Exod. 32.20.

[71] What passage does Egeria have in mind? Is she referring to Exod. 32.20 ("And laying hold of the calf which they had made, he burnt it, and beat it to powder, which he strowed into water, and gave thereof to the children of Israel to drink")? Or is she referring to an event which took place at Raphidim (Exod. 17.6: "Behold I will stand before thee, upon the rock Horeb; and thou shalt strike the rock, and water shall come out of it so the people may drink. Moses did so . . .")? It is possible that guides transposed the locale of the Raphidim miracle because of the "Horeb" (*Choreb*) in Exod. 17.6 (on which, cf. n. 46 above). On other transpositions of locales, cf. nn. 1 and 5 above, and n. 145 below.

[72] Cf. Num. 11.24 f.

[73] Cf. Num. 11.4 and n. 5 above.

[74] On the place called The Burning, cf. Num. 11.1 ff. The event referred to occurred after the Israelites had departed from Sinai.

[75] The "rain" of manna and quail is recorded in Exod. 16.13 ff.,

and Exod. 16.35 says "the children of Israel ate manna forty years." The first "rain" occurred not at Mount Sinai, but in the desert of Sin, before the Hebrews came to Raphidim and Sinai. Another supply of quail, after the departure from Sinai, is recorded in Num. 11.31 f.

76 *affectio vestra*, a phrase used repeatedly by Egeria (cf. chs. 7, 17, 20, 23, 24). On the various terms she used for her addressees, and on their significance, cf. n. 43 above and Intro. pp. 8–11. Although Blaise 48 does not cite *affectio vestra* as a form of address (Egeria uses the phrase in the nominative, as the subject of verbs in the third person, and in one instance in the accusative; she does not use it in the vocative), he does list it as a term of love among Christians, at times synonymous with *amor*, in other texts having a more perfunctory meaning. On *caritas* and *dilectio* as the principal terms expressing love-charity among Christians, cf. Pétré, *op. cit.* in n. 21 above, 25–100. C. Mohrmann. *Die altchristliche Sondersprache in den Sermones des hl. Augustin. I. Lexikologie und Wortbildung* (Latinitas christianorum primaeva 3, Nijmegen 1932) 53, lists among the terms of address found in the writings of St. Augustine *charitas vestra*, *dilectio vestra*, and *sanctitas vestra*. *Affectio vestra* as a term of address is not found in Augustine, but it is analogous in meaning to the terms he uses. My translation follows that of Pétré: "Votre Charité."

77 Cf. Num. 9.1–5.

78 Cf. Exod. 40.15–32.

79 On the Graves of Lust, cf. n. 5 above. At this point the pilgrims had returned to the place where they had first entered the valley, as described in ch. 1.

80 The *in nomine Dei*, "in the name of God," here is another illustration of the incorporation of the language of prayer and devotion into the speech patterns of the Christian. Cf. n. 40 above. The present phrase appears frequently in the *Diary* (cf. chs. 12, 17, 18, 21, 22, etc.), and similar phrases are scattered throughout the text (e.g., *in nomine Christi Dei nostri* in chs. 9, 18, 19, 23).

81 This passage is a type of humility *topos*, consonant with the nature of the work and the pious attitude of the author. A striking example will be found in ch. 23, at the conclusion of the narration of the journeys, and Egeria expresses similar feelings at

other points (e.g., in ch. 16). On the humility *topos* in patristic and medieval Christian literature, cf. E. R. Curtius, *European Literature and the Latin Middle Ages* (Bollingen Series 36, New York 1953) 83 ff.

CHAPTER 6

[82] On Pharan, cf. n. 16 above.

[83] *inde maturantes*, literally "hurrying forth from there." In translating the phrase I have followed Pétré *Journal* 119: "partant de bonne heure."

[84] *sicut et superius dixi*. The resting station referred to in this sentence is not further specified. In fact, this entire chapter lacks precise detail, and it must be presumed that the author described the stages of the journey in the missing pages of the manuscript. Using the account of Peter the Deacon (cf. Intro. pp. 16 f.), we can establish the most likely stages of her return journey. For commentary on these stages, cf. Bludau 8 f.; Devreese, *op. cit.* 209 ff.; Meistermann 53–81; Lagrange, "De Suez à Jérusalem par le Sinaï," RBibl 5 (1896) 618–41. Meistermann is particularly valuable, for he relates both the text of Peter the Deacon and this chapter to the sites mentioned in Exod. 16 and Num. 33. It is likely that Egeria's party proceeded down the Wadi Feiran and the Wadi Mokatteb until they came to Magharah. According to Meistermann, it is a 12-hour journey from Pharan to Magharah, which he identifies with the biblical Dapha, mentioned in Num. 33.12 as one of the two encampments of the Israelites between the desert of Sin and Pharan. Although never a permanent Egyptian settlement, it was the center of mining operations and possessed an ancient well and a dike to trap downpours. It is reasonable to suppose that pilgrims would have stopped here to replenish their water supply.—The phrase "in the desert of Pharan" (*in desertum Pharan*) can be explained by a passage in Peter the Deacon (CCL 175.102 f.). He calls the desert of Pharan a valley, six thousand feet in width and even greater in length, where there had been much excavation and where Hebrew inscriptions could be seen (*unumquodque autem cubiculum est descriptum lidteris hebreis*). He mentions that the place had an abundant water supply.

[85] Bludau (16) believes that this resting station is to be found at the Ras abu Zanimeh, a promontory jutting into the Red Sea.

Peter the Deacon (CCL 175.102) mentions a station which *iusta mare est*. Below the promontory is the plain of el Markha, the biblical desert of Sin. It is undoubtedly in this area of the Ras abu Zanimeh and the plain of el Markha that Egeria's encampment is to be found.—The reference to a resting station *quae erat iam super mare* may be an allusion to Num. 33.10.

[86] *via enim illic penitus non est*. On the absence of a road here, cf. Löfstedt 170.

[87] The reference in this paragraph to a return by the children of Israel to the area of the Red Sea probably is due to a misinterpretation of the meaning of Num. 10.12, where it is stated that the Israelites, on leaving Sinai, arrived in the desert of Pharan. In the context of the Pentateuch, the term "desert of Pharan" refers to the northern half of the Sinai peninsula, where the Israelites wandered for forty years. Egeria and her guides, however, understood the expression in the narrow sense indicated by Peter the Deacon (cf. n. 84 above). Since the Israelites did not retrace their route from Egypt, it would be presumed that on leaving the spot which Egeria's guides had told her was the desert of Pharan the Israelites would have taken a route different from that she took. In fact they did not return this way at all.

[88] For the remaining stages of the journey to Clysma, cf. Intro. pp. 16–21. From the Ras abu Zanimeh our author proceeded to the Wadi Charandel, where she found the resting station of Arandara, the site of the biblical Elim. From there a three-day journey would take her through the desert of Sur to Clysma.

Chapter 7

[89] The toponymic and scriptural notes for chs. 7–9 are heavily dependent on the two previously cited studies of Ziegler and on two studies which base their interpretations of the route of the Exodus on the Christian tradition of the 4th century, particularly as reflected in Egeria's account of her travels, thus serving as extensive commentary on our text: C. Bourdon, "La route de l'Exode, de la terre de Gesse à Mara," RBibl 41 (1932) 370–92 and 538–49, and A. Servin, "La tradition judéo-chrétienne de l'Exode," *Bulletin de l'Institut d'Egypte* 31 (1948–49) 315–55. These authors differ on the precise interpretation to be given the data furnished by Egeria. The notes given here, since their only purpose is to furnish a commentary on her data, will only inci-

dentally allude to the discussion concerning the precise locations of the sites mentioned in Exodus and their bearing on the controversy over a northern or southern route.

[90] The fortress of Clysma (Clesma), the ruins of which lie at Kom el Qolzum, slightly to the north of modern Suez, was a port for ships trading with India. It was founded under Trajan to replace the Ptolemaic city of Arsinoe. In situating the crossing of the Red Sea at Clysma, Egeria was simply reflecting the general Christian tradition of her day. Those contemporary scholars who favor a southern route tend to situate the crossing south of the Bitter Lakes. Advocates of that position generally postulate that the Red Sea originally extended far to the north of its present northern end. Albright, *From the Stone Age to Christianity* 14, summarizes the view of those defending the northern route and a crossing at the Papyrus Marsh, or Reed Sea, south of the Mediterranean: "Again, our Sinai Expedition of 1947–48 was able to prove that the 'southern' route of the Exodus across Suez was impossible and that the only possible route is that described in Exodus and fixed by recent finds, from the neighborhood of Tanis (Zoan, Raamses) to the Wadi Tumilat (Pithom), and then back to the coast near Baal-Zephon (Tahpanhes, Greek Daphne) and across the Papyrus Lake (as the Egyptians called the Hebrew 'Lake of Papyrus' or Reed Sea) into the Peninsula of Sinai." Cf. Moritz, "Klysma," RE 11.881.

[91] Gessen, the Hebrew Gošen, is mentioned several times in Genesis (45.10; 46.28, 34; 47.1, 4, 6; 50.8). The expression *terra Arabiae, terra Gesse* is a paraphrase of the LXX for Gen. 45.10 or 46.34 (cf. the Greek texts: ἐν γῇ Γέσεμ Ἀραβίας, or Ἀραβίᾳ). The translators of the LXX, obviously well acquainted with the geography of Hellenistic Egypt, frequently added to Hebrew names the terms current in their day. Egypt was divided into forty-four administrative districts or Nomes, twenty in Lower Egypt and the remainder in Upper Egypt. From Ptolemaic to Byzantine times the twentieth Nome was known as Arabia, with its capital at Pi-Sopd, the present-day village of Saft el-Henneh. The land of Gessen comprised undoubtedly a much larger area, perhaps the whole region between the Pelusiac or easternmost branch of the Nile and the desert to the east. Strabo, *Geographica* 4.5, understood *terra Arabiae* to designate such an expanse of territory. Egeria, however, uses the

term in the restricted sense of the Nome of Arabia. Cf. Meistermann 5 ff.; Lesetre, "Gessen," DB 3.218–21.

⁹² This is a paraphrase of one of several biblical texts, e.g.,
Gen. 47.6 ("make them dwell in the best place, and give them
the land of Gessen") or 47.11 ("in the best place of the land, in
Ramesses").

⁹³ The Latin text has *cata mansiones monasteria*. Van Oorde
131 gives for *monasteria* in this passage *castellum, statio militum*.
On the *cata mansiones*, cf. Löfstedt 175, where *cata* is interpreted
as having a sense analogous to that of the Romance language
forms *chacun, cada uno*, and *caduno*.—For an indication of
Egeria's social position seen in her obtaining military escort, cf.
Intro. pp. 8 f.

⁹⁴ The sense of the passage is clear. The Hebrews did not
follow a straight line, but veered to the left and the right, and
often backtracked. This is most likely a personal observation
rather than a specific scriptural allusion.

⁹⁵ The name Epauleum (Epauleos), possibly meaning "swamp
house," is found in the LXX for Exod. 14.2 (ἀπέναντι τῆς
Ἐπαύλεως, to translate "over against Phihahiroth") and 14.9.
In the catalogue of mansions given in Num. 33, the LXX translates Phihahiroth with either Ἐπιρώϑ or Εἰρώϑ. The location
of Epauleum-Phihahiroth, as is the case for virtually all sites
mentioned in Exodus, is disputed. For those who hold to
a northern route, such as Albright, "Pi-hahiroth . . . is thus to be
located not too far from modern Qantara"; cf. W. F. Albright,
"Exploring in Sinai," BASOR 109 (1948) 5–20, esp. 15. Partisans
of a southern route, however, are at odds on fixing the site of
Epauleum-Phihahiroth, and thus differ on where Egeria might
have been shown this place. Bludau 18 suggested the Egyptian
port of Pikeheret, five miles southwest of Ismailia; Meistermann
25 f., somewhere to the northwest of the Bitter Lakes; Servin,
art. cit. 340, at Byr-Soueys, three miles north of Suez; Bourdon,
art. cit. 545, at the Tell Abou Hassan, fifteen miles north of Suez.
Bourdon bases his identification on Egeria's specific statement
that she was shown Epauleum only after reaching the first resting
station-fortress.

⁹⁶ I again follow Erkell 41 in translating *de contra*. It should
be noted, however, that in the present instance Egeria seems to
be paraphrasing Scripture (cf. Exod. 14.2 or Num. 33.7), and in
that case *de contra* would correspond to "over against" or

"facing." Pétré translates here "d'en face." On the other hand, the previous usages of *de contra* (cf. nn. 20 and 65 above) tend to confirm Erkell's suggestion.

[97] Magdalum, a semitic term (also Magadilou or Migdol), designates a type of fortification used in southern Syria and adopted by the Pharaohs to strenghten the eastern frontier. Cf. Meistermann 27. In Egeria's day a Roman fortress stood on the site that she called Magdalum. Bourdon, *art. cit.* 543 ff., associates it with the Roman-Byzantine outpost at Tell Abou Hassan. In the two scriptural passages which speak of Magdalum, it is associated with Phihahiroth and Beelsephon; cf. Num. 33.7 and Exod. 14.2 ("Let them turn and encamp over against Phihahiroth, which is between Magdal and the sea, over against Beelsephon"). Servin, *art. cit.* 340, attempts to associate it with a site near Clysma. It is apparent, however, that the site of Magdalum indicated by Egeria's guides lay at one resting station from the port city.

[98] The manuscript has either *et ioebelsepon* or *et loebelsepon*. I have translated here the emended text as given in Franceschini-Weber: *et loco Belsefon.*—Beelsphon (Baal-Zephon, "God of the north wind") should be located in the vicinity of Phihahiroth and Magdalum, but Egeria situates it a second fortress beyond the migdol of Tell Abou Hassan. Bourdon and Servin intrepret differently her description of the place as a plain beside a mountain above the sea. For Bourdon, it is a narrow plain lying between the Djebel Geneffe and the southeastern shore of the Bitter Lakes. For Servin, it is the plain between Djebel Ataqa and the Gulf of Suez. Bourdon, *art. cit.* 545, identifies Egeria's second fortress as the Roman outpost of Fayed, thirty miles north of Clysma. For Albright, *art. cit.* 15 f., Beelsephon lies on the site of the modern Tell Defneh, the ancient Tahpanhes-Daphne, southeast of Tanis.

[99] Cf. Exod. 14.10.

[100] The Latin text reads: *Oton . . . quod est iuxta deserta loca.* Oton is the Vulgate Etham; the spelling here is derived from the LXX's Ὀθόμ or Βουθάν. The topographical detail given here faithfully reflects the Greek text of Exod. 13.20 and the *Onomasticon* 141. It was at Oton-Etham that the Hebrews made their second camp site and changed direction in their march. Servin, *art. cit.* 332–5, cites two copies of a map dating from the

time of Ptolemy that show Etham situated for the geographers of Late Antiquity on the northern shore of the Bitter Lakes. Bourdon, *art. cit.* 391 f., identified it with a fortress (a *Khtm* or *Khatem*, meaning a wall or line of fortifications) near Serapeum, an important road center in the same area.

[101] Soccoth is mentioned in Exod. 12.37 and 13.20 and in Num. 33.5 f., and it was the first camp of the Hebrews. E. Naville, *The Store City of Pithom and the Route of the Exodus* (Egyptian Exploration Fund, London 1885) 5, states the problem posed by Soccoth succinctly: "Thuku (sc. Soccoth) was a region, then a district, then it became the name of the chief city or capital of the district. . . . The list of Nomes gives either Pithom or Thuku as the capital of the 8th Nome of Lower Egypt." Albright, *art. cit.* 15 f., and "The Archaeology of the Ancient Near East" in *Peake's Commentary on the Bible* (ed. M. Black and H. Rowley, London 1962) 58–65, states that "Succoth was at Heroopolis, modern Tell el-Maskhuta." However, the Tell el-Maskhuta cannot be the site of Egeria's Soccoth (cf. nn. 103 and 105 below). Servin, *art. cit.* 329–33, suggests a site, originally proposed by de Lesseps, on the southeast shore of Lake Timsah, at the entrance of the valley of Saba byar, near the Roman-Byzantine city of Thaubastum. Since she speaks of Oton and Soccoth in the same sentence, Egeria may have been shown their reputed sites close to one another. Servin's identification has the advantage of placing them in the same general area.

[102] Cf. Exod. 12.43.

[103] Phithom is mentioned in Exod. 1.11 as one of the two store cities or tabernacles built by the Hebrews at the command of Pharaoh. Albright, "The Archaeology of the Ancient Near East" 63, identified the Phithom of the Exodus with Tell er-Retabeh, located in the Wadi Tumilat, nine miles to the west of Tell el-Maskhuta. However, when Naville excavated the latter site, he identified it as Phithom, and he cited Egeria's text, at that time just recently discovered, as evidence of where it was understood to be in Late Antiquity. In the LXX, Phithom is translated by Heroopolis ('Ηρώων πόλις). Egeria calls Phithom a fortress and situates it next to Heroopolis, a point which can be very easily explained. The Romans had their outpost on the site of Phithom, whereas the town of Heroopolis lay a short distance away (cf. Meister-mann 15 and Naville, *op. cit. passim*). On Phithom, cf. H.

Cazelles and J. Leclant, "Pithom," DB Suppl. fasc. 42 (Paris 1967) 4 ff.

[104] Egeria doubtless means that she had here entered Egypt proper by crossing into the 8th Nome, the Heroopolitan, with its capital at Tell el-Maskhuta. The "lands of the Saracens" were the area lying to the east; cf. n. 45 above.

[105] "Heroopolis" = *Heroum civitas*. Cf. *Onomasticon* 95: *Eroum civitas in Aegypto, ad quam Iosep occurrit patri suo Iacob.* Farther on in the text Egeria uses a slightly different form, *Hero*, which is the name she would have heard from local inhabitants. At Tell el-Maskhuta, Naville discovered two inscriptions which clearly mark it as the site of Heroopolis.

[106] The allusion to Joseph meeting his father at Heroopolis is a reflection of the LXX for Gen. 46.28 f. (where substituted for "Gessen" is "Heroopolis in the land of Ramesses") as well as of the *Onomasticon* (cf. n. 105 above). Ziegler *Schrift* 195 cites the *Vetus Latina* for Gen. 46.29: *ad Heroum civitatem in terra Ramesse.*

[107] . . . *nunc est come, sed grandis, quod nos dicimus vicus.* *Come* is a transliteration of the Greek κώμη, which Egeria glosses with its Latin equivalent, *vicus.*

[108] *martyria*, a word used frequently in the text to designate commemorative shrines over tombs of martyrs. Cf. Van Oorde 126 f.; Souter 244; Bechtel 131.

[109] Sixteen Roman miles to the west is the Tell el-Kebir, which marked the boundaries of the land of Gessen.

[110] It was not a branch of the Nile but the fresh-water canal, mentioned by Strabo, *Geographica* 17.25, which linked the Nile to the Red Sea via the Bitter Lakes.

[111] E. Naville, *The Shrine of Saft el-Henneh and the Land of Goshen* (Egyptian Exploration Fund, London 1888) *passim*, identified the city of Arabia with the Egyptian village of Saft el-Henneh, some 30 miles west of Tell el-Maskhuta, near the modern Egyptian city of Zagazig. Arabia was the Graeco-Roman name of the city of Pi-Sopd, which the Egyptians originally called Kes or Kesem. It was the capital of the Nome of Arabia and, as Egeria's references to a bishop of Arabia in the following chapters indicate, it was an episcopal city. Cf. Bourdon, *art. cit.* 371 f., n. 1; Servin, *art. cit.* 323; Meistermann 5 ff.

[112] Cf. Gen. 47.5 f. Egeria's wording differs substantially from that of the Vulgate.

CHAPTER 8

[113] Ramesses is mentioned in Exod. 1.11, along with Phithom, as a store city built by the Hebrews. It is also mentioned as the point of departure for the Exodus (cf. Exod. 12.37 and Num. 33.3). Montet's excavations at Tanis (cf. P. Montet, "Tanis, Avaris et Pi-Ramses," RBibl 39 [1930] 5–28) have convinced partisans of the northern route of the Exodus that Ramesses was located at Tanis, present-day So'an. Cf. Albright, "The Archaeology of the Ancient Near East" 63. However, Egeria's Ramesses must be sought in the Wadi Tumilat, but its location is in doubt. Bourdon situates it at Saft el-Henneh itself. The mileage figure given by Egeria would seem to exclude locating it farther east in the Wadi Tumilat, at Tell el-Kebir, as Naville, *op. cit.* 20, had proposed, or at Tell er-Retabeh, as was suggested by F. Petrie.

[114] The two giant figures certainly were not of Moses and Aaron, but of the Pharaohs or some Egyptian gods. At the Tell er-Retabeh Petrie found two colossal statues, one of Ramesses II and the other of the god Thum, the titular god of Phithom. However, at Arabia-Pi-Sopd Naville had discovered two statues, one of Ramesses II and the other of Pharaoh Nectanebo.

[115] Substantial evidence that the site of Ramesses shown to Egeria lay near Arabia-Pi-Sopd was uncovered by Naville in a fragment he found in Vienna which had come from Saft el-Henneh and refers to the cult of the sycamore tree. Naville contends (*op. cit.* 11–14) that Egeria offers proof that the veneration of the tree "was yet surviving, though in Christian garb." The curative powers that the people associated with the tree belonged to the sycamore symbol of ancient Egypt, and Naville cites texts to show that the sycamore was regarded as a life-giving tree: "To his fathers, the lords of the abode of the sycamore. The sycamore is green, its boughs put forth their green leaves, the land is green in all its extent, the residence of this god is green every day. . . . The lords of the abode of the sycamore, perfecting Egypt in its appearance, renewing the abode of the sycamore, making it wholly afresh, all the land was in joy."

[116] The expression *dendros alethiae* (Greek: δένδρος ἀληθείας) and its Latin meaning, *arbor veritatis,* obviously came from the bishop, and this passage in no way reflects a knowledge of Greek by Egeria.

[117] *senior vir, vere satis religiosus ex monacho. . . .* In chs. 19 and 20 it is mentioned that bishops were selected from among the monks. Van Oorde 77 gives several meanings to the phrase *ex monacho*, and suggests that in this passage it signifies *ut decet monachum esse*, "as it befits a monk to be."

[118] There is no statement in Scripture that Pharaoh entered Ramesses or that he burned the city. This was perhaps a local Christian legend to explain the barrenness of the plain.

CHAPTER 9

[119] Epiphany marked the feast of the Nativity in the East, and in ch. 25 Egeria describes the liturgy of the feast of the Epiphany in Jerusalem. The reference to a vigil service to be held in the church here finds a parallel in the procession to the grotto of the Nativity in Bethlehem, where the church of Jerusalem celebrated the Epiphany vigil. To express the idea of holding the vigil service Egeria uses the verb *agere: vigiliae agendae erant.* On *agere* as a term to designate liturgical action, cf. Bastiaensen 39–48.

[120] On Egeria's visit to the Thebaid, see Intro. pp. 15 ff. The Upper Thebaid was a great monastic center. St. Pachomius, founder of the cenobitic life, had established himself at Tabennisi near Denderah.

[121] This was the main highway to Pelusium. In its final stretches, it ran near the Pelusiac branch of the Nile, and it is that branch of the river that Egeria is referring to in the following sentence.

[122] These allusions to the fertility of the countryside may reflect scriptural texts (e.g., Num. 13.3 and Deut. 11.10) as well as personal observation.—On the importance of the large estates (the *fundi*, the term used here by Egeria, or *massae* and *potestatae*) in the economy and social structure of Late Antiquity, cf. F. Lot, *The End of the Ancient World and the Beginning of the Middle Ages* (New York 1953) 128–34.

[123] In the Arezzo manuscript, Tanis is spelled either *Tatnis* or *Tathnis*, while Peter the Deacon's account (CCL 175.100) has *Taphnis*. Except for Bernard, editors and commentators see in *Tatnis-Tathnis* the city of Tanis, the ruins of which have been excavated by P. Montet (cf. n. 113 above). Tanis was on the Tanitic branch of the Nile, but outside the boundaries of the

land of Gessen (cf. n. 91 above). It served as the capital of the Hyksos Pharaohs and probably of Ramesses II. Under Roman and Byzantine rule it was an important port for trade with the East. Bernard, *op. cit.* 24 n. 1, contended that the spelling in the Arezzo manuscript may have been a scribe's error for *Taphnis* (*Daphne*), which lies 16 miles southwest of Pelusium, and where Petrie, at Tell Defenneh, uncovered "Pharaoh's house in Tahpanhes." Egeria's route then would have been along the right bank of the Pelusiac branch of the Nile. Cf. H. Kees, "Tanis," RE² 4.2175-8.

[124] There is no statement in Scripture that Moses was born at Tanis. In Ps. 77.12 (and similarly verse 43) there is reference to the "wonderful things" Moses did "in the land of Egypt, in the field of Tanis." Since Pharaoh's capital was at Tanis and Pharaoh's daughter rescued Moses, Egeria may herself have concluded that Moses was born there. Or her statement may have been based on a local tradition she heard from guides.

[125] No account of Egeria's visit to Alexandria has survived. Peter the Deacon (CCL 175.277 f.) has a passage devoted to Alexandria, but it is borrowed from Bede's *De locis sanctis* (CCL 175.251-80).

[126] Pelusium, Σαίν in the LXX, was called Permum by the Egyptians. It is first attested in the 7th century B.C., and it is mentioned in Ezech. 30.15 f. It was both a port and a major Egyptian frontier fortress. Under the Roman empire, Pelusium attained its greatest economic importance and in the Byzantine era was the capital of the province of Augustamnica Prima. An important Christian center, it was a bishopric; Rufinus, *Hist. monach.* 22 f. (ML 21.459 f.), speaks of it as a flourishing monastic center. After the Moslem conquest, it was known as Farmea, and under this name it is mentioned by the Frankish pilgrim Bernard, who visited it *ca.* 870 (cf. Tobler-Molinier, *Itin. latina bellis sacris anter.* 313). Today called Tell-Farama, it is 26 miles southeast of Port Said. Cf. H. Kess, "Pelusion," RE 19.407-15.

[127] On the return journey, Egeria undoubtedly followed the coastal road. The various resting stations, too many to enumerate here, can be found in F.-M. Abel, "Les confins de la Palestine et de l'Egypte sous les Ptolomées," RBibl 48 (1939) 207-36 and 530-48, and RBibl 49 (1940) 55-75 and 224-39.

[128] By *Aelia* is meant the colony of *Aelia Capitolina*. In 135 A.D., Hadrian ordered Jerusalem to be rebuilt as a Roman

colony following the destruction of the Jewish city during the revolt of Bar Kokhba. Jerusalem was known officially by this name until the Arab conquest. According to Bludau 20, *Aelia* was from the family name of Hadrian and *Capitolina* was in memory of Jupiter Capitolinus, in whose honor a pagan shrine was erected on the site of the Jewish temple. Cf. W. F. Albright, *The Archaeology of Palestine* (Baltimore 1949) 166 ff.

CHAPTER 10

[129] By "Arabia" Egeria here means *provincia Arabia*, established by Trajan following the conquest of the Nabatean kingdom in 106 A.D. The province encompassed the Hellenistic cities of the Decapolis which lay to the east of the Jordan, in the biblical land of Moab. An excellent history of the province is given in R. Aigrain, "Arabie," DHGE 3.1159-339, where there is a detailed map showing its boundaries after the reorganization of the provinces by Diocletian. For Mount Nebo, which lay within the borders of the province of Arabia, Egeria uses the form Nabau, found in the LXX (Deut. 32.49 f.) and in the *Onomasticon*. The name has been preserved since antiquity in the Djebel Neba, a mass of rocky mountains lying 11 miles east of the northern shore of the Dead Sea. It is generally agreed that among the mountain peaks of the Djebel Neba is to be found the biblical Mount Nebo. Three names are given in Scripture: Abarim, Phasga, and Nebo. Meistermann 299 succinctly relates them to one another: "Le Mont Nébo n'est donc qu'un sommet du Phasga, montagne qui appartient à la chaîne des monts Abarim à l'orient de la mer Morte." A major commentary on Egeria's chs. 10-12, describing the pilgrimage to Nebo, is given by F.-M. Abel, "L'exploration du sud-est de la vallée du Jourdain," RBibl 40 (1931) 214-26 and 375-400. Cf. also H. Leclercq, "Nébo," DACL 12.1065-71.

[130] Cf. Deut. 32.49 f. The text as given in the Arezzo manuscript here follows closely the LXX but differs from both the Greek text and the Vulgate in the name of the mountain, having Arabot rather than Abarim. Ziegler *Schrift* 171 attributes the difference to a copyist's error, a confusion with the phrase *Arabot Moab* in Egeria's quotation from Deut. 34.8 a few sentences below. *Arboth Moab*, the plains of Moab (cf. Num. 22.1, 31.12, 33.48, and 36.13; Deut. 34.8), was the name formerly

given to a section of the Jordan valley encompassed within the Wadi Nimrin, the river, and the Dead Sea. Cf. Abel, "L'exploration du sud-est . . ." 223.

[131] *Deus noster Iesus, qui sperantes in se non deseret.* Meister 370 cites the phrasing here as a biblicism. For a possible source, cf. Judges 13.17.

[132] Cf. Jos. 3–4.

[133] Cf. above, n. 67.

[134] Cf. Jos. 22.10–34. Ziegler *Schrift* 182 remarks that Egeria uses here *ara*, the term generally reserved in Scripture to describe a pagan altar. It is found only once in the Vulgate New Testament, in Acts 17.23, where the reference is to the altar "to the unknown God." The Latin translators of the LXX generally followed their models in distinguishing the altar of the true God (*altare*) from the idolatrous altar (*ara*). The controversy described in Jos. 22 centered on a mistaken belief that the altar there in question was sacrilegious, and it may be that *ara* was used (the Vulgate has *altare*) in Egeria's Bible text.

[135] Livias (*Libiada* in the Arezzo manuscript) was the name given to Beth-Haram (Betharan in Jos. 13.27) by Herod Antipas, who hoped to curry favor with Augustus by renaming the city in honor of the emperor's second wife, Livia, in the first years of the Christian era. Hoping later to flatter her son Tiberius, the new emperor, Herod renamed the city Julias after 14 A.D., when the empress had changed her name to Julia. In spite of evidence in Josephus, *Antiquities* 27.2, for use of the new name, Livias was employed exclusively from the 2nd century to the Arab conquest. The site of Livias is today known as Tell er-Rameh, and in this name Abel, "L'exploration de sud-est . . ." 219–22, sees a linguistic affinity across the centuries with Beth-Haram, which in the 10th century was called Bait-ar-Ram. Of minor importance until Herod fortified it and popularized it as a winter residence and spa, Livias was modernized by Antipas and became a road center known for its agricultural products and palms. The reputation of its waters continued into Byzantine times. Its first known bishop, Letoios, was present at the Council of Ephesus.

[136] The area around Livias was identified by Egeria's guides with the *Arboth Moab*, or plains of Moab, where the Israelites had their camps before crossing the Jordan (cf. n. 130 above). The language here—*Campus enim ipse est infinitus subter montes*

Arabiae super Iordanem—may have been modeled on Num. 33.47 f. Is it possible that *montes Arabiae* is an error for *montes Abarim?*

[137] Cf. Deut. 34.8, where, however, the period of mourning is given as 30 days. Egeria's text is a near-literal translation of the LXX, except on the length of mourning. Bechtel 155 assumed that Egeria's "forty days" was, "doubtless, a mistake of memory." Ziegler *Shrift* 172 f., however, cites the *Vetus Latina* (the *Cod. Lugd.*) for Num. 20.30, describing the mourning period for Aaron: *Et ploraverunt Aaron XL diebus omnis domus Israhel.* (The Vulgate for Num. 20.30 has *triginta diebus.*) Ziegler also gives additional evidence on a 40-day mourning period, particularly in Greek-speaking areas.

[138] *post recessum Moysi.* Löfstedt 273 ff. considers *recessus* and the verb *recedere*, which Egeria uses in ch. 20, as specifically Christian terms for death and dying.

[139] Cf. Deut. 34.9.

[140] Cf. Deut. 31.24.

[141] Cf. Deut. 31.30, 32.1–43. For "of the whole assembly of Israel" Egeria has *totius ecclesiae Israhel.* This is the only passage in the *Diary* where *ecclesia* is used to refer to the "congregation of Israel."

[142] Cf. Deut. 33.

[143] The texts referred to are undoubtedly those cited in the preceding few notes. On the practice of reading the "appropriate" text from Scripture, cf. above, n. 52.

[144] *deinde legeretur lectio ipsa de codice.* Bastiaensen 91 shows that both *legere* and *lectio* are applied to readings from Scripture. *Codex* was the customary term for a copy of the Scriptures.

[145] Scripture records two occasions on which the Israelites complained about a lack of water and Moses struck a rock to bring forth water, once at Raphidim (cf. Exod. 17.1–7), and once at Cades (cf. Num. 20.1–13); but it mentions no such occurrence in the encampment in the plains of Moab. On transpositions of events, cf. nn. 5 and 71 above. Both Theodosius and Anthony of Piacenza (CCL 175.121 and 134) refer to an incident such as that recorded by Egeria, but by the 6th century the site had been transferred to Livias itself and the waters of the spa were called *termae* (i.e., *thermae*) *Moysi: civitas . . Liviada . . in quo loco sunt termae ex se lavantes, quae vocantur Moysi* (CCL 175.134). The tradition of a spring on the way to Mount Nebo

continues to this day in the name of one of the wadis, Ayoun Mousa, the precise location of which can be seen in a detailed map with the article of E. Power, "The Site of the Pentapolis," *Biblica* 11 (1930) 4. Abel, "L'exploration du sud-est . . ." 375 f., confirms in part the accuracy of Egeria's remarks, for a short distance from the stone marking the sixth mile of the Roman road from Livias to Hesebon a path running parallel to the Ayoun Mousa leads to mountain springs. Bastiaensen 148 had suggested that the ordinal *sexto*, "sixth," was used for the cardinal and that the sense of the *Diary* text was that the path was to be followed for six miles.

[146] Abel, "L'exploration du sud-est . . ." 375, believed that he had located the site of this church in a group of ruins called *el-Meshed* (literally, "the martyrium" or "shrine").

CHAPTER 11

[147] Probably meant here is one of the two passages cited in n. 145. Cf. also n. 71 above.

CHAPTER 12

[148] The mountain on which Egeria was and which she called Nebo was the Ras Siagha, over two miles west-northwest of the mountain peak today called En Nebo. Regarding the church on Mount Nebo, see J. Saller, "L'église du mont Nébo," RBibl 43 (1934) 120–27, and *The Memorial of Moses on Mount Nebo* (Publications of the Studium Biblicum Franciscum 1, Jerusalem 1941).

[149] Deut. 34.6. Where the Vulgate has *et non cognovit homo sepulcrum eius*, Egeria has *sepulturam illius nullus hominum scit*.

[150] Translating here the text as given in Franceschini-Weber: *Nam memoria illius, ubi positus sit, in hodiernum ostenditur.* The Arezzo manuscript has *in hodie non* instead of *in hodiernum;* on the emendation, cf. Löfstedt 216 f. An explanation of the apparent contradiction between Deut. 34.6 (". . . and no man hath known of his sepulchre [*sepulcrum;* as noted in n. 149, Egeria uses *sepulturam*] until this present day") and the statement that Moses' grave was shown to Egeria was offered by Geyer. He distinguished the *sepultura*, understood in the abstract sense of a burial to which no man was a witness, from the *memoria*, a

grave site or tomb. Some editors, Heraeus and Pétré, have accepted the manuscript reading. However, the full context of the statement and the emergence of a legend *ca.* 430, describing how a shepherd was shown the grave site in a vision, would seem to support Löfstedt's emendation and Geyer's comments on *sepultura* and *memoria.* On the legend of the shepherd, cf. Abel, "L'exploration du sud-est . . ." 376 f., and H. Leclercq, "Nébo," DACL 12.1070 f. For a discussion of the passage, cf. Ziegler *Schrift* 173 f.

[151] Translating here the text as emended by Geyer (CSEL 39.53): *sicut enim nobis a maioribus, qui hic manserunt, ubi positus sit ostensum est.* The Arezzo manuscript lacks the words *positus sit.*

[152] *et sic cepimus egredere de ecclesia.* I have generally translated the periphrastic *coepi* with an infinitive by the preterite of the verb in question. Here, however, Egeria and her party had not yet left the church, as is apparent from the following sentences.

[153] *Vidimus etiam de contra non solum Libiadam.* . . . I have consistently translated the phrases *de contra* and *e contra* in this chapter by "in the distance." Cf. above, n. 20.

[154] For the panorama of the Promised Land seen by Moses, cf. Deut. 34.1-4. On the phrase "land of promise," *terra repromissionis,* cf. Heb. 11.9.

[155] Egeria is cited by two opposing camps as a witness to the location of the biblical Pentapolis of Sodom, Gomorrha, Adama, Seboim, and Segor (cf. Gen. 14.2). She is quoted by E. Power, "The Site of the Pentapolis," *Biblica* 11 (1930) 23-62 and 149-82, who believes that these cities were in the northern region of the Dead Sea country, and also by Abel, who defends the more traditional site near the southern shore. Abel insists that the reader should remember that at the beginning of the tour Egeria was facing west, then she looked to the south, or to her left, and then to the north, or to her right.

[156] This passage has been the subject of much controversy with regard to the location of the site that Egeria states could be seen from the Ras Siagha. Jerome, *Onomasticon* 153, equates Segor with Bala, a biblical synonym for the city of Segor (cf. Gen. 14.2 and 8), and with Zoara, a Byzantine city which the mosaic of Madaba placed near the southeastern shore of the Dead Sea. It is

universally agreed that this latter site could not have been seen by an observer in Egeria's position. Ziegler *Onomastikon* 78 f. expresses the belief that Egeria must have been shown a place near the northern shores of the Dead Sea. L. Heidet, "Ségor," DB 5.1561–5, refers to C. R. Condor, who held that the name Segor persisted in Tell es-Saghur, about eight miles northeast of the Dead Sea and very close to Tell er-Rameh, the ancient Livias. Abel, "L'exploration du sud-est . . ." 384, argues that Egeria's guides were indicating the general direction in which the city was to be sought and were not pointing it out to her. He cites the description of the panorama from Mount Sinai at the end of ch. 3 of the *Diary* as a parallel passage.

[157] *Nam et memoriale ibi est.* The word *memoriale*, used only once in the *Diary*, is glossed by Geyer (CSEL 39.407) with *memoria*. Pétré *Journal* 143 n. 3 suggests that it was probably a commemorative monument.

[158] Egeria here uses *titulus* and a few lines later uses *columna* in referring to the στήλη ἁλός of the LXX for Gen. 19.26. For the various translations in the Vulgate, the *Vetus Latina*, and the Fathers, cf. Ziegler *Schrift* 184.

[159] Bludau 25 cites several Christian authors who spoke of the pillar of salt as still being visible in their day: Clement of Rome, Justin Martyr, and Irenaeus.

[160] A further complication is introduced by this reference to the bishop of Segor. Are we to assume that this bishop was present with Egeria and was the ordinary of a near-by see? Or are we to accept the hypothesis of Abel, "L'exploration du sud-est . . ." 384, that she may have received this information from him in Jerusalem? Abel, *ibid.* 387 f., insists on identifying the see of Segor with the see of Zoara, for the latter was the only bishopric bordering the Dead Sea.

[161] *Esebon . . . quae nunc appellatur Exebon.* Hesban, the modern name for Hesebon, lies about seven miles northeast of the Ras Siagha. In Meistermann 278–81 there is a brief notice with a chart. Originally a Moabite city, it was captured by Sehon and made the capital of the Amorrhites, but following the Israelite invasion came under the control of the tribes of Ruben and Gad. It had ceased to have a Jewish population until Alexander Janneus (106–79 B.C.) restored it with a Jewish colony. After its conquest by Placidius, one of Vespasian's generals, it flourished as a

Roman city named Esbus. Both the Hebrew and Roman names are given by Jerome, *Onomasticon* 85: *Esebon civitas Seon regis Amorraeorum in terra Galaad . . . porro nunc vocatur Esbus, urbs insignis Arabiae.* The form *Exebon* given by Egeria appears in no other text. Ziegler *Onomastikon* 76 states that there is no possibility that that form could have evolved from *Esebon.*–The principal scriptural references to Sehon and Og are in Num. 21.21–35 and Deut. 2.24–3.11.

[162] *Safdra* is the spelling in the Arezzo manuscript and in Franceschini-Weber. All other editors give Sasdra. Under neither spelling is there a reference to such a city in Scripture or in the *Onomasticon.* Two cities are mentioned in Deut. 1.4 as residences of King Og, Astaroth and Edrai, and the latter was the site of Og's defeat at the hands of the Israelites. Bludau 25 assumes that Sasdra is Edrai, the Byzantine city of Adraa, located 30 miles east of the southern tip of the Sea of Galilee in the district of Hauran. Jerome, *Onomasticon* 85, mentions it as the place where Og was slain: *ubi interfectus est Og rex Basan. . .; nunc autem est Adra insignis Arabiae civitas in vicesimo quarto lapide a Bosra.* Abel, "L'exploration du sud-est . . ." 385 n. 1, suggests that the form *Sasdra* may have resulted from a misunderstanding on Egeria's part of the phrase *polis Asdra.* The form *Asdra* would be explained as a result of a contamination of *Adras* by *Astaroth,* since the two names are found together in the *Onomasticon.* Cf. Ziegler *Onomastikon* 77 f. For scriptural references to Edrai, cf. Num. 21.33 and Deut. 3.10.

[163] The name Phogor (Egeria has *Fogor;* Jerome, *Onomasticon* 170, gives *Fogo*) appears in Num. 23.28 ("mount of Phogor"), Deut. 3.29 and 4.46 ("the temple of Phogor"), and Deut. 34.6 ("in the valley of the land of Moab over against Phogor"). With none of these passages does Egeria's explanatory phrase, *civitas regni Edom,* "a city of the kingdom of Edom," which is a direct quotation from the *Onomasticon,* seem pertinent. As Ziegler *Onomastikon* 75 f. points out, however, there are references to five Phogors in Scripture and the *Onomasticon.* Two of these five are located by Eusebius and Jerome in the neighborhood of Mount Nebo, one being described as a mountain in Moab near Livias (cf. *Onomasticon* 168), the other being the city of Bethfogor (cf. *Onomasticon* 48), mentioned as Bethphogor in Jos. 13.20. Ziegler states that Bethfogor (Bethphogor) is the

Phogor to which Egeria's guides referred. According to Ziegler, however, either the guides or Egeria erred in adding the *civitas regni Edom*, a phrase which the *Onomasticon* applied to a quite different Phogor, one located far to the south in the land of Edom. This latter Phogor (Phau) is mentioned in Gen. 36.39 and 1 Par. 1.50.—Abel, "L'exploration du sud-est . . ." 385 f., offered a different explanation. He saw the phrase *Fogor . . . civitas regni Edom* as having been forged from two entries in the *Onomasticon*: *Dannaba super montem Fogor in septimo lapide Esbus*, and *Dannaba civitas Balac filii Beor regis Edom*.

[164] Agrispecula (*specula* = "lookout," "watch-tower," "height," or "summit"; *agri* = "of the field") is a translation of 'Αγροῦ σκοπία in Num. 23.14 in the LXX. Cf. Num. 23.14 in the Vulgate: *in locum sublimem, super verticem montis Phasga.*—Egeria took the name (the Arezzo manuscript has *agrisecula;* Gamurrini emended to *agri specula*) from the *Onomasticon* and borrowed liberally from the explanatory notice given there. Her text reads: *Sane illa parte montis, quam dixi sinistra, quae erat super mare Mortuum, ostensus est nobis mons precisus valde, qui dictus est ante Agrispecula. Hic est mons, in quo posuit Balac filius Beor Balaam divinum ad maledicendos Israhel filios. . . .* The *Onomasticon* 13 reads: *Agrispecula mons Moabitarum, in quem adduxit Balac filius Beor Balaam divinum ad maledicendum Israel super verticem, qui propter vehemens praeruptum vocatur excisus, et imminet mari mortuo haud procul ab Arnone.*—Abel, "L'exploration du sud-est . . ." 226, suggests that Agrispecula is the present-day Tal'at es-Safa, and forms part of the complex of mountains in which Mount Nebo was situated. Abel, *ibid*. 386 f., also suggests that in mentioning the episode of Balaam and Balac after the allusions to Og and Sehon, Egeria was actually following the order of presentation in the *Onomasticon*, where the entry on Agrispecula follows immediately after the entry on Og and Adraa.

[165] Balac was the son of Sephor (cf. Num. 22.2), and Balaam was the son of Beor (cf. Num. 22.5). In calling Balac the son of Beor, Egeria was clearly following the entry in the *Onomasticon* quoted in the immediately preceding note. Cf. Ziegler *Schrift* 184.

[166] Cf. Num. 22–24.

Chapter 13

[167] *ad regionem Ausitidem accedere.* For the Land of Hus (cf. Job 1.1) the LXX and the *Onomasticon* 143 use Ausitis, a term which appears in the Vulgate in Jer. 25.20.

[168] *propter visendam memoriam sancti Iob gratia orationis.* On the phrase *sancti Iob,* cf. Tob. 2.12 and also n. 6 above. The pious intent of Egeria's travels is made evident in the phrase *gratia orationis;* in her *Diary* the displacement of the devout is always explained as being for the purpose of prayer. Cf. the reference in ch. 23 to the visit of Marthana to Jerusalem, *ubi illa gratia orationis ascenderat.*

[169] On the length of time required for the journey, see Wistrand 3–6 and also n. 191 below.

[170] This sentence is geographically self-contradictory. In a brief but incisive article, P. Dhorme, "Le pays de Job," RBibl 29 (1911) 102–7, shows how two separate traditions were the sources for Egeria's clearly impossible statement. The tradition reflected in the first half of her statement—*Carneas autem dicitur nunc civitas Iob, quae ante dicta est Dennaba*—would situate Job's homeland in the district of Hauran in the Trachonitis. The Byzantine and later the Arab tradition, following Josephus' statement that Hus, son of Aram (cf. Gen. 10–23), had founded Damascus and the Trachonitis, sought the land of Hus in this area. An early interpretation had identified Job with Jobad, king of Edom (cf. Gen. 36.33), and confusion arose between Δεννάβα, the capital of Idumea, and the Δανάβα located in Hauran. The names of both places were translated by Jerome as *Dennaba.* R. Aigrain, "Arabie," DHGE 3.1177, quotes from Clermont-Ganneau, *Recueil d'archéologie orientale* 6 (1894) 137–44, who shows that the area around Dennaba, the present-day edh-Dhuneibeh, is full of reminiscences concerning Job: at Scheikh Sad there is Job's stone, the Sajgrat Eyyoub; not far from there are the baths of Job, Hamman Eyyoub; and less than a mile away is the convent of Job, Deir Eyyoub, the site of his tomb. While the Arabs situated Job's tomb at Nawa, the *Onomasticon* mentions a tradition putting it at Καρναείν, the former Ασταρὼθ Καρναείν, a few miles south of Nawa. It is this tradition that Egeria accepted and thus sought for

Job's tomb in the upper Jordan valley.—The second half of
Egeria's statement here—*in terra Ausitidi, in finibus Idumeae et
Arabiae*—reflects another tradition, one pointing to a locale south
of the Dead Sea in northwest Arabia, where John Chrysostom
knew of a "dunghill of Job."

[171] The Latin text has *turbae aliquantae commanent*. Geyer
(CSEL 39.418) suggested that *turbae* here was the equivalent
of *catervae monachorum*, a meaning which *turbae* has in ch. 49
of the *Diary*: *incipiunt se undique colligere turbae, non solum
monachorum*. . . . (The reading *turbae* in ch. 49 is an emendation by Cholodniak of the manuscript reading *ubi*.) Bludau 26
interpreted the *turbae aliquantae* here as referring to piles of
rubble. Bernard, however, considers *turbae* here to be an error
for *tumbae*, a word which was used only a few lines earlier:
*monticulus non satis grandis, sed factus sicut solent esse tumbae
sed grandis*. I accept Bernard's interpretation and have translated
accordingly.

[172] This apparently matter-of-fact statement raises two inter-
related questions that ultimately may be insoluble: the identification of Sedima and the location of the town that Egeria was
told was Melchisedech's city of Salem. C. Kopp, "Salem," LTK
9.261 f., summarizes the various opinions on the identification of
the city of Melchisedech in the patristic tradition. Egeria's guides
obviously did not identify Salem with the historical Jerusalem,
as do Josephus (cf. his *Ant.* 1.10), Jerome (cf. his *Quaest. in
Gen.* in ML 23.959), and modern commentators, but with a
locale in the upper Jordan valley, near Ennon, a site associated
in the New Testament with the ministry of John the Baptist (cf.
n. 180 below). According to the *Onomasticon* 41, Ennon lay to
the south of Scythopolis (the modern Beisan), and nearby was
a town of Salem, eight miles from Scythopolis and bearing the
name Salumias (*Onomasticon* 153: *In octavo quoque lapide a
Scythopoli in campo vicus Salumias appellatur*). Jerome, *Ep.*
73.7, also refers to a city near Scythopolis which in his day was
called Salem (*oppidum iuxta Scythopolim, quod usque hodie
appellatur Salem*) and where the ruins of the palace of
Melchisedech could be seen. Lévesque, "Salem," DB 5.1371 f.,
remarks that Jerome "a placé la capitale de Melchisedech au nord
de la Palestine, parce qu'il l'a confondue avec Salim, près
d'Ennon." This is very like the Salem which Egeria visited and
which she called Sedima.—Apart from Egeria's citation of the

name in this chapter of her *Diary*, there is no extant reference to a city of Sedima. Ziegler *Onomastikon* 79 f. has suggested that Egeria's "Sedima" may be a corrupt form of Sichem (via the forms Sicima, Secima). In addition to referring to the Salem near Scythopolis, the *Onomasticon* 153 also refers to a Salem which is to be identified with Sichem, the modern city of Nablus (*Salem, civitas Sicimorum, quae est Sichem*), and Ziegler conjectures that Egeria may have confused a form reflecting the local pronunciation of Salem with the name Sichem-Sicima, which she would have found in the *Onomasticon*, and thus created the identification Salem-Sedima.

[173] Franceschini-Weber emended the manuscript here to read *opu Melchisedech*, calling attention to the wording in ch. 15 of the *Diary: ecclesia, quae appellatur opu Melchisedech.* . . . Commentators are not in agreement on what Greek word is meant by *opu*. Gamurrini had suggested ὄρος, "mountain." Bechtel 128 concurred, seeing the *opu* here as illustrating the confusion between the Latin letter P and the capital Greek rho. Heraeus suggested that *opu* stood for ὅπου, "where," so that *opu Melchisedech* would mean "where Melchisedech [sacrificed]" (note that a few words later Egeria does have *locus ubi optulit Melchisedech*). Heraeus also cited a suggestion of Th. Mayr that *opu* should be *topu*, which would be the Greek τόπου (τόπος), so that the phrase would be "the place of Melchisedech."

[174] Cf. Gen. 14.18.

CHAPTER 14

[175] The passage read here probably was that mentioned in n. 174 above, or Gen. 14.18–20, the verses of which refer specifically to Melchisedech, or perhaps all of Gen. 14.

[176] *qui ipsi loco preerat*. Although the *preerat* (*praeerat*) here would seem to have much the same sense as the *deputabatur* in ch. 3 (*qui ipsi ecclesie deputabatur*, "who was assigned to the church"), the meaning "to be in charge of" for *praeesse* fits the present context very well.

[177] *advenientem sanctum Abraam*.

[178] *si quis subito iuxta sibi vult facere domum*. For the interpretation of *subito iuxta* as meaning "right nearby," cf. Erkell 50.

[179] I have used the Vulgate form of this Elamite king's name, though Egeria used the form given in the LXX and the *Onomasticon* (cf. Ziegler *Onomastikon* 82 and *Schrift* 185), Codollagomor (*quod Ollagomor* in the Arezzo manuscript). P. Dhorme, "Abraham dans le cadre de l'histoire," RBibl 40 (1931) 506–14, discusses in detail the expedition of the four kings narrated in Gen. 14.1–17, and shows that Codorlahomor is an Elamite name, *KudurLagamar*, the second element of which, *Lagamar*, was the name of an Elamite goddess. Egeria's reference to Chodorlahomor as "king of nations" is probably due to inaccurate recollection of Gen. 14.1 and 9, where the description "king of nations" belongs to Thadal, whom Dhorme equates with Tudhalias, king of the Hittites.

Chapter 15

[180] John 3.23 speaks of John the Baptist's mission at Ennon near Salim. In identifying this Salim with Salem Egeria was following the *Onomasticon* 153 (cf. n. 172 above), and it was reasonable for her to seek the site of John's second mission near the city of Melchisedech. According to Kopp, *art. cit.* 261, the site was a short distance southwest of Salim and the stream is called Ain ed-Deir.

[181] *ubi parebat fuisse operatum sanctum Iohannem Baptistam.* In translating this phrase I have interpreted *fuisse operatum* as referring to the administration of baptism. Cf. Bastiaensen 52–7. This is the only place in the *Diary* where the verb *operari* is used in a liturgical or ritualistic sense. The noun *operatio* appears twice, both times in ch. 24, where I have translated it by "ritual." Cf. the *Index verborum et locutionum* in CCL 176.728: *operatio = actio liturgica*. Cf. also n. 283 below.

[182] *cepos tu agiu Iohanni, id est quod vos dicitis latine hortus sancti Iohanni.* The phrase *cepos* (*copos* in the Arezzo manuscript) *tu agiu Iohanni* is a transliteration of the Greek κῆπος τοῦ ἁγίου Ἰωάννου. On this passage, cf. Intro. p. 6.

[183] "by candlelight" = *ad candelas*. Meister 388 and Löfstedt 244 take the *ad* here as standing for *cum* and interpret the phrase to mean "with candles." Bechtel 137, however, thought that the phrase here meant "at candlelight," that is, "at vespers."

CHAPTER 16

[184] According to Bludau 29, Thesbe is probably the present-day Chirbet el-Istib, approximately eight miles north of Jabbok, lying to the east of the Jordan in the biblical land of Galaad, as mentioned in 3 Kings 17.1. The remains of a chapel called the *mar eljas* are found there. In referring to the cave where Elias sat, Egeria is associating an episode that occurred at Mount Horeb (cf. 3 Kings 19.9 and also n. 50 above) with the upper Jordan country.

[185] *et ibi est memoria sancti Gethae, cuius nomen in libris Iudicum legimus.* Cf. Judges 11 and 12.1–7. Both Bludau 28 and Ziegler agree that the form *Getha*, found nowhere except in this text, is a scribe's error for *Jepte*, which appears in one of the fragments published by Dom de Bruyne, *op. cit.* 482: *ibi et jacet jepte.* Judges 12.7 gives his burial place as the city of Galaad, thought to be Maspha (cf. Judges 11.11). Bludau cites an Armenian calendar which calls the Saturday preceding the second Sunday after the Transfiguration the Saturday of the Holy Patriarchs, and which gives "saint" Jephtha place along with Barac (cf. Judges 4), Gedeon (cf. Judges 6–8), Samson and Heli (cf. 1 Kings 1–4). On the expression *in libris Iudicum*, cf. Ziegler *Schrift* 166.

[186] *monasterium cuiusdam, fratris nunc, id est monachi.* This is the reading in Franceschini-Weber and apparently also the reading of the manuscript of Arezzo. All editors except Cholodniak and Bernard have accepted this reading. Cholodniak gave *nunni* for *nunc*, and further emended *nunni* to read *nonni*, genitive of *nonnus*, "monk."

[187] Cf. 3 Kings 17.3–6. For the name of the stream, the Vulgate has *Carith*, the LXX has Χορράθ. The name given in the *Onomasticon* of Eusebius 174 is Χορρά, but Jerome gives *Corrath*. The location of site is in dispute. Wilson, *op. cit.* 147, suggested the valley of the Yarmuk, one of the chief tributaries of the Jordan.

[188] Bludau 31 identifies this mountain with Mount Hermon of the Anti-Lebanon range. In Late Antiquity, Phoenicia had been constituted a separate province, and the Hermon mountain mass lay astride this province and its eastern neighbor, *Augusta*

Libanensis, the capital of which was Damascus.—"In the distance" = *e contra*. Cf. n. 20 above.

[189] One of the fragments discovered by Dom de Bruyne clearly belongs to the leaf missing here: *in eo loco ubi Job sedebat in stirliquinio, modo locus mundus est per girum cancellis ferreis clusum et candela vitrea magna ibi lucet de sera ad serum* ("on that spot where Job sat on a dunghill, there is now a bare spot surrounded on all sides by iron railings, and a large glass lamp burns there from night to night"). Cf. Job 2.8. M. Le Cour Grandmaison and B. Billet, "Le pèlerinage au fumier de Job et la date de la *Peregrinatio Aetheriae*," RSR 48 (1960) 460–5, have used this fragment in an attempt to fix 387 as a *terminus ante quem* for Egeria's journey. They contend that this fragment describes the pilgrimage site at an early stage when there was only "an empty place" surrounded by a railing, whereas John Chrysostom, *Hom. ad pop. ant.* 5 (MG 49.69), in what is generally admitted to be one of the sermons delivered during the Lenten season of 387, is supposed to be describing a more developed pilgrimage site, marked by a statue of Job. Lambert, "L'*Itinerarium Egeriae* vers 414–416" 60, arguing for a slightly later date for Egeria's journey, remarks that neither the stone of Job nor the legend of the grotto is mentioned in the *Onomasticon* in Jerome's translation of 392 or in the sermon of John Chrysostom.—De Bruyne also assigned another fragment to this lost leaf: *Fontem vere ubi testa saniam radebat, quater in anno colorem mutat, primum ut purulentum habeat colorem, semel sanguinem, semel ut fellitum, et semel ut limpida est* ("where the bricks surround a spring whose color changes four times a year; it has first a pus-like color, then the color of blood, next that of bile, and finally it becomes crystal clear").

[190] On Carneas, cf. n. 170 above. Bludau 30 f. remarks that it is generally considered to be either Tell Achtera or Tell el-Achari, in the vicinity of the modern village of Schech Sad. R. Aigrain, "Arabie," DHGE 3.1177, remarks that the reference to a bishop at Carneas is the only allusion to its being an episcopal center.

[191] *regressi sumus in Ierusolimam, iter facientes per singulas mansiones, per quas ieramus tres annos.* Wistrand 3–6 recommends that the phrase *tres annos* be suppressed as not in accord with the facts. He argues that by the author's own testimony the journey to the site of Job's tomb required eight days. He further

contends that it was unlikely that on her way to Jerusalem three years earlier Egeria had come by way of Carneas. He also notes that the statement about returning through the *mansiones* by which she had come is a standard phrase (cf., e.g., the concluding statements of chs. 9 and 12) into which she may here have inadvertently slipped a phrase which appears at the beginning of the following chapter.

CHAPTER 17

[192] The term "Mesopotamia of Syria" is used in Gen. 28.2, 5, and 6 to designate the region of Haran, where Abraham settled after leaving Ur of the Chaldees and where Jacob sought a wife. It is Egeria's farthest destination. Roman control over Mesopotamia was sporadic and incomplete. Trajan in 115 conquered the area and created two provinces, Mesopotamia and Assyria, but his successors were unable to hold this territory. In 195 under Septimius Severus its northern half was brought under Roman control and called Mesopotamia, but Roman authority was repeatedly disputed by the Parthians and Sassanians. In the administrative reorganization of the empire during the 4th century, it was divided into two provinces, Mesopotamia, with its capital at Amida, and a southwestern segment, Osrhoene, with Edessa as its capital. It was the latter province that Egeria visited.

[193] On the renown and importance of Mesopotamian monasticism, see Besse, *op. cit.* 14 ff.

[194] On the shrine of St. Thomas, cf. nn. 204 and 206 below. The apostle was particularly revered in Edessa, where his relics had been transferred from India, according to the apocryphal *Acts of Thomas.* Bludau 30 cites A. Vith, *Der heilige Thomas der Apostel Indiens* (Aachen 1925) 59 and 88, who believes that the transfer took place long before 233, the date given in the Latin *passio.* The feast of the transfer is celebrated on July 3. According to Syriac tradition, it was St. Thomas who sent Thaddaeus, one of the seventy disciples, to found the church in Edessa. An apocryphal text, the so-called *Doctrina Addei,* ascribed to Thaddaeus (Addai in Syriac), was probably written *ca.* 400 A.D. A partial English text was published by W. Cureton, *Ancient Syriac Documents* (London 1864) and a complete translation was provided by G. Phillips, *The Doctrine of Addai the Apostle* (London 1876). Cf. Quasten *Patr.* 1.140–3.

[195] Eusebius, *Hist. eccl.* 1.13, has the earliest known reference to the legend of the correspondence between Christ and King Abgar V, called Uchama (i.e., "the Black"), who ruled the kingdom of Osrhoene from 4 B.C. to 7 A.D., and again from 13 to 50 A.D. Eusebius translated the Syriac texts of the letters into Greek, and the correspondence was popularized in the West by Rufinus' translation of Eusebius after 403. Augustine, *Contra Faustum* 28, denied the existence of any authentic letters of Christ, and the Gelasian Decree declared the letters apocryphal. H. Rahner, "Abgar," LTK² 1.43, fixes the origin of the legend in the early period of Christianity at Edessa, under its first Christian king, Abgar IX (179–216), who probably converted to Christianity around 206. For a summary of the religious history of Edessa, see H. Leclercq, "Edesse," DACL 4.2058–110; R. Janin, "Edesse," DHGE 14.1421–4.

[196] Antioch was a major political and economic center from the time of its foundation in the Hellenistic era. On the religious history of the city, cf. C. Karalevskij, "Antioche," DHGE 3.563–703.

CHAPTER 18

[197] Septimius Severus was the first emperor to begin the subdivision of the provinces that was to characterize imperial administration in the late empire, dividing *ca.* 194 the province of Syria into *Syria magna*, or *Syria Coele*, with Antioch as its capital, and *Phoenicia*. Between 381 and 399 *Syria Coele* (*Sirie Celen* in the Arezzo manuscript) was further subdivided into *Syria prima* and *Syria secunda*, but the older name probably continued to be used to describe the entire area.

[198] The manuscript has *Augustophratensis*, which was probably a colloquial form for *Augusta Euphratensis*, sometimes referred to simply as *Euphratensis*. Originally comprising that segment of *Syria Coele* which bordered the Euphrates, it had been erected into a separate province *ca.* 341. Hierapolis (the manuscript has *Gerapolim* in this sentence, *Ierapolim* a little farther on in this paragraph) lay along the main highway from Antioch to the Euphrates and was the center of an Oriental religion, the cult of Atargatis. It was a metropolitan see; one of its bishops, Alexander, attended the Council of Ephesus, and another, Stephen, the Council of Chalcedon. Also known as Bambuke and Mabbug, the site of its extensive ruins is today called

Membij. Cf. B. Kötting, "Hierapolis," LTK² 5.321 f.; W. Ruge, "Hierapolis," RE 8.1404 f.

¹⁹⁹ Gen. 15.18.

²⁰⁰ This comparison of the Rhone and the Euphrates is one of the points cited by those who hold Egeria's homeland was Gaul. See Intro. p. 10. Bludau 236 f. states that the swiftness of the Rhone was a *topos* in late Latin verse, and he cites Ausonius, Lucan, and Claudian as referring to the treacherous current of the Rhone.

CHAPTER 19

²⁰¹ Bathnae (*Batanis* in the manuscript), which the Arabs called Sarug (today Seroujd), was located in the province of Osrhoene in the neighborhood of Edessa. Ammianus Marcellinus 14.3 stated that it was the center of an annual September fair which probably coincided with a religious festival. Ziegler *Schrift* 193 states that in referring to a scriptural mention of Bathnae, Egeria may have been confusing the Mesopotamian city with Ecbatana in Persia.

²⁰² Egeria uses the term *confessor* only three times, and only in reference to bishops she met in Mesopotamia—at Bathnae, Edessa, and Carrhae. In each case the term in linked with *monachus*. Cabrol 173 and Bludau 252–5 attempted to link the title of confessor to the repercussions of the Arian persecution under Valens (364–378) in northeast Syria. Bouvy, *op. cit.* 520, believed that he could identify the three bishops in question as Abraham of Bathnae, Eulogius of Edessa, and Vitus of Carrhae, each of whom was present at the Council of Constantinople in 381. B. Botte, "Confessor," ALMA 16 (1942) 137–48, suggested that the term was used for defenders of the faith against Arianism, while Meister 358, in view of his late dating of the text, saw these bishops as anti-Monophysite champions. Lambert, "L'*Itinerarium Egeriae* vers 414–416" 58 f., interpreted *confessor* as Hispanic Latin for a monk or ascetic specifically assigned to recitation of the divine office; cf. also his "Egeria, soeur de Galla" 25 n. 5. Lambert identifies two of the bishops as Rabboula of Edessa and Abraham of Carrhae. All such identifications depend, of course, on the date assigned. G. Morin, "Un passage énigmatique de s. Jérôme contre la pèlerine espagnole Eucheria?" RB 30 (1913) 183 n. 6, doubts that Egeria's use of *confessor* can be used to date her *Diary*.

²⁰³ On Bathnae as a military center, cf. V. Chapot, *La frontière de l'Euphrate* (Paris 1907) 305.

²⁰⁴ The wording here, *ad ecclesiam et ad martyrium sancti Thomae*, has been cited in support of several opposing theories concerning the date of the *Diary*. The discussion has centered on the precise meaning of the *et* here. Gamurrini, Geyer, Deconinck, and Kruger interpret it disjunctively, thus having Egeria visit two separate buildings. Baumstark, Morin, and Meister interpret the *et* conjunctively, taking the *ecclesiam* and the *martyrium* as referring to a single building. The first group of critics date Egeria's pilgrimage in the period 378–389, while the second group must date it after 394. The chronicle of Edessa states that the sarcophagus of St. Thomas was transferred to the great church dedicated to him on August 22, 394 (the 27th Ab of the year 705 of the Seleucid era). For a summary of the question, see Bludau 246–51.

²⁰⁵ Probably from the apocryphal *Acts of Thomas*, which date from the 3rd century and which were probably written in Syriac by a member of the Bardaison sect at Edessa. Cf. Quasten *Patr.* 1.139 f.; F. L. Cross, "Acts of Thomas," ODC 1351.

²⁰⁶ *nova dispositione*. The cathedral church of Edessa, which had suffered greatly from the floods of A.D. 201 and 303, had been reconstructed between 313 and 324, and it is generally assumed that it was to this church, also called the Old Church, that the relics of St. Thomas were transferred in 394. Bludau 34 and 248 f. suggests that *nova dispositione* refers in fact to a structure dedicated to St. Thomas but separate from the cathedral; he asserts that it was this structure which received the apostle's remains. Meister 345 f. states that the phrase aptly describes the new church built under Justinian in 525.

²⁰⁷ The area around Edessa was filled with monastic cells. Cf. Besse, *op. cit.* 15; L. Fliche and H. Martin, edd., *Histoire de l'Église depuis les origines jusqu'à nos jours* 1 (Paris 1936) 347.

²⁰⁸ Cf. n. 202 above.

²⁰⁹ The reference here is to the summer residence of the rulers of Edessa located within the city. Farther on Egeria mentions the winter palace constructed in the citadel and protected from the ravages of flooding.—Abgar was a traditional name for the kings of Edessa, and Egeria is alluding here to Abgar V. Cf. n. 195 above; also H. Leclercq, "La légende d'Abgar," DACL 1.87–97; L. J. Tixeront, *Les origines de*

l'église d'Edesse et la légende d'Abgar (Paris 1888); R. Duval, *Histoire politique, religieuse et littéraire d'Edesse* (Paris 1892); F. L. Cross, "Legend of Abgar," ODC 5.

[210] *in cuius Aggari vultu parebat de contra vere fuisse hunc virum satis sapientem et honoratum.* On the phrase *de contra* as used by Egeria, cf. n. 20 above. The phrase can hardly be translated here by "at a distance."

[211]Pétré *Journal* 164 f., n. 3, suggests that these phrases may have been borrowed from the letters alleged to have been exchanged between Abgar and Christ. Cf. n. 195 above.

[212] It was customary for successive kings of Edessa to bear the names of Abgar and Magnus, which is Egeria's form of the name Ma'nou. Abgar V was succeeded by his son Ma'nou, who ruled from 50 to 57 A.D. The first Christian king of Edessa, Abgar IX, was followed on the throne by Ma'nou IX.

[213] Edessa bore the name of *Callirhoe* ("beautiful flowing") because of its fountains and pools, especially the one containing the fish dedicated to the goddess Atargatis. According to the chronicle of Edessa, the river Daican (or Skirtos) traversed the city and was fed by twenty-five streams. Duval, *op. cit.* 9, cites Procopius, *De aedificiis* 3, who describes how Justinian constructed a canal to divert the excess waters of the Daican following the flood of 525. Meister 358 thought that Egeria's failure to mention the river indicated that her visit took place after that canal was built; but Deconinck, *art. cit.* 437 f., suggests that if Meister's dating of the visit were correct, the bishop would scarcely have failed to refer to so recent an event as the building of the canal. Deconinck, who argues for an earlier dating, conjectures that Egeria either was badly informed or visited the city during a dry spell. Cf. Bludau 250 f.; H. Leclercq, "Edesse," DACL 1.2059.

[214] On the edge of the eastern frontier, Edessa was undoubtedly the site of numerous Persian attacks. In A.D. 260, the Sassanians defeated the Roman legions commanded by the emperor Valerian near Edessa. Cf. R. Ghirshman, *Iran* (Pelican Books 1953) 292.

[215] H. Leclercq, "La légende d'Abgar," DACL 1.92, contrasts Eusebius' version of the legendary correspondence with that in the later *Doctrina Addei* (cf. above, nn. 194 and 195). The promise mentioned here in the *Diary* does not appear in Eusebius, but forms the conclusion of Christ's letter in the

Doctrina Addei. However, it is doubtful that Egeria was acquainted with that latter work, for she does not refer to its account of a picture of Christ. See following note.

[216] P. Devos, "Egérie à Edesse. S. Thomas l'Apôtre. Le Roi Abgar," AB 85 (1967) 381–400, does not agree with the generally held opinion that the promise of God referred to by the bishop here was part of a late development of the Abgar legend. Devos contends that Egeria visited Edessa in 384 and that the account given in her *Diary* is an authentic reflection of the primitive stage of the legend.

[217] This is the winter palace which was located on the citadel. It was probably constructed after the summer palace within the city to avoid the floods. Cf. Pétré *Journal* 169 n. 1.

[218] On the importance of the Latin translation of the correspondence in determining the date of Egeria's pilgrimage, cf. Intro. p. 13. The first known Latin translation of Eusebius, that of Rufinus, appeared in 403. The "more extensive" text mentioned by Egeria presumably was one including the promise of Christ referred to above (cf. nn. 215 and 216).

CHAPTER 20

[219] Carrhae, the site of the defeat of the Roman legions under Crassus in 53 B.C. by the Parthians commanded by Surena, was the biblical city of Haran, where the household of Abraham lived before entering Chanaan (cf. Gen. 11.31 f.). Located south of Edessa, it was an important fortress city in the province of Osrhoene in the 4th century. It was constantly changing hands between the Romans and the Sassanians and had been captured by Sapor II in A.D. 359–"As far as Carrhae"=*usque ad Carris.* The name by which the city was known to Graeco-Latin writers was *Carrae* or *Carrhae.* Except in the phrase *a Charris* in ch. 21, in subsequent references to the city Egeria uses the form *Charra* (once *Carra*), which, she states, was the name given in Scripture. *Charra* is a transliteration of the form used in the LXX for Gen. 11.31 f., 12.4, etc. In the *Onomasticon* 171 we find Χαρράν and *Charran* (*Charran civitas Mesopotamiae trans Edessam, quae usque hodie Carra dicitur*). Χαρράν is the Greek transcription for the Hebrew Haran. Wherever Egeria uses the form *Charra*, I have translated it with the Vulgate form, "Haran." Cf. R. Janin, "Carrae," DHGE 11.1123 f.; K. F.

Kramer, "Charres," LTK² 2.1024; A. Legendre, "Haran," DB 3.424–7.

²²⁰ Cf. Gen. 12.1, which in the Vulgate reads: *Egredere de terra tua et de cognatione tua et de domo patris tui et veni in terram quam monstrabo tibi.* Neither the LXX nor the *Vetus Latina* has Haran (Charran) in this passage. Bludau 35 and 226 and Ziegler *Schrift* 175 suggest that Egeria intended to write *Chanaan* instead of *Charran*, or else that in her text of the Scriptures *Charram* had been substituted for *terram.*

²²¹ Cf. n. 202 above. In addition to the suggestions there noted on the identify of this bishop, Deconinck, *art. cit.* 445, suggested the name of Protogenus, the companion in exile of Eulogius of Edessa.

²²² Cf. Gen. 24.15–27. For the name of Abraham's servant Egeria has Eleazar, which is probably a corrupt form of Eliezer, the name of Abraham's steward mentioned in Gen. 15.2. Cf. Ziegler *Schrift* 186.

²²³ There is no mention of a St. Helpidius in any martyrology. Palladius, *Hist. Laus.* 48 (= ACW 34.130 f.), mentions a Cappadocian monk named Elpidius with whom he lived for a time in caves near Jericho around 388. For a St. Elpidio, see AASS Sept 1 (1868) 378. Bludau 36 believes that the Helpidius mentioned by Egeria was a local saint of Carrhae who probably died during the persecution of Christians under Sassanian King Sapor II (310–380). Egeria gives his feast day as April 23. M. L. McClure and C. L. Feltoe, *The Pilgrimage of Etheria* (Translations of Christian Literature, Series 3: Liturgical Texts, London 1919) 37 n. 1, note that the ancient Syriac martyrology (411/412) as presented by Lietzmann mentioned Helpidios and Hermogenes as martyrs in Melitene in Cappadocia. The date of their feast is given as May 3.

²²⁴ *etiam et illos maiores.* In translating this phrase I have followed the interpretation given in Bastiaensen 20. Cf. n. 32 above. For a passage in which *maiores* means monks of an earlier generation, cf. n. 151 above. Regarding the monks around Carrhae, cf. Sozomenus, *Hist. eccl.* 6.39 (MG 67.1391–5).

²²⁵ *propter memoriam sancti Abrahae.* The word *memoria* is used five times in chs. 20 and 21, in each case with its late meaning of *memoriale* or *monumentum.* Egeria uses the word in earlier passages to refer to a tomb or a grave. Here, however, she is not saying that the tomb of Abraham was located at Carrhae,

but rather only that a "memorial," a church commemorating his presence, could be visited there.

[226] *quoniam tales sunt ut et virtutes faciant multas.* Near the end of this chapter is the phrase *quae mirabilia fecerint.* I have interpreted *virtutes* here in the sense of *mirabilia.* Mohrmann, *Die altchristliche Sondersprache in den Sermones des hl. Augustin* 121 f., gives a similar interpretation to the term. For the sense of the word *virtus* in Egeria, Van Oorde 214 gives *miraculum.* Pétré *Journal* 175 n. 2 states: "Il peut désigner soit les 'miracles' accomplis par ces saints personnages, soit la manière extraordinaire dont ils vivaient." Cf. also Bayard, *Le latin de s. Cyprian* (Paris 1902) 94.

[227] Egeria's comment on the religious complexion of Carrhae is corroborated by the testimony of others. Carrhae remained a predominantly pagan city until Justinian; cf. Procopius, *De bell. pers.* 2.13. Theodoret, Hist. *rel.* 4.18 (MG 82.1159), refers to Carrhae under the emperor Valens (364–378) as "savage" and "full of thorns of paganism," although a bishop had been installed there under Constantius (337–361). Janin, *art. cit.* 1124, suggests that the strong influence of the cult of the moon-god may have hampered the progress of Christianity. Bishop Abraamius (Abraham) is credited with apostolic zeal in spreading Christianity there early in the 5th century; cf. Theodoret, *Hist. rel.* 17 (MG 82.1420–5).

[228] *pro memoria illius.* Egeria wishes to say that the Christians reverenced the place where Abraham lived, where the church now stood in memory of him.

[229] On Nachor and Bathuel, cf. Gen. 22.20–23. Nachor was the brother of Abraham; his son Bathuel was father of Laban the Syrian.

[230] Cf. Gen. 11.31.

[231] Cf. Gen. 24. The Scriptures do not specifically state that Abraham's servant came to Carrhae (Haran), but rather that he "went on to the city of Nachor." Albright, *From the Stone Age to Christianity* 236, distinguishes the two cities: "The city of Nahor, mentioned as the home of Rebekah's parents in Gen. 24.10, figures often as Nakhur in the Mari tablets as well as in more recent Middle-Assyrian documents; it seems to have been located below Harran in the Balikh valley, to judge from both the Mari references and the Assyrian records of the seventh century B.C., where Til-Nakhiri, 'the Mound of Nakhuru,' is

the name of a town (with Assyrian vowel harmony) in the Harran district." Egeria's statement on the presence of Nachor at Haran probably was based on such passages as Gen. 27.43 and 29.4 f.

[232] Cf. Gen. 11.31.

[233] *Scriptura canonis.* This is the only use of *canon* in the *Diary.* Ernout 296 states that *canon* came into use in the 4th century to designate the list of books recognized by the Church as divinely inspired. Ernout cites an analogous use of the Greek source-word in Cicero, *Fam.* 16.17: *tu qui κανών esse meorum scriptorum soles.*

[234] Cf. Gen. 28. For the expression "Laban the Syrian," cf. LXX for Gen. 25.20. The Vulgate for Gen. 25.20 reads: . . . *Rebeccam filiam Bathuelis syri de Mesopotamia, sororem Laban.* H. W. Klein, "Zur Latinität des *Itinerarium Egeriae* (früher *Peregrinatio Aetheriae*). Stand der Forschungen und neue Erkenntnismöglichkeiten," *Romanica: Festschrift Gerhard Rohlfs* (Halle 1958) 243–58, states that the *Vetus Latina* had two examples of the phrase "Laban the Syrian," in Gen. 31.20 (*celavit autem Jacob Laban Syrum ne diceret ei quod recederet*) and 31.22 (*Nuntiatum est Labae Syro tertio die quod recessisset Jacob*).

[235] Cf. Gen. 29.2–10.

[236] *locus ille Chaldaeorum*, a reminiscence of Gen. 11.28.

[237] By "Persia," Egeria means the kingdom of the Sassanians, which succeeded the Parthian empire. It lasted from 208 to 651, when it was destroyed by the Arabs.

[238] On Nisibis as an important Christian religious and intellectual center, cf. H. Engberding and P. Krüger, "Nisibis," LTK² 7.1010.

[239] Five days would appear to be correct for the journey from Carrhae to Nisibis, but the same amount of time cannot be correct for the journey from Nisibis to Ur, if the bishop was referring to the site of the biblical Ur agreed upon by most archaeologists and ancient historians, who identify it with the present-day ruins at Mugalyar in southern Iraq. F. Hommel, *Die altisraelitische Überlieferung in inschriftlicher Beleuchtung* (Munich 1907) 212 and 293, had suggested a more northerly Mesopotamian site, perhaps at Arpakschad (Arpachiya), north of the ruins of Nineveh. Wilson, *op. cit.* 147, says of Ur: ". . . five stations beyond Nisibis, which is apparently the place,

not yet identified, mentioned by Ammianus Marcellinus, as a 'castle' existing in his day between Atrai (el Hadhr) and Nisibis." The question of Egeria's Ur is probably insoluble.

²⁴⁰ One of the arguments proposed by Gamurrini for dating the *Diary* in the late 4th century was based on this passage: *sed modo ibi accessus Romanorum non est, totum enim illud Persae tenent.* Gamurrini gave to *modo* here its classical meaning of "recently"; since Nisibis had come under definitive Sassanian control only after the death of the emperor Julian through Jovian's treaty with Sapor II in 363, Gamurrini concluded that our author's journey must have taken place not long afterwards. Meister 342 took *modo* here as equivalent to *nunc*, "now," and buttressed his argument with other passages of the *Diary* where this meaning of *modo* is beyond dispute. Löfstedt 240–4 supported Meister's interpretation. While Deconinck, *art. cit.* 438, and Bludau 251 f. accepted *nunc* as the meaning of *modo* here, they continued to defend a 4th-century date for the *Diary;* they argued that *modo* coupled with a verb in the present tense referred to a situation which was not considered irremediable, and hence the usage here would have been amply justified in the 4th century, but scarcely possible in the 6th century after 150 years of Sassanian hegemony.

²⁴¹ For *orientalis*, "eastern," Geyer (CSEL 39.69) suggested *Syria orientalis*. Pétré *Journal* 179 n. 2 cites *terram orientalem* in Gen. 29.1 as referring to the region around Haran.

²⁴² *sive qui iam recesserant.* Cf. n. 138 above.

²⁴³ *sive etiam qui adhuc in corpore sunt.* Cf. the phrasing in 2 Cor. 12.3: *sive in corpore, sive extra corpus.* Ch. 23 of the *Diary* concludes with these words: . . . *sive in corpore, sive iam extra corpus fuero.*

²⁴⁴ *gesta monachorum maiorum.* Pétré *Journal* 179 understood *maiores* as referring to monks of yore. I have here once again followed the interpretation of Bastiaensen 20. Cf. nn. 32, 151, and 224 above.—For the types of *gesta* Egeria may have heard about, see Besse, *op. cit.* 501–33, who describes "le merveilleux dans la vie des moines orientaux."

CHAPTER 21

²⁴⁵ Cf. Gen. 29.2–10.

²⁴⁶ Bludau suggested that Fadana may have survived as a place

212 NOTES ON PAGES 86-87

name in the form *Tell-feddan*, a mound of ruins located to the west of Carrhae; also that the name may be derived from *Padan-Aram*, the term translated in Gen. 25.20 and 28.2, 5, and 6 by "Mesopotamia" or "Mesopotamia of Syria." According to Albright, *From the Stone Age to Christianity* 237, *Padan-Aram* means "plains of Aram."

[247] Cf. Gen. 31.19 and 30.

CHAPTER 22

[248] Tarsus, the chief city of Cilicia, was established as the province's capital by Pompey in 67 B.C., and was the seat of a Stoic school of philosophy. It was the birthplace of St. Paul (cf. Acts 21.39).

[249] Isauria was established as a separate province during the reorganization of the empire by Diocletian (284–305) from territory carved out of western Cilicia and southern Lyaconia.

CHAPTER 23

[250] For a brief notice on this city, cf. A. M. Schneider, "Pompeipolis," RE 21².2043 f. The earliest archaeological remains of the city date from the middle of the 2nd century. There is evidence of a Christian presence there late in the 3rd century. Pompeipolis was a suffragan see of Tarsus.

[251] Pliny the Elder, *Naturalis historia* 5.92, refers to Corycus, located near the modern Korghos, as a city of Cilicia, but in Egeria's day it was within the borders of the province of Isauria. For an extensive treatment of the Christian archaeology of Corycus with numerous illustrations, see E. Herzfeld and S. Guyer, *Monumenta Asiae Minoris antiqua* 1: *Meriamlik und Korykos* (Publications of the American Society for Archaeological Research in Asia Minor, Manchester 1930). Cf. also Juthner, "Korykos," RE 11².1451 ff.

[252] Seleucia, the modern Selefkeh, originally within the province of Cilicia, lay within the boundaries of Isauria in the 5th century. It was founded by Seleucus Nicator (312–281 B.C.) on the banks of the river Calycanos.

[253] The feast of St. Thecla, virgin and martyr, is celebrated in the Western church on September 23 and in the East on September 24. According to the apocryphal *Acts of Paul and Thecla*

(cf. below, n. 257), she was converted by St. Paul during his mission to Iconium (cf. Acts 13.51 and 14). Tradition placed her tomb at Meriamlik, three miles from Seleucia, where a shrine stood in her honor. Cf. H. Delahaye, "Les recueils antiques de miracles des saints 7: les miracles de ste. Thècle," AB 44 (1925) 49–57; F. Cabrol, *La légende de ste. Thècle* (Paris 1895); J. Gwyn, DCB 4.882–96.

[254] Marthana is the only contemporary mentioned by name in the *Diary*. A Marthana, presumably the same person, is mentioned in Basil of Seleucia's *De vita ac miraculis s. Theclae virginis martyris Iconiensis* 2.30 (MG 85.617). See Intro. pp. 14 f.; also Bludau 267. On the title "deaconess," cf. F. L. Cross, "Deaconess," ODC 377 f.; H. Leclercq, "Diaconesse," DACL 4.725–33.

[255] *haec autem monasteria aputactitum seu virginum regebat.* Used nine times in the *Diary*, the term *aputactitae* (from the Greek ἀποταχτῖται) refers to both men and women, as is evident from a statement later in this chapter (*visis etiam sanctis monachis vel aputactites, tam viris quam feminis*) and another in ch. 28 (*aputactite, viri vel feminae*). The verb ἀποτάσσεσθαι is used once in the New Testament with the meaning "to renounce"; in Egyptian monastic literature the term ἀποτασσάμενοι means *monachi* or "anchorites," and the verb ἀποτάσσεσθαι is equal to *monachari*. Egeria seems to be reporting the word *aputactitae* to her correspondents as a local term for monks and nuns. A. Lambert, "Apotactites et Apotaxamenes," DACL 1.2604–26, believes that the terms *monachi, monazontes* (cf. n. 266 below), and *aputactitae* all had the same general meaning, but with *aputactitae* reserved for those whose life was more austere, whose practices of fast and abstinence were more rigorous. Because in late Latin *vel* is frequently used without any disjunctive force (cf. Löfstedt 197–201), it cannot be determined whether Egeria identifies *aputactitae* with the *monachi* or distinguishes between them.

[256] On the reputation of the Isaurians as bandits, cf. Ammianus Marcellinus 14.2.

[257] Presumably a reference to the *Acts of Paul and Thecla*, originally part of the larger *Acts of Paul*, probably written before 190 by a priest of Asia Minor. Cf. Quasten *Patr.* 1.130–3; F. L. Cross, "Acts of Paul and Thecla," ODC 1032; B. Kötting, "Thekla," LTK 10.18 f.

[258] This station, the name of which is variously spelled

Mansocrenas, Mansucrinae, and *Mopsucrene,* was on the road from Tarsus to the Cilician Gates. Cf. W. Ruge, "Mopsukrene," RE 16.250 f.

²⁵⁹ F. Wotke, "Peregrinatio ad loca sancta," RE Suppl. 7.875–85, believes that Egeria followed the same route as that described in the *Itinerarium Burdigalense* (CCL 175.1–26). Her route then would have been across the Taurus mountains to Podandus and Faustinopolis, northward to Tyana, Archelais, and Ancyra (modern Ankara), then westward to Juliopolis and Nicaea, northward to Nicomedia, and westward again to Chalcedon, opposite Constantinople. The pilgrim of Bordeaux gives 61 Roman miles from Chalcedon to Nicomedia, 258 miles from there to Ancyra, and 343 miles from Ancyra to Tarsus.

²⁶⁰ The feast of St. Euphemia is celebrated on September 16, the reputed date of her martyrdom in 303 or 304 at Chalcedon, where an impressive basilica was erected over her grave (see AASS Sept. 5 [1755] 255–86). The Council of Chalcedon was held in this church in 451. Meister 350 argued that the adjective *famosissimum,* "very famous," referred to the fame the church had acquired from the Council of Chalcedon, and thus pointed to a relatively late date for the *Diary.* Egeria appears, however, to attribute the fame of the church to its association with St. Euphemia. On Euphemia, cf. A. P. Frutag, LTK 3.1184 f.; H. Leclercq, "Euphémie," DACL 5.745 f.; A. M. Schneider, "Sankt Euphemia und das Konzil von Chalkedon," in A. Grillmeier and H. Bacht, edd., *Das Konzil von Chalkedon* 1 (1951) 291–302. On Chalcedon, cf. H. Leclercq, "Chalcédon," DACL 3.90–130.

²⁶¹ This may be a reference to the shrine or *martyrium* dedicated to the apostles which was built by Constantine. Cf. Eusebius, *Vita Const.* 4.58 (MG 20.1209).

²⁶² Ephesus was the capital of the proconsular province of Asia. Renowned in antiquity for the cult of Artemis (Diana), Ephesus was an early Christian center, the scene of one of St. Paul's missions, and, according to tradition, the home of the aged St. John. The most famous shrine built on the traditional site of St. John's burial was constructed by Justinian in 540. The Third Ecumenical Council was held in Ephesus in 431. Cf. P. Antoine, "Ephèse," DB Suppl. 2.1076–1104.

²⁶³ Cf. n. 243 above.

CHAPTER 24

[264] An account of the daily and Sunday services described by
Egeria is given in Cabrol 31–68 and Bludau 43–67. The first
office to be described here is the nocturnal or pre-dawn vigil,
called nocturns, which resembles the office of matins. On the
origin and nature of this service, cf. Intro. pp. 28 f. and n. 134
to the Intro. The precise hour of this service is difficult to
determine. Leclercq, "Bréviaire," DACL 2.1283, states that this
office began two or three hours before sunrise, and the time
would therefore have varied from season to season—around 1 a.m.
in the summer and as late as 5 a.m. in the winter. Hanssens, *op.
cit.* 88, mentions that Benedict set the 8th hour of the night (*ca.*
2 a.m.) and Columba the middle of the night (*ad medium noctis*)
for the service. As Cabrol 37 indicates, the office took place *a
primo gallo usque ad mane*, which generally meant between
midnight and 3 a.m. Hippolytus, *Canons* 27, states that at
cockcrow prayers were always said in church in obedience to
evangelical counsel (cf. Mark 13.35).

[265] On the Anastasis, cf. Intro. p. 24 and n. 111 to the Intro.

[266] These transliterated Greek terms designate ascetics who
were closely connected with the liturgical life of Jerusalem. This
is the only example of *parthene* in the text, but *monazontes* is
used nine times, almost exclusively in direct reference to the
liturgy of Jerusalem. Bludau 45 cites Conybeare on *monazontes:*
"of solitaries, of virgins, both men and women." Cabrol 37 n. 2
quotes Dom Toutté, who insisted that Cyril of Jerusalem understood the term to refer to monks dwelling in cities. Bastiaensen
20 sees *monazontes* as practically a synonym for *monachi.*

[267] Bastiaensen 23 f. cites this passage as an indication that
Egeria both came from and wrote for a monastic milieu. On
laicus, "lay," cf. L. de la Potterie, "L'origine et le sens primitif
du mot 'laic,'" *Nouvelle revue théologique* 80 (1958) 840–53.—
As Egeria's description indicates, the service referred to here was
essentially one for religious. The Fathers, however, frequently
admonished both the secular clergy and the laity to join the
monks at such vigils. Cf. Basil, *Ep.* 207 *ad clericos Neocaesariae*
(MG 32.760–5), and John Chrysostom, *In ps. 133 expos.* (MG
55.386). Both Socrates, *Hist. eccl.* 6.8 (MG 67.687–91), and

Sozomenus, *Hist. eccl.* 8.7 (MG 67.1535–38), speak of John Chrysostom's inauguration of a Saturday as well as a Sunday night vigil during the Arian controversy in Constantinople.

[268] *maturius vigilare.* Pétré translates: "faire cette vigile matinale." However, both Van Oorde 213 and Anglade 121 state that the phrase here (as also the *maturius vigilantes* in ch. 4) refers to early rising and is not synonymous with *vigilias agere,* "to hold a vigil."

[269] *dicuntur ymni et psalmi responduntur, similiter et antiphonae.* The expression *dicuntur (h)ymni* is used frequently by Egeria in her descriptions of the liturgy. Löfstedt 282–5 sees *dicere* as a late Latin synonym for *canere* or *cantare.* C. Butler, *Regula* 217 n. 1, remarks: *nulla prorsus distinctio sensus est apud sanctum Benedictum inter verba: 'dicere, canere, cantare, modulare, psallere.'* "—The precise meaning of *psalmi responduntur, similiter et antiphonae* is not clear.

[270] As usual, Egeria does not specify either the number of hymns or the particular hymns sung. A. Baumstark, *Festbrevier und Kirchenjahr der syrischen Jakobiten* (Paderborn 1910) 141–7, contrasts with comparative tables the Jerusalem vigil and the Greek Orthos, the Roman matins and the Jacobite church's night office. Basil, *Ep.* 207.3 (MG 32.764), says that Ps. 50 was sung daily at the vigil.

[271] *incipiunt matutinos ymnos dicere.* This marked the beginning of the *officium matutinum,* which corresponds to our lauds. Cf. Benedict, *Regula* 8: *matutini [sc. psalmi], qui incipiente luce agendi sunt, subsequantur [sc. hora vigiliarum].* Jerome, *Ep.* 22.37 (= ACW 33.173), calls this hour of prayer *diluculum,* "daybreak," "dawn." Epiphanius, *Expos. fid.* 23 (MG 42.829), also refers to "morning hymns," ἑωθινοὶ ὕμνοι. Cassian, *Inst.* 3, lists Pss. 62, 118, and 148 as standard hymns for lauds.

[272] Called *spelunca* by Egeria, this is the site of the Holy Sepulchre itself, located at the center of the Anastasis.—In the following, "from within the railings" = *de intro cancellos.* It is probable that there were columns supporting a conical roof, and between the columns iron grilling.

[273] Bludau 49 f. states that we have here commemorations for the living and the dead which resemble the mementos of the Mass. The names of those to be commemorated were written on tablets or diptychs. Egeria does not elaborate on these prayers, but in the *Apostolic Constitutions* 8.35 we find an extensive litany

in which the deacon calls for prayers for the whole world, the church, the bishops, priests, deacons, the sick, travellers, the dead. On the ritual at vespers, cf. n. 279 below.

[274] *omnes ad manum ei accedunt.* This phrase occurs frequently in the text. J. H. Srawley, *The Early History of the Liturgy* (2nd ed. Cambridge 1947) 102 f., n. 2, compares Egeria's *ad manum accedere* with the προσελθεῖν ὑπὸ χεῖρα in canon 19 of the Synod of Laodicea (363) with reference to the blessing at the withdrawal of catechumens, of penitents, etc.

[275] *ac sic fit missa.* Egeria uses *missa* 72 times, most frequently, as here, to describe the ritual of dismissal from a liturgical office. According to F. J. Dölger, "Zu den Zeremonien der Messliturgie. III. *Ite, missa est* in kultur- und sprachgeschichtlicher Beleuchtung," *Antike und Christentum* 6 (1940) 81–132, esp. 95–9, the *Itinerarium Egeriae* is a pivotal text in the development of the meaning of *missa* from "dismissal" to "Mass." Dölger cites several passages in the *Diary* where *missa* is used to designate a sort of religious service, indeed the Mass itself (cf. below, n. 332). The earliest commonly accepted text in which *missa* = "Mass" is in Ambrose, *Ep.* 20 (ML 16.995), written in 385: *Ego tamen mansi in munere, missam facere coepi. Dum offero . . . et orare in ipsa oblatione Deum coepi.* C. Mohrmann, "Missa," *VC* 12 (1958) 67–92, an article largely dedicated to the *Itinerarium Egeriae*, considers *missa* a stylized term, almost a cliché, used to designate a set of ill-defined rites constituting the elaborate dismissals characteristic of the Eastern liturgies; according to Mohrmann, in only a few passages in the *Diary* has it the general but vague meaning of some sort of religious service.

[276] On the absence of a mention of a liturgical office at the third hour except in Lent, see Intro. pp. 28, 34. I have avoided using the technical terms "sext" and "nones" to translate *hora sexta* and *hora nona*, since there is no set stylized form for them in the text, which has alternately *hora sexta, ad sexta,* and *ad sextam.*

[277] For the contents of these offices we must rely on contemporary or slightly later texts. Cassian, *Inst.* 2.5 and 3.3, mentions three Psalms for sext and nones in the East.

[278] Egeria's transliteration of the Greek λυχνικόν, the counterpart of which in the Western liturgies was very well known to her, as evidenced by her frequent use of *lucernare, lucernarium, hora lucernae. Lucenarium* means "candlelight"; I follow Souter

236, who gives "vespers" as its equivalent. Férotin 390 f. states that the Spanish church surpassed all others in the importance it accorded to the *lucernarium* in its liturgy.

[279] *kyrie eleyson, quod dicimus nos: miserere Domine.* Egeria's text here suggests that her addressees might not have been familiar with the Greek phrase, but would have been familiar with the practice of *preces feriales.* Bludau states that the *Kyrie eleison* response was common throughout Asia Minor, in Jerusalem, and at Antioch. The *Apostolic Constitutions* 8.35 refers to the people, especially the children, responding with *Kyrie eleison.* This is a more elaborate ceremony than the morning commemorations (see n. 273 above). Cf. Jungmann, *Pastoral Liturgy* 180 ff.; B. Fischer, *"Litania ad laudes et vesperas.* Ein Vorschlag zur Neugestaltung der Ferialpreces," *Liturg. Jahrbuch* 1 (1951) 53-74.

[280] *Et postmodum de Anastasim usque ad Crucem cum ymnis ducitur episcopus.* On the *ad Crucem,* cf. Intro. pp. 24 f. and n. 113 to the Intro. Baumstark, *Liturgie comparée* 46 ff., considers this procession to the Cross and the conclusion of the vespers service there to have exercised a great influence on several other liturgies, citing, e.g., the station *ad crucem* on certain major feasts at the monastery of St. Gall from the 9th to the 11th centuries and the station *ad fontes* for the ancient vespers service at Rome.—The phrase *cum ymnis ducitur episcopus* recurs frequently in the text. I have generally translated the phrase as here, supplying the passive verb with an indefinite subject. Cf. Van Oorde 7-11.

[281] *post Crucem.* Cf. Intro. p. 25 and n. 114 to the Intro.

[282] "candelabra" = *cereofala.* Cf. Bechtel 137 and Souter 46.

[283] Just as Egeria made no mention of the distinctly monastic office of prime, so also she makes no reference to a compline service.—Both at the beginning and at the end of her account of the daily service of prayer at the Anastasis Egeria uses the word *operatio* (*Ut autem sciret affectio vestra, quae operatio singulis diebus cotidie . . .* at the beginning of this chapter, and here: *Haec operatio cotidie per dies sex ita habetur . . .*). Bastiaensen 92-5 discusses whether *operatio* may not have already acquired in Egeria's time a meaning similar to the phrase *opus Dei,* the monastic ritual of prayer at fixed hours of the day; Bastiaensen does not suggest that *operatio* had become a technical formula like *opus Dei,* but that it may have been consciously

employed to describe one aspect of the liturgy, the services of prayer held at various hours on weekdays.

[284] *ac si per pascha.* This phrase occurs frequently in the text. It is practically a stereotyped expression to signify a large crowd. On the construction *per pascha* for "at Easter," see Bastiaensen 170 ff.

[285] "in the forecourt" = *in basilica.* I have in this instance given "forecourt" for *basilica,* because Egeria is using the word here to describe the atrium or inner court between the Anastasis and the Martyrium. Cf. her ch. 37 for a description of the Ante Crucem. The word *basilica* is used two other times in the *Diary,* once again in this chapter and once in ch. 25, and in both of these instances the word refers to the church of the Anastasis (*tota basilica Anastasis* and *de basilica Anastasis*).

[286] For the various interpretations of the nature of this service, see Intro. p. 30 and n. 137 to the Intro.

[287] Differently from on weekdays, the bishop arrives at the opening of the office and precedes the people into the Anastasis. On the nature of the office Egeria describes here, see Intro. pp. 31 f. and nn. 138 and 139 to the Intro.

[288] *dicitur et tertius psalmus a quocumque clerico.* Bastiaensen 12-15 remarks that *clericus* and *clerus* have a variety of meanings in this text. Generally, the words are used for all ecclesiastics of less than episcopal rank, but in this passage the *quocumque clerico* means a member of one of the minor orders below the diaconate, a meaning the word *clerus* appears to have in Augustine, *Contra Emer.* 1: *cum Deuterius episcopus . . . cum Alypio . . . et ceteris episcopis in exedram processissent, praesentibus presbyteris et diaconibus et universo clero ac frequentissima plebe.*

[289] The Psalms sung may have been the three that conclude the Psalter, Pss. 148-150.

[290] Egeria does not mention censers and incense in connection with the weekday service. "Censers" here = *thiamataria.* Cf. *thymiamateria* in Jer. 52.19 and *thymiateria* in 2 Par. 4.22.

[291] The aptness of such a reading on Sundays is obvious in view of the fact that the Gospels put the Resurrection on the first day of the week (cf. Mark 16.2; Luke 24.1; John 20.1). Baumstark, *Liturgie comparée* 44 f., compares the Jerusalem rite of the *Resurrectio Domini* with the practice of having the abbot or chief minister read a Gospel text either at the morning or evening

office in the Benedictine Rule and in other liturgies. Cf. also Cabrol 53.

[292] *tantus rugitus et mugitus.* Meister 370 considers this phrase a biblicism and cites Job 3.24 (*antequam comedam, suspiro; et tanquam inundantes aquae, sic rugitus meus*) and Mal. 2.13 (*operiebatis lacrymis altare Domini, fletu, et mugitu*). This phrase is used again by Egeria in her account of Holy Week.— Baumstark, *Liturgie comparée* 44 n. 1, believes that the Scripture reading on Sundays must have also included a section of the narrative of the Passion, and that this would account for the expressions of sorrow.

[293] Bludau 62 states that from the time of the bishop's departure until daybreak an office resembling lauds was celebrated at the Anastasis by the monks. For contrary views, see Intro. p. 31.

CHAPTER 25

[294] "they assemble for the liturgy" = *proceditur.* Bastiaensen 26–39 cites *procedere* and the noun *processio* as key liturgical terms used by Egeria to designate the celebration of Mass; he identifies 18 examples of *procedere* used with this sense. Duchesne, *op. cit.* 512, had already identified *oblatio* and *procedere* as the specific terms used by Egeria to designate the Mass. Mohrmann, "Missa" 76 f., distinguishes *oblatio* from *procedere:* "*Procedere* se rapporte à une synaxe liturgique, il ne désigne pas la célébration eucharistique (*oblatio*) comme telle. C'est plutôt l'acte de s'assembler du *populus* (processionnellement? avec les célébrants?) et dans tous les textes d'Égérie la traduction la meilleure me semble être: 'on se réunit pour le synaxe liturgique.' " It is in this latter sense that I have translated *procedere.* For the thesis that *procedere* (*processio*) and *offerre* (*oblatio*) are identical in meaning in Egeria, cf. A. Coppo, "Una nuova ipotesi sull'origine di *Missa*," EL 71 (1957) 225–67. Mohrmann sees a basic speech pattern in which *procedere* occurs: an impersonal passive followed by *in* with the ablative (*in ecclesia maiore* in the present instance) or the indeclinable noun *Syon,* and frequently balanced by a verb alluding to the eucharistic sacrifice, e.g., *agere* or *fieri* (in this passage Egeria's sentence concludes with *fiunt omnia secundum consuetudinem que ubique* [Geyer and Franceschini-Weber: *qua et ubique*] *fit die dominica;* on the liturgical sense of *agere* and *fieri,* cf. nn. 34

and 119 above). Bastiaensen distinguishes three separate contexts in which *procedere* appears in the *Diary:* for the Sunday morning service at the Martyrium, for the Wednesday and Friday service at the Church of Sion, and for the morning service on feast days and during octaves. Bastiaensen sees *oblatio* as reserved for those services in which only the Eucharist is celebrated (cf. above, n. 34), and gives *procedere* the role of introducing the solemn Jerusalem liturgy consisting of scriptural readings, sermons, and the eucharistic sacrifice. Ernout 306 accepted *procedere* in Egeria as meaning simply "avancer, former un cortège, une procession." Coppo sees *processio* as referring to an offertory procession, while Bastiaensen takes it to mean an assembling of the people to assist at Mass. With respect to the *processio* and *procedunt* in ch. 26 (cf. below, n. 315), Cabrol 79 n. 1 says the words do not refer to liturgical processions, but are simply terms used to indicate that the faithful in a group come to this or that church.

²⁹⁵ Leclercq, "Bréviaire," DACL 2.1268, believes that the *missa catechumenorum* and *missa fidelium* are clearly distinguished, the one occurring at the Martyrium, the latter at the Anastasis. Pétré *Journal* 71 f. concurs. Bludau 63–6 cites numerous liturgists, including Baumstark, Jungmann, Duchesne, and Bäumer, who hold that the Eucharist was celebrated at the Martyrium (cf. n. 298 below). While Baumstark prefers daybreak, Jungmann fixes the celebration at the third hour.

²⁹⁶ *Sane quia hic consuetudo sic est, ut de omnibus presbyteris, qui sedent, quanti volunt, predicent, et post illos omnes episcopus predicat.* On the evolution of the meaning of *praedicare,* cf. Bastiaensen 96–9 and C. Mohrmann, *"Praedicare—Tractare—Sermo.* Essai sur la terminologie de la prédication paléochrétienne," *La maison Dieu* 39 (1954) 97–107. On the practice of having more than one sermon, see Duchesne, *op. cit.* 59, who cites Jerome as evidence that there were sermons by several priests, and then the bishop's address. For the practice at Antioch, see John Chrysostom, *Hom.* 33 *in Act.* 1 (MG 60.243).

²⁹⁷ *intra cancellos martyrii spelunca (speluncae). Martyrium* when used with reference to the Basilica of the Holy Sepulchre specifically designates the major church, the church directly on Golgotha, and never refers to the Anastasis. I have translated the word *martyrium* here in its general sense of "shrine."

²⁹⁸ The Arezzo manuscript reads: *Primum aguntur gratiae Deo,*

et sic fit orationem pro omnibus. Wistrand 13–21 has proposed this emendation: *Primum aguntur gratiae Deo, et sic fit oblatio, item facit orationem pro omnibus.* It is this latter reading that I have translated. This passage is critical in discussions on whether or not Mass was celebrated on Sundays in the Anastasis. Löfstedt 290 ff. had dealt with the problem of *fit orationem,* which various editors had attempted to resolve with either *facit orationem* (Heraeus) or *fit oratio* (Geyer, Pétré); Löfstedt accepted the manuscript reading and justified it as an impersonal passive with the accusative retained for the object. However, Cabrol had already raised a more important question, suggesting that the *aguntur gratiae Deo* referred here to the celebration of Mass, for *actio gratiarum* is a paraphrase of the Greek εὐχαριστία. Bludau 65 f. interpreted *aguntur gratiae* as referring to a post-Communion act of thanksgiving at the Anastasis. For a discussion of the question in the context of the *Diary* as a whole, see Intro. pp. 31 f.

[299] Following the Peace of Constantine, Sunday Mass, celebrated in the primitive Church before dawn, was offered at the third hour (mid-morning). No mention is made here of an office on Sunday at the sixth hour or the ninth hour; on this question, see n. 324 below.

[300] Bludau 67 remarks that Egeria's frequent references to the usage of hymns, prayers, and readings appropriate to the feast being celebrated and to the place of observance suggest that such practice was new to her. Bludau cites in this connection Sidonius Apollinaris, who praised bishop Mamertus for ordering for the feasts of the year readings fitting for each period.

[301] *una tantum die dominica, id est quinquagesimarum per pentecosten.* The juxtaposition of *quinquagesimae* and *pentecosten,* two essentially synonymous terms, occurs again in ch. 41. While Egeria uses *quinquagesimae* alone in referring to Pentecost, she uses the loan-word from the Greek only in conjunction with the Latin equivalent. On the use of both terms by Christian authors of the 4th and 5th centuries, cf. Bastiaensen 132–51.

[302] The break in the text at this point leaves Egeria's sentence incomplete, and the meaning of the word *missa* here is moot. The Latin text immediately prior to the break reads: . . . *in Syon proceditur, sicut infra annotatum invenietis, sic tamen in Syon ut, antequam sit hora tertia, illuc eatur, fiat primum missa in ecclesiam maiorem.* Pétré *Journal* 201 translates *missa* here

by "messe" ("ayant auparavant célèbré la messe à l'église majeure"). However, there is a passage in ch. 43 with similar wording in which the author refers to an early dismissal in the Martyrium so that everyone may be at the Church of Sion by the third hour, and in this latter passage it is clear that *missa* = "dismissal."

Wistrand 9 f. believes that at this point Egeria went on to describe the Wednesday and Friday celebration of Mass at the Church of Sion at the ninth hour. See Intro. p. 32 and also n. 329 below. References to the Wednesday and Friday liturgy at the Church of Sion will be found in chs. 27, 41, and 44.

[303] Where the text resumes Egeria is describing the return of the procession from Bethlehem following the vigil service in the church of the Nativity for the feast of Epiphany. It may be presumed that the vigil itself was described in the missing part of the text, where Egeria may also have presented an introduction to the liturgical year. For the processional refrain, cf. Matt. 21.9. On the celebration of Epiphany, cf. Intro. pp. 33 f.

[304] *ea hora, qua incipit homo hominem posse cognoscere.* Cf. Ruth 3.14: *Surrexit itaque antequam homines se cognoscerent mutuo.*

[305] *Ministerium autem omne genus aureum gemmatum profertur illa die.* Bechtel 110 and 134 gives for *ministerium* "treasure" or "furniture" of a church, and he sees in this passage "a striking example of the adverbial accusative" ("every kind of service of gold and jewels").

[306] *sub presentia matris suae.* On the sense of the phrase, cf. Bastiaensen 178 ff.

[307] *fit ergo prima die missa in ecclesia maiore, quae est in Golgotha.* What meaning should be given to the stylized expression *fit missa* here? Certainly Mass was celebrated on so important a feast as Epiphany, but it is not so clear that Egeria is here using *missa* in the sense of "Mass." We do observe, however, a parallel to the Sunday liturgy: the service begins in the Martyrium, is concluded in the Anastasis, and lasts several hours. Pétré *Journal* 205 translates: "On célèbre donc le premier jour de la fête, la *messe* à l'église majeure. . . ." Bludau 68 f. states that the Mass of the Catechumens was definitely celebrated in the Martyrium, followed by either the Mass of the Faithful or an act of thanksgiving in the Anastasis. Mohrmann, "Missa" 82, does not accept the equation of *missa* to "Mass" in this passage.

[308] *Per triduo ergo haec omnis laetitia . . . celebratur.* I follow Cabrol 76 f., n. 4, who interprets this passage to mean that Mass was offered. Bastiaensen 152 ff. lists *laetitia* among the words used by Egeria to designate liturgical ceremonies: "Il est bien évident que chez elle aussi se fait sentir la tendance qui fléchit le sens de *laetitia* 'joie publique' vers celui de 'fête publique.' *Laetitia* se réfère toujours aux solennités liturgiques, et accouplé à *celebrare*, il va être quasi sans réserve synonyme de *sollemnitas*."—An equivalent phrasing is found in chs. 26 and 48: *cum summo honore celebrantur.* Cf. Bastiaensen 156–60.

[309] On the church of the Eleona, see Intro. p. 26 and n. 119 to the Intro.

[310] On the Lazarium, see Intro. p. 24 and n. 110 to the Intro.

[311] On the Church of Sion, see Intro. p. 25 and n. 117 to the Intro.

[312] *ad Crucem.* On the various liturgical services held at the Cross, cf. Intro. pp. 24 f. and nn. 113 and 114 to the Intro., and for a different order of stational churches during the Easter octave, cf. ch. 39 of the *Diary* and n. 406 below.

[313] *in ecclesia in Bethleem.* The reference is to the church of the Nativity; cf. ch. 42 of the *Diary: in ecclesia in Bethleem, in qua ecclesia spelunca est ubi natus est Dominus.*

CHAPTER 26

[314] *quadragesimae de epiphania. Quadragesimae* here refers to the feast we call Candlemas, or the Purification of the Blessed Virgin, or the Presentation of Jesus in the Temple. The feast evidently had no proper name in Egeria's day and was apparently still unknown in the West, for she emphasizes *hic celebrantur.* On the Christocentric character of the feast, cf. Intro. p. 34. The argument in Meister 361 that reference to the Feast of the Purification dated the text after the reign of Marcian (450–457), when there was a definite Marian accent in the celebration of the feast, is irrelevant, as Deconinck, *art. cit.* 440, has shown. On the genesis, development, and spread of the feast, see Bludau 89–93.—For a discussion of the other usages and meanings of *quadragesimae* in the *Diary*, cf. nn. 320, 323, and 422 below; Bastiaensen 132–51; Van Oorde 161 f.

[315] *eadem die processio est in Anastase, et omnes procedunt.*

On the significance of *procedere* generally in the text, cf. n. 294 above. The use here of the noun *processio* and of *procedere* in the active voice raises the question of whether there was a real procession, an early Candlemas rite. Bastiaensen 36 rejects such an interpretation and translates: "Ce jour-là on se réunit à l'église de l'Anastasis et tous viennent de chez eux et sont présents à l'église." Moreover, as Baumstark, *Liturgie comparée* 166 f., has shown, the procession with candles was not introduced until the middle of the 5th century by Ikelia.

[316] *cum summa laetitia.* In the preceding sentence, "with the greatest solemnity" = *cum summo honore.* Cf. n. 308 above.

[317] Cf. Luke 2.22–40. Though Egeria states that the Presentation occurred "on the fortieth day" (*quadragesima die*), the Gospel does not say this. However, cf. Lev. 12.2–5.

[318] *aguntur sacramenta.* This is the only place in the *Diary* where the word *sacramentum* and the liturgical formula *agere sacramenta* appear. On the meaning, cf. Bastiaensen 82 f. and C. Mohrmann, "*Sacramentum* dans les plus anciens textes chrétiens," in *Études sur le latin des chrétiens* 233–44.

CHAPTER 27

[319] *dies paschales. Pascha* and the adjective *paschalis* are used in the *Diary* in five different senses, according to Bludau 120 f.: (1) to refer to Lent (as here); (2) to designate Holy Week (*septimana paschale*, ch. 30); (3) to refer to the Easter vigil rites (*vigiliae paschales*) and to Easter itself (*per pascha*); (4) to specify the Easter octave (*dies paschales* and *octo dies paschae*, ch. 39); and (5) to mean Passover (*lex paschae*, chs. 5 and 7).

[320] The full sentence reads in the text: *Nam sicut apud nos quadragesimae ante pascha adtenduntur, ita hic octo septimanae attenduntur ante pascha.* Though *quadragesimae* is used by Egeria as a technical term for Lent (cf. n. 323 below), it is here the equivalent of *quadraginta dies.*

[321] This reference to an 8-week Lent has been the subject of extensive commentary and some controversy. On the problem relative to this passage, cf. Cabrol 135–9; Bludau 94–108; Meister 350–5; Deconinck, *art. cit.* 433–6. On the question of fasting in general, cf. Baumstark, *Liturgie comparée* 215–21; H. Leclercq, "Jeune," DACL 7.2481–501; E. Vacandard, "Carême," DTC 2.1724–50.—Meister based his argument for a 6th-century dating

for the *Diary* largely on the observance of an 8-week Lent, a practice which he believed could not have antedated Patriarch Peter's proclamation of a 7-week fast for the year 532. Deconinck, while admitting that no specific ecclesiastical ordinance for an 8-week Lent is known to have been issued in either the 4th or the 5th century, argued that the diversity of practice in the Greek and Latin churches would have allowed for an 8-week fast in Jerusalem at the time of Egeria's visit there. Bludau cites Epiphanius, *Expos. fid.* 22 (MG 42.828), and John Chrysostom, *Hom.* 17 *de statuis ad populum Antiochenum* (MG 49.179), as referring indirectly to an 8-week fast.

The Lenten fast evolved over several centuries. The earliest Easter fast was limited to Good Friday, and then was extended to include Holy Saturday, the *biduana*. Irenaeus (cf. Eusebius, *Hist. eccl.* 5 [MG 20.501]) states that some recommended one, others two, still others three days of fast before Easter, while still others fasted uninterruptedly for forty hours. By the 3rd century a week-long Holy Week fast had become standard. The concept of a forty-day fast developed in imitation of the fasts of Christ, Moses, and Elias, and such a fast was incorporated gradually during the 4th century with the older Holy Week period of fasting. The theoretical distinction between the two was still maintained; cf. John Chrysostom, *Hom.* 30 *in Gen.* 11.1 (MG 53.273). Both the interpretation of the τεσσαρακοστής (*quadragesimas*) and the manner of allotting the number of fasting days per week differed. Sozomenus, *Hist. eccl.* 1.7 (MG 67.1477), describes a 7-week period of five days a week in the orbit of the Syrian church. A 6-week Lent was observed in Alexandria. Socrates, *Hist. eccl.* 5.22 (MG 67.632), speaks of a 3-week Lent at Rome. Cassian even reinterpreted the idea of *quadragesimae* to mean a period equivalent to one tenth of a year. The greatest pressure for the extension of fasting came of course from the monastic milieu, and at times the heterodox movements reinforced this. Cf. Tertullian, *De ieiunio* 2 (ML 2.956).

[322] The nonobservance in the East of a fast on Saturdays, except for the Saturday before Easter, is attested also by other sources. Cf., e.g., the *Apostolic Constitutions* 5. Basil the Great, *Hom.* 1 *de ieiunio* (MG 31.181 and 189), specifically mentions a 5-day week of fasting. According to Gregory of Nyssa, *Or. adv. eos qui castigationes aegre ferunt* (MG 46.309), Saturdays and

Sundays were treated like "brothers," and John Chrysostom, *Hom.* 11 *in Gen.* 2 (MG 53.92), speaks of two days of the week on which the body rests from fasting.

323 *remanent dies quadraginta et unum qui ieiunantur, quod hic appellant eortae, id est quadragesimas. Eortae* is a transliteration of the Greek ἑορταί (the ordinary meaning of which would be "feasts," "festivals"), and evidently in Egeria's day it was in Jerusalem the current word to describe Lent. It is surprising that at no time does Egeria mention the normal Greek word, τεσσαρακοστή.

324 The manuscript reading here, *dominica enim die nona fit*, was emended by Duchesne by the insertion of a *non* after *nona*. I have translated the text as emended by Duchesne. Geyer (CSEL 39.78) and Franceschini-Weber (CCL 175.73) reproduce the original reading of the manuscript. Duchesne's change seems to me justified in view of the absence elsewhere of reference to an office at the sixth or ninth hours on Sunday.—Near the beginning of ch. 25 above a similar emendation was made by Gamurrini in an analogous construction involving the impersonal verb form *fit*. He inserted a *non* before *fit* so that the text would read: *et ideo ante quartam horam aut forte quintam missa non fit.* There also I have translated the text as emended.

325 To designate the days of the week from Monday through Friday, Egeria uses the ecclesiastical terminology: *secunda feria, tertia feria*, and so forth, what Augustine, *In Ps.* 93.2, called the *ritus loquendi ecclesiasticus*. She never employs the more hieratic and formal *feria secunda, feria tertia*, and so forth, but always uses the popular forms, which eventually developed into the names of the week in Portuguese (e.g., *segunda feira*, "Monday"). Cf. R. Bahr, "Zu den romanischen Wochentagsnamen," *Romanica: Festschrift Gerhard Rohlfs* (Halle 1958) 26–56, esp. 35–42. Bastiaensen 82 f. doubts that any argument for the putative Galician homeland of Egeria should be sought in the correspondence of her terminology for the days of the week with the modern Portuguese terms.

326 On a service at tierce or the third hour during Lent, cf. Intro. pp. 28, 34.

327 For a discussion of fasting on Wednesdays and Fridays, see Bludau 108 ff. The earliest evidence for a Wednesday and Friday fast is found in the *Didache* 8.1 (= ACW 6.19), but Tertullian, *De ieiunio* 2 (ML 2.956), reminds us that observance of that fast

was a matter of free choice (*ex arbitrio, non ex imperio.*) Third-century texts, however, indicate that the fast had become obligatory and that it was justified as a commemorative penance for the betrayal and passion of Christ, as reflected in the *Apostolic Constitutions* 5.14: *quarta feria et sexta feria iussit Dominus ieiunare; illa quidem propter proditionem, haec vero propter passionem.* Epiphanius, *Expos. fid.* 22 (MG 42.825), mentions an obligatory fast on Wednesdays and Fridays which lasted until mid-afternoon. On the customary service at Sion at the ninth hour, cf. Intro. pp. 32, 34.

[328] This passage has always presented difficulties. The manuscript reads here: *Nam si fortuito in quadragesimis martyrorum dies evenerit quarta feria aut sexta feria atque ad nona in Syon proceditur.* Bludau 108 believes the reading here is corrupt. While the need to correct the manuscript by substituting a negative for the *atque* seems clear, the emendation proposed by Gamurrini and Geyer, replacing *atque* with *neque*, has not met with universal approval. Heraeus tried to restore the manuscript by suppressing the controversial *atque* and by inserting after *sexta feria* the following: *penitus nemo ieiunat, tunc nec.* The passage would then translate: "If by chance during Lent a martyr's feast day happens to fall on a Wednesday or a Friday, no one fasts at all, and then no one goes to Sion at the ninth hour." Heraeus' proposal can probably be justified in view of the specific reference in ch. 41 of the *Diary* to a morning service at Sion during Eastertide, when there was no fasting in Jerusalem. Franceschini-Weber (CCL 175.74) propose *aeque* for *atque*, and the passage would then mean that regardless of whether it was the feast day of a martyr the people assembled for the liturgy at the ninth hour. It would seem more likely, however, that on a martyr's feast day the same order of Wednesday service would have prevailed as during a period of no fasting, and I have, therefore, translated the passage as emended by Gamurrini and Geyer.

[329] In spite of the rather awkward manner in which these important facts are presented, it is clear that the liturgical office of the ninth hour was customarily held throughout the year at the Church of Sion on Wednesdays and Fridays. Moreover, Egeria provides additional evidence that in the 4th and 5th centuries in Jerusalem Mass was offered normally three times a week, on Sundays, Wednesdays, and Fridays, as we already know

from Epiphanius, *Expos. fid.* 22 (MG 42.825). Egeria's text makes it clear that the hour of celebration varied. On a ferial day, when the daily fast was observed until the evening meal, Mass was offered during the service at the ninth hour; on a feast day, when everyone was dispensed from fasting, it was offered earlier in the day, presumably at the Church of Sion. In her ch. 41, where she describes briefly the practices during Eastertide, when there was no fasting, Egeria refers to a morning service at the Sion on Wednesdays and Fridays. Cf. n. 420 below. Wistrand 8 ff. believes that Egeria had already referred to the Wednesday and Friday services at Sion in the lost portion of ch. 25 (cf. n. 302 above). Wistrand cites Egeria's ch. 44, which recapitulates the normal weekly ritual resumed after Pentecost, to confirm that on Wednesdays and Fridays the ninth hour service was always held at the Church of Sion. The distinctive feature of the Lenten service on these two days was the omission of the sacrifice, presumably because the fast was not to be broken by the more rigorous ascetics (cf. n. 335 below).

[330] . . . *fit missa lucernaris in Anastase et ad Crucem. Missa autem lucernari.* . . . This is one of the few places where Egeria combines *missa* with either an adjective or a genitive that refers to a particular religious service. Other examples will be found in chs. 38 (*missa vigiliarum*), 39 (*post missa lucernarii . . . de Anastase*), and 44 (*missa fiat matutina*). Bludau 50 suggests that *missa* in this present passage has the meaning of a religious service rather than simply the rites of dismissal. The translation "vespers service" would seem to be justifiable here by analogy with the *missa vigiliarum* in ch. 38 (generally interpreted to mean either "vigil service" or "vigil Mass") and in view of the construction with the ablative of place *in* which, rather than place *from* which. In ch. 39, on the other hand, I have interpreted *missa* as "dismissal," since *missa lucernarii* there is followed by *de Anastase*.

[331] On the all-night vigil on Friday, cf. Baumstark, *Liturgie comparée* 133. This Friday night watch culminated in morning Mass. For other examples of such a vigil preceding Saturday morning services, cf. Jungmann, *Pastoral Liturgy* 115.

[332] This is one of the most significant passages in the text: *Missa autem, quae fit sabbato ad Anastase, ante solem fit, hoc est oblatio, ut ea hora, qua incipit sol procedere, et missa in Anastase facta sit.* As Dölger, *art. cit.* 99, indicated, the general word

missa is being explained by the specific, technical term *oblatio*, and has thereby practically acquired the meaning of the eucharistic sacrifice or Mass: "Hier haben wir im ersten Teil das Wort *missa* im Sinne von Gottesdienst oder eucharistischer Gottesdienst, denn das Wort *missa* wird durch *oblatio* erklärt." Pétré *Journal* 213 translates *missa* here "messe," and then extends this meaning to the next five uses of the word in the concluding lines of ch. 27, since they all refer to the Saturday morning service. Mohrmann, "Missa" 86, rejects the equation *missa* = "Mass" here; cf. above, n. 275.

333 . . . *hi, quos dicunt hic ebdomadarios.* This is the only chapter in which Egeria uses the word *ebdomadarius*, though in ch. 28 she has *hi qui faciunt ebdomadas* and *qui non possunt facere integras septimanas ieiuniorum.* A Greek loanword, *ebdomadarius* (*hebdomadarius*) appears in Cassian, *Inst.* 4.28, where it designates the one who acted as community bursar or steward for the week. Ernout 295 believes that the word developed in the environs of Jerusalem to describe those who fasted uninterruptedly from the Sunday meal until after Mass on Saturday.

334 *ut citius absolvant.* According to Meister 375, the verb *absolvere* here should be understood as *absolvere ieiunium: Subaudiendum est "ieiunium" cui isti per totam septimanam astricti fuerunt. Itaque proximum abest ab Italice "asciolvere" quod vim prandendi, i.e., ieiunium solvendi habet.*

CHAPTER 28

335 Bludau 112–5 summarizes the development of the continuous fast in the early Church, particularly among the ascetics. "Overfasting," called *superpositio* (cf. the Greek ὑπερθέσις), the practice of uninterrupted fasting over a period of several days, probably had its origins in the primitive Church's Easter vigil fast, during which some Christians fasted for forty consecutive hours, from the evening meal on Good Friday until the Easter morning service (cf. n. 321 above). The optional nature of such fasting is emphasized by Dionysius of Alexandria, who describes how in the 3rd century some ate no food during the six days of the Holy Week fast, whereas others might fast for two, three, or four days without interruption, and still others might have one meal a day. Palladius, *Hist. Laus.* 43 and 48 (= ACW 34.119 and 130 f.), describes two monks, Adolius ("in

Lent he would eat only every five days") and Elpidius ("eating only on Sundays and Saturdays"), whose fasting practices were similar to those of Egeria's *hebdomadarii*.

[336] *post missa.* The same phrase is used twice more in this chapter, but both times in conjunction with a genitive of the place (*post missa Anastasis* and *post missa ecclesiae*), so there is no doubt that in each of those cases *missa* is to be understood in the sense of *dismissio*, "dismissal." It is possible that in the present passage Egeria was using *missa* for "Mass," but there is doubt on this and hence I translate the word here also by "dismissal."

[337] Cf. n. 255 above.

[338] *de sera ad seram*, literally "from evening to evening."

[339] On the optional nature of "overfasting," cf. Bludau 108–112 and Deconinck, *art. cit.* 432–6.

[340] . . . *ut nec panem, quid liberari non potest, nec oleum gustent, nec aliquid, quod de arboribus est, sed tantum aqua et sorbitione modica de farina.* The Latin is faulty and the passage is very obscure. Most editors have sought to emend the core of the difficulty—*panem, quid liberari non potest*—by reconstructing *quid liberari* according to some more logical syntactical pattern: *quod librari* (Gamurrini, Geyer), *quod liberari* (Meister, Bludau), *qui delibari* (Heraeus, Pétré), *quo liberari* and *qui liberari* (Franceschini). Löfstedt, surprisingly, does not deal with the question. Meister 378 interpreted *liberari* in the sense of the French "livrer," and the reference then would be to bread which could not be delivered to a rigorous community of ascetics during Lent. Recent scholarship on this passage has tended to focus on precisely what type of bread might have been forbidden during Lent. R. Weber, "Note sur *Itinerarium Egeriae*, XXVIII,4," VC 12 (1958) 93–97, J. G. Preaux, "Panis qui delibari non potest," VC 15 (1961) 105–15, and O. Prinz, "Philologische Bemerkungen zu einer Neuausgabe des *Itinerarium Egeriae*," ALMA 30 (1960) 143–53, have all concentrated on this difficult passage. Preaux (111) insists that it was not bread as such that was forbidden in Lent, but rather a certain type of bread, bread made with yeast or honey.

[341] The CCL edition retains the original manuscript reading both here (*Quadragesimarum sic fit, ut diximus*) and in the initial phrase of ch. 29 (*Et completo earum septimanarum*). In both passages it has proved difficult to interpret the genitives (*quadragesimarum* and *septimanarum*). Meister 383 and Löfstedt

301 f. interpreted them as temporal constructions involving in each case the ellipsis of the ablative *tempore*. In translating the two passages I have adopted this interpretation. However, several editors have assumed that there were lacunae in the two passages. With regard to the final sentence of ch. 28, Gamurrini posited a lacuna at the beginning of the sentence and he added the nominative *ieiunium*. The sentence would then be translated: "The Lenten fast is observed just as we have said." Geyer and Heraeus adopted Gamurrini's proposal, adding only an *ergo* as a connective with the preceding sentence. Cholodniak proposed emending both passages so that they would refer specifically to the first week of Lent. He filled the supposed lacuna at the beginning of the final sentence of ch. 28 by adding *ac prima quidem septimana*, so that the passage in translation would read: "And the first week of Lent is observed just as we have said." In the initial phrase of ch. 29 he changed *earum septimanarum* to read *ea iam septimana*. That passage would then be translated: "As this week comes to an end." For another interpretation of how this latter passage should read, see the immediately following note.

CHAPTER 29

[342] Bludau 117 attempted to fill in the supposed lacuna in the manuscript at this point (cf. n. 341 above) by completing the sentence to accord with the total context of the chapter: "At the end of the seventh week of Lent there is a service in the church of the Lazarus in Bethany."

[343] *offeret episcopus et facit oblationem.* The Latin text appears redundant, for *offerre* and *faceret oblationem* are synonymous. It is possible that by *offeret episcopus* Egeria intends to say that the bishop is the celebrant, and she then uses *facit oblationem* to state specifically that he offers the sacrifice.

[344] *Archidiaconus*, "archdeacon," a term taken over literally from the Greek, appears first in Optatus of Miletus (*ca.* 370). The word came into general use in the 4th and 5th centuries. Mohrmann, *Die altchristliche Sondersprache in den Sermones des hl. Augustin* 80, cites the *Itinerarium Egeriae*, Sermons 302 and 303 of Augustine, and canon 17 of the Synod of Carthage (398), as among the earliest texts attesting to the adoption of *archidiaconus* into Latin.

[345] On Lazarus Saturday, cf. Intro. p. 35 and n. 162 to the Intro.; also Cabrol 83–7. Theodosius (CCL 175.123), writing *ca.* 530, states that the ceremony at Bethany took place on Palm Sunday (*ante pascha dominico*).

[346] Cf. John 11.18.

[347] Cf. John 11.29.

[348] The reading here may have been of the single verse cited above, John 11.29, or of a longer passage, such as John 11.19–32.

[349] John 12.1.—In the preceding, "the Pasch is proclaimed" = *denuntiatur pascha*. This phrase makes it clear that the commemoration of Holy Week has begun.

[350] In thus explaining the motive for this ceremony at Bethany six days before Christ's arrest, Egeria calls attention to the representational nature of the ceremony and again illustrates how so much of the seasonal liturgy took form in the Jerusalem milieu. Cf. Intro. p. 33.

CHAPTER 30

[351] For the notes concerning Holy Week, I have drawn frequently on Thibaut, Bludau 119–48, and H. Leclercq, "Semaine sainte," DACL 15.1151–85. Cf. also Intro. pp. 35–40.

[352] For "Holy Week" Egeria has *septimana paschale* (cf. n. 319 above), but she also gives the name generally employed in the East, *septimana maior*, "Great Week." For examples of the expression "Great Week," cf. John Chrysostom, *Hom. in magna hebdomada* (MG 55.519), and the *Apostolic Constitutions* 8.

[353] *Propterea autem Martyrium appellatur, quia in Golgotha est, id est post Crucem, ubi Dominus passus est, et ideo Martyrio.* In the first 23 chapters of the *Diary, martyrium* referred to a martyr's shrine. Here Egeria is stating that the building at the site of Golgotha is a *martyrium* because of Christ's death there.

[354] On the grotto referred to here, cf. n. 364 below. On the Eleona, to which there are frequent allusions in the following chapters, cf. Intro. p. 26 and n. 119 to the Intro.

CHAPTER 31

[355] Bludau 112 and Cabrol 92 state that this ceremony at the Eleona, lasting about two hours, was a local rite and does not correspond to any present-day liturgical office. On the Palm

Sunday procession, cf. Intro. pp. 35 f. and nn. 167–169 to the Intro.
[356] On the Imbomon, cf. Intro. p. 25 and n. 118 to the Intro.
Whenever she speaks of the Imbomon, Egeria adds: *id est in
eo loco, de quo ascendit Dominus in caelis.* The church of the
Imbomon was octagonal in shape and had an opening in its roof
over the reputed site of Christ's Ascension.
[357] Matt. 21.9. The Gospel accounts of Christ's entry into
Jerusalem (Matt. 21.9; Mark 11.8 ff.; Luke 19.36 ff.; John 12.12
f.) do not specifically mention children bearing palms and
branches. Matt. 21.15, however, does mention "children crying
in the temple, and saying, 'Hosanna to the Son of David.' " Cyril
of Jerusalem, *Catechesis* 10.19, refers to a palm tree in the valley
from which the children took branches to greet Christ. The
Pilgrim of Bordeaux (CCL 175.17) also mentions such a tree, so
evidently this had become a local tradition: *in monte Oliveti,
vallis, quae dicitur Iosafath . . . a parte vero dextra est arbor
palmae, de qua infantes ramos tulerunt et veniente Christo sub-
straverunt.*
[358] Regarding the children being borne on their parents'
shoulders, cf. Thibaut 15 n. 1.
[359] *et sic deducetur episcopus in eo typo, quo tunc Dominus
deductus est.* Cabrol 94 n. 2 interprets this to mean that the
bishop, like Christ, rode on a donkey.
[360] *. . . pedibus omnes, sed et si quae matrone sunt aut si qui
domini, sic deducunt episcopum.* Cabrol 94 n. 2 proposed changing the *omnes, sed et* to read *omnis sedit,* so that the meaning
then would be that each of the distinguished ladies and men of
importance rode on mounts and did not walk. While the
matronae and *domini* may have ridden in the return procession
from Bethlehem, this does not seem likely here.

CHAPTER 32

[361] Cabrol 96 notes that on Monday, Tuesday, and Wednesday of Holy Week there were two departures from the usual
routine in the celebration of the daily afternoon services. The
office of the ninth hour was held in the Martyrium; it was longer
than usual and included appropriate scriptural readings (*lectiones
etiam aptae diei et loco leguntur*). Vespers was also celebrated in

the Martyrium rather than in the Anastasis and at the Church of the Cross. It should be emphasized that following the dismissal from the Martyrium there was a procession to the Anastasis, where there was a ritual similar to the concluding ceremonies of daily vespers at the Cross.

[362] In translating this sentence I have followed the slight change in the text proposed by Wistrand 21 f. The manuscript reads: *sic est ergo, ut nocte etiam fiat missa ad Martyrium.* Wistrand suggests *iam* for *etiam*.

[363] *in ecclesia, quae est in monte Eleona.* Cf. above, n. 119 to the Intro.

[364] The congregation goes to the grotto of the ".Teaching of Jesus," located beneath the sanctuary of the church of the Eleona and measuring about 23 feet in length and 5 feet in width. Prior to the construction of the Constantinian church on the Mount of Olives, Eusebius, *Demonst. evang.* 6 (MG 22.458), mentioned that a grotto was pointed out where Christ revealed to His disciples the mysteries of the end of the world. Eusebius, *De laud. Const.* 9 (MG 20.1361), refers to it as one of the three "mystical grottoes" embellished by Constantine. Christ's eschatological discourse, recorded in Matt. 24 f., was delivered two days before the Pasch (cf. Matt. 26.1 f.), or, according to tradition, on Tuesday of Holy Week.

[365] Matt. 24.4.

CHAPTER 34

[366] Cf. Matt. 26.14 ff.; Mark 14.10 f.; Luke 22.3–6. According to Bludau 130, the Greek Typicon, reflecting a 9th-century liturgy, states that on each day from Monday to Thursday one of the Gospels was read by the arch-priest. This probably refers to selected readings of the Passion.—On the reaction of the people to the reading of the Gospel, described in the following sentence, cf. n. 292 above.

CHAPTER 35

[367] The "as usual," *iuxta consuetudinem*, refers here to the Lenten practice mentioned above in n. 361. On the Holy Thursday ritual, cf. Intro. pp. 36 ff.

[368] Mass was offered twice on Holy Thursday in Jerusalem, once at the Martyrium and again at the Post Crucem, the small roofed-in chapel behind the Cross at the southeast angle of the great atrium (cf. Intro. p. 25 and n. 114 to the Intro.). Cabrol 98 believed that the second Mass, behind the Cross, commemorated the institution of the Eucharist. The 5th-century Armenian Lectionary also prescribes a Mass at the Martyrium as well as a Mass *before* the Cross. The scriptural readings indicated in the Armenian Lectionary pertain either to the prefiguration of the sacrifice or to the sacrifice itself, e.g., 1 Cor. 11.23–32 and Matt. 26.20–39. John Chrysostom, *De prod. Iud.* 1.1 (MG 49.373 and 380), speaks of everyone receiving Communion at Antioch on Holy Thursday. The Gelasian Sacramentary (ML 74.1095–1104) describes three Holy Thursday Masses in Rome, the *missa reconciliationis, missa chrismatis,* and *missa ad vesperum.* Although Egeria makes no mention of the blessing of the oils or the *mandatum,* both ceremonies were known in the 4th and 5th centuries; cf. Bludau 131 f. and Cabrol 97 n. 1. For the ceremonies of Holy Thursday in Jerusalem, cf. also H. Leclercq, "Jeudi saint," DACL 15.1456–67.

[369] At the conclusion of the Mass at the Cross, the Armenian Lectionary mentions a station at Sion. Bludau 131 f. concluded that this indicated a third Holy Thursday Mass at the Church of Sion. Thibaut 44, however, states that a Mass there is not specifically prescribed, but only the scriptural texts that had been read earlier at the Martyrium. The Armenian Lectionary then prescribes a vespers service at the Mount of Olives, consisting of psalmody, prayers, and readings, concluding with a reading of John 13.31–18.1, the Holy Thursday discourse of Christ to the apostles.

[370] This ceremony commemorated the Holy Thursday discourse of Christ to His apostles. Matt. 26.30 and Mark 14.26 state that after the Last Supper, Christ and the apostles went to the Mount of Olives. Local tradition apparently associated the Mount of Olives, and in particular the grotto of the "Teaching of Jesus," with the Holy Thursday discourse. The Armenian Lectionary also mentions that this ceremony was followed by a procession to the Imbomon. As scriptural texts for this station the Armenian Lectionary lists Ps. 118 and Luke 22.39–46.

CHAPTER 36

[371] Luke 22.41.

[372] *In eo enim loco ecclesia est elegans.* According to Thibaut 32 f., the procession returned to the church of the Eleona. Thibaut bases his conclusion on a literal interpretation of "stone's throw" in Luke 22.41 (the Eleona was only 200 feet from the Imbomon) and on the Armenian Lectionary, which indicated the next station to be the room of the apostles, that is, the grotto of the Eleona. The scriptural site of Christ's Agony in the Garden, however, is the garden of Gethsemani. Cabrol 23, therefore, identified the church referred to here with the grotto of the Agony on the lower slopes of the Mount of Olives, and Bludau 133 f. situated the church at the base of the mountain. This would be in accord with the *Onomasticon* 75: *Gethsemani, locus ubi Salvator ante Passionem oravit. Est autem ad radices montis Oliveti, nunc ecclesia desuper aedificata.* The reference here is to the church of Gethsemani, excavated in 1920 on the site of the Crusaders' church of the Holy Saviour. For a description of the church, cf. Thibaut 34–40; also Vincent-Abel, Jérusalem 2.301–7 and 1007–13.

[373] Cf. Matt. 26.41 and Mark 14.38. The reading prescribed for this station in the Armenian Lectionary is Mark 14.33–42.

[374] Thibaut puts this station of Gethsemani in the immediate vicinity of the church of Gethsemani mentioned in n. 372 above. Bludau 133 f. believes the procession had moved only a short distance into the garden of Gethsemani from the previous station. According to Thibaut, in the 13th century two separate chapels marked the sites of Christ's prayer in the garden and His arrest, the first being the Crusaders' church of the Holy Saviour, the other being a chapel hewn from the rock and called Gethsemani.

[375] The candles may have had both a functional and a symbolic purpose. John 18.3 notes that the party which came to arrest Christ carried "lanterns and torches."

[376] The reading prescribed in the Armenian Lectionary for the station in Gethsemani is Matt. 26.36–56. Other possible readings would be Mark 14.41–52, Luke 22.47–53, and John 18.2–12. Anthony of Piacenza (CCL 175.137) attests that in the 6th century a church dedicated to the Virgin Mary and a grotto with

three places for lying down were located on the site of the arrest. It should be noted that Egeria mentions no church here.

³⁷⁷ The gate in question is the so-called "Sheep Gate" of Jerusalem, the *Probatica Porta*, also called in Christian times "St. Stephen's Gate." It was located not far from the pool called "Probatica, which in Hebrew is named Bethsaida" (John 5.2).

³⁷⁸ Thibaut 41 notes that the procession did not follow the route of Christ on the night of the Passion, but proceeded to the site of the Crucifixion. The Armenian Lectionary lists three stations after that in Gethsemani: at Golgotha, at the "Palace of the Judge," and once again at Golgotha.

³⁷⁹ Cf. Matt. 27.2–26; Mark 15.1–15; Luke 23.1–25; John 18.28–19.16.

CHAPTER 37

³⁸⁰ The Pilgrim of Bordeaux, writing in 333, reported that the pillar at which Christ was scourged was still on the site of Caiphas' house on the eastern slope of Mount Sion: *In eadem ascenditur Sion et paret ubi fuit domus Caifae sacerdotis et columna adhuc ibi est, in qua Christum flagellis ceciderunt* (CCL 175.16). The column was later moved to the Church of Sion, and Theodosius (CCL 175.118), writing in the 6th century, says that it had been borne there at God's command (*iusso Domini*) and that a pilgrim could see the imprint of Christ's hands, arms, and fingers on the column.

³⁸¹ *Et sic ponitur cathedra episcopo in Golgotha post Crucem, quae stat nunc.* Thibaut 91 n. 1 questions the meaning of this passage. It is clear that the ceremony took place in the chapel known as the Post Crucem. Thibaut considers that the relative *quae* probably refers to the Cross which stood on the reputed site of the Crucifixion.—On the rite of the *adoratio crucis*, cf. Intro. p. 38.

³⁸² Thibaut 85–90 refers to the Chapel of the Relics, which was located behind the Cross and served as a repository for the cross that was to be venerated. The 6th-century account of Anthony of Piacenza (CCL 175.139) states that the cross was brought out of the chapel into the atrium for veneration. From Egeria's account, the veneration apparently took place in her day in the small chapel itself.—The discovery of the True Cross took place in the third or fourth decade of the fourth century (cf. n. 488

below), and frequent references to it will be found in works of the 4th and 5th centuries. Cf., e.g., Ambrose, *De obitu Theod.* 46 (ML 16.1402); John Chrysostom, *Hom.* 85 *in Iohan.* (MG 59.461); Paulinus of Nola, *Ep.* 31.5 f. (= ACW 36.130 ff.). For further references, see the note of P. G. Walsh in ACW 36.328 n. 11.

[383] Cf. Matt. 27.38; Luke 23.38; John 19.20. Anthony of Piacenza (CCL 175.139) states that he saw the inscription, held it in his hand, and kissed it.

[384] Bludau 140 cites Procopius, *De bell. Pers.* 2, who refers to a Syrian who once stole a large piece of the Holy Cross and brought it to Apamea, where it was long venerated. In 4th-century Jerusalem there was a special priest, the Staurophylax, charged with guarding the relics of the Cross. Baumstark, *Liturgie comparée* 159, calls attention to a similar feature of the *adoratio crucis* rite of the Dominicans and of some Benedictine communities, namely, the standing of two deacons on each side of the crucifix.

[385] On the ring of Solomon and the phial, cf. Bludau 143. According to legend, the ring revealed to Solomon the past, present, and future. It is mentioned in the Babylonian Talmud in the story of Solomon and Asmodeus (*ca.* A. D. 500). Anthony of Piacenza (CCL 175.139) and the author of the *Breviarius de Hierosolyma* (CCL 175.110) also refer to the ring and the phial.

[386] The manuscript is defective at this point, and I have translated the emended text as given in Franceschini-Weber: . . . *anulum de hora plus minus secunda; ac sic ergo.* . . . This is essentially the correction proposed by Cholodniak. The Arezzo manuscript has a blank space with room for about twelve letters after *anulum*, then there are three words, *minus secunda feria* (though the *feria* has been erased), and then there is another blank space with room for about seven letters. Gamurrini, Geyer, and Heraeus made no attempt to restore the manuscript reading.

[387] Cf. ch. 35 and n. 368 above.

[388] This *locus subdivanus* is the Ante Crucem, on which cf. Intro. p. 24 and n. 112 to the Intro. In ch. 24 it is referred to as a *basilica*, or "forecourt."

[389] The Armenian Lectionary states that everyone gathered at Golgotha at noon, and that from then until the tenth hour there was a service of Psalms, scriptural readings, and prayer. Eight Psalms were sung; after each Psalm there was a reading

from the Old and the New Testament. There were readings from Matt. 27.3–53, Mark 15.16–41, Luke 23.32–49, and John 19.25–37. Prayer and genuflection followed each Psalm.

[390] Cf. John 19.30.

[391] There appears to be a brief lacuna in the manuscript at this point, and I have translated the text as emended in Franceschini-Weber: . . . *statim omnes in ecclesia maiore ad Martyrium conveniunt et.* . . . The Arezzo manuscript lacks the *conveniunt et.* Geyer suggested that *procedunt et* may have been the reading.— As Bludau 145 f. notes, there was no afternoon liturgy on Good Friday. He cites Innocent I, *Ep. 25 ad Decent.* 4: *isto biduo sacramenta penitus non celebrari.* According to John Chrysostom, *Hom. de coemet. et de cruce* 3 (MG 49.397), a eucharistic sacrifice was held in Syria at the graveyard. The Mass of the Presanctified, however, apparently was unknown before the 7th century in Rome; cf. P. Salmon, *Le lectionnaire de Luxeuil* 1 (Rome 1944) 88. Thibaut 105–9 notes that the Georgian Canonarian of the 7th century provided for a Mass of the Presanctified in Jerusalem for that period. The service held at the Martyrium was limited to the singing of Psalms and readings from Scripture. A vespers service may also have been held (cf. above, chs. 32–34).

[392] Cf. John 19.38.

[393] Translating here the text as emended by Wistrand 12, following the suggestion of Cholodniak: *Hoc autem lecto fit oratio, benedicuntur cathecumini sic fideles ac sic fit missa.* The Arezzo manuscript lacks the *sic fideles ac.* Wistrand believes that our author inadvertently omitted a reference here to the blessing of the faithful.

[394] Egeria does not mention whether the vigil concluded with the morning office. The Saturday morning Lenten Mass (cf. chs. 27–29 above) would be excluded, but one would expect some reference to a formal conclusion to this vigil. It should be noted that in ch. 38, which describes what took place on Holy Saturday, a service is mentioned for the third and sixth hours.

CHAPTER 38

[395] Augustine, *Sermo* 219 (ML 38.1088), refers to the Easter vigil as the "mother of all holy vigils," and the Second Coming of Christ was associated with the hour of the vigil service by

early Christians; cf. Lactantius, *Div. inst.* 7 (CSEL 19.644), and Jerome, *Comment. in Matt.* 4.25 (ML 26.184). For a discussion of the Easter vigil service, cf. Intro. pp. 38 ff. and n. 183 to the Intro.

[396] "neophytes" = *infantes*, a technical term used for the newly baptized. In ch. 47, Egeria designates the newly baptized as *neofiti*, a word in use in Christian Latin since the time of Tertullian. Mohrmann, *Die altchristliche Sondersprache in den Sermones des hl. Augustin* 130, has shown that *infantes* is more frequently used by Augustine, who in his *Sermo* 228.1 (ML 38.1101) explains the significance of the term: *Qui paulo ante vocabantur competentes, modo vocantur infantes. . . . Infantes dicuntur, quia modo nati sunt Christo, qui prius nati fuerant saeculo.* The term was still used to refer to adults in the 9th century, as is evident from the *Missale mixtum* (ML 85.467): *Neophyti omnes, etsi aetate senes, infantes appellabantur. Hinc octavae Paschae, apud Sanctum Augustinum octavae infantium appellantur, quotquot enim baptizati erant, utpote regenerati, novam vitam ingressi erant.*

[397] The baptistery had been built beside the church of the Anastasis and is mentioned by the Pilgrim of Bordeaux: . . . *basilica facta est, id est dominicum, mirae pulchritudinis habens ad latus excepturia, unde aqua levatur, et balneum a tergo, ubi infantes lavantur* (CCL 175.17). Cf. also Vincent-Abel, *Jérusalem* 2.138–44. When the neophytes emerged from immersion in the baptismal fonts, they were clothed in white linen tunics which signified that they had been made clean inwardly; cf. Augustine, *Sermo* 223.1 (ML 38.1092). On the baptismal service, cf. also Intro. pp. 39 f.

[398] According to Bludau 147 f., the procession to the Anastasis was analogous to a procession of the newly baptized to a *consignatorium*, where confirmation was administered. The *Testamentum Domini*, like Egeria's *Diary*, makes no mention of a *consignatorium*, but it does speak of confirmation being administered in the church; cf. Quasten, "Ostervigil im *Testamentum Domini*" 94.

[399] According to Weller, *op. cit.* 47 f., the portion of the vigil continued by the faithful while baptism was being administered "developed into a form which eventually became the Office of Matins for Easter, with invitatory, three psalms, followed by the

Gospel of the Resurrection according to St. Mark and concluding with a homily by the bishop."
[400] *Et post facta missa vigiliarum.* On the translation, cf. Dölger,
art. cit. 98; Bludau 50; also n. 330 above. Egeria makes no specific mention of the First Communion of the newly baptized
which completed the triple sacramental initiation of new Christians during the Easter vigil.

CHAPTER 39

[401] Most editors have accepted the reading of the Arezzo manuscript here: *Sero autem illi dies paschales sic attenduntur . . .* ,
which would mean that on Easter and during the Easter octave
the services were held at a late hour. Wistrand 22 ff. rejected
sero on the grounds that it does not provide a smooth transition
from the preceding chapter and it does not seem to be in accord
with the sense of the present section of the *Diary*, for in what
follows Egeria mentions daily morning services in the stational
churches of Jerusalem. Developing an earlier suggestion of
Cholodniak, who had proposed *sex* for *sero*, Wistrand proposed
the change be to *octo*. Though there is no paleographic basis for
emending *sero* to *octo*, the change could be justified in view of
the repeated references in this section to the eight days of the
Easter octave. Furthermore, Egeria has numerous similar transition passages introduced by a number and a noun of time. I
have adopted Wistrand's proposal and translated accordingly.

[402] "The liturgy" = *missae*. This is the only place in the *Diary*
where the nominative plural *missae* occurs. The word apparently
refers here to the totality of the services held, and not specifically
to the celebration of Mass. My choice of "liturgy" to translate
missae is based on the striking parallels between the construction
employed here and that used elsewhere by Egeria in stating that
the usual ceremonies were being performed. Egeria's wording
here is: *et ordine suo fiunt missae per octo dies paschales, sicut et
ubique fit per pascha.* Elsewhere she has: *et fiunt omnia secundum consuetudinem, qua et ubique fit die dominica* (ch. 25); *et
ordine suo aguntur omnia . . . ac sic per pascha* (ch. 26);
aguntur . . . quae et toto anno dominicis diebus fiunt (ch. 27).

[403] On the celebration of Easter and its octave, cf. Bludau
150–4; the 5th-century Armenian Lectionary in Conybeare, *op.
cit.* 524; also Intro. pp. 40 f.

[404] The embellishments of the stational churches during the octave of Epiphany were described by Egeria in ch. 25.

[405] *quia dies paschales sunt.* Cf. above, n. 319.

[406] For the order of the stational churches during the octave of Epiphany, which differed somewhat from that described here for the Easter octave, cf. ch. 25 of the *Diary.* During the Epiphany octave, on the fifth day the station was at the Lazarium, on the seventh day it was at the Anastasis, and on the eighth day it was at the Cross. On the service *ante Crucem* on the Saturday of the Easter octave, cf. above, n. 112 to the Intro.

[407] "lunch" = *prandium*, the meal taken by the Romans around noon. Egeria stated in ch. 27 that on Sundays during Lent this meal was eaten at the fifth hour (*ca.* 11 a.m.).—On the development of *prandere* as a technical term meaning "not to fast," an antonym of *ieiunare*, cf. Bastiaensen 130 f.

[408] I.e., *infantes.* Cf. above, n. 396.

[409] Such a procession to the Eleona is mentioned in the Armenian Lectionary, but it is there restricted to Easter Sunday, Easter Thursday, and Low Sunday.

[410] *post missa lucernarii, id est de Anastase.* Cf. above, n. 330.

[411] Cf. John 20.19–25.

[412] Cf. John 20.25.

CHAPTER 40

[413] *statim post sexta.* Pétré *Journal* 245, translates: "après l'office de la sixième heure." However, Egeria at no time mentions a Sunday office at the sixth hour, and if Duchesne's emendation of the text in ch. 27 (cf. above, n. 324) is correct, she specifically excludes a service on Sunday at the ninth hour. With rare exception (cf. ch. 41 and n. 419 below), the services at the sixth and ninth hours are always linked together.

[414] "in the Eleona" = *illic*, which for clarity I have translated by its referent.

[415] *octavis paschae.* The same phrase is used at the beginning of this chapter, and in both cases I have translated it "on the octave of Easter." Here, however, the expression may have a somewhat different sense, and it may be an echo of John 20.26: "And after eight days. . . ."

[416] Cf. John 20.26–29.

CHAPTER 41

⁴¹⁷ *A pascha autem usque ad quinquagesima, id est pentecosten.*
Cf. above, n. 301.
⁴¹⁸ On the absence of all fasting and all signs of penance during
this period, cf. Bludau 154. Tertullian remarks in his *De corona*
3: *Die dominico ieiunium nefas ducimus vel de geniculis adorare:
ea immunitate a die paschae in pentecosten usque gaudemus.*
⁴¹⁹ In this listing of daily services at the Anastasis, Egeria does
not mention an office of the ninth hour. However, in ch. 44, in
summarizing the ritual after Pentecost, she does list a service at
the ninth hour.
⁴²⁰ The comment on no fasting on Wednesdays and Fridays
may appear redundant in view of the statement at the beginning
of this chapter that no one fasted between Easter and Pentecost.
However, Egeria is here offering an explanation for a service
during Eastertide at Sion in the morning instead of at the ninth
hour (mid-afternoon), the hour at which it would have been
held at all other times throughout the year except on the feast
day of a martyr. Cf. above, nn. 328 and 329.
⁴²¹ *fit missa ordine suo.* On the translation here of *missa* by
"divine service," cf. Bludau 50; Dölger, *art. cit.* 98; Mohrmann,
"Missa" 80 ff.

CHAPTER 42

⁴²² *Die autem quadragesimarum post pascha.* On other usages
of *quadragesimae* in the *Diary*, cf. n. 314 above and the references there cited. Bludau 154–61 and Bastiaensen 141 f. cite
several 4th-century texts to show that *quadragesima* was used to
designate the feast of the fortieth day after Easter. (For a similar
use of the Greek τεσσαρακοστή, cf. S. Salaville, "La Tessarakoste
du 5ᵉ canon de Nicée," *Echos d'Orient* 13 [1910] 65, and
"Tessarakoste, Ascension et Pentecôte au IVᵉ siècle," *Echos
d'Orient* 32 [1929] 257.) Cf. Augustine, *Sermo* 267.3 (ML
38.1230): *Quando celebravimus quadragesimam, recolite, quia
commendavimus vobis Dominum Iesum Christum ecclesiam suam
commendasse et ascendisse. Quadragesima* as a term for the feast
of Ascension was rapidly replaced in ecclesiastical Latin by

ascensio, and *quadragesima* then was confined to designating Lent.

⁴²³ Whether this means there was a separate celebration of the feast of the Ascension has been disputed. Cabrol 121 ff. insisted that the Ascension was commemorated on Pentecost Sunday, and an afternoon station at the Imbomon on Pentecost lends support to his theory (cf. n. 439 below). Dekkers, *art. cit., passim,* has suggested that the anomaly of a special Ascension celebration in Bethlehem can be explained by the coincidence in the year 417 of Ascension Day (i.e., the fortieth day after Easter) and the Feast of the Dedication of the Basilica of the Nativity. J. G. Davies, *art. cit.* 98, contends, however, that "it will be evident from . . . the Fathers' teaching about the Ascension that to Christians of the 4th century and before the celebration of that festival at Bethlehem would occasion no surprise and would in fact be regarded as most fitting." Davies further states that prior to the construction of the Imbomon a tradition of celebrating Ascension in Bethlehem could have developed and this would very likely have been maintained for some years after the construction of the church between 370 and 378. Cf. Intro. pp. 41 f. and n. 198 to the Intro.

⁴²⁴ I.e., the Basilica of the Nativity.

⁴²⁵ *Alia die autem, id est quinta feria quadragesimarum.* The Latin is awkward, but the sense is clear. In translating here, I have interpreted the genitive *quadragesimarum* as equivalent to *die quadragesimarum.*

⁴²⁶ *celebratur missa ordine suo.* Cf. n. 421 above.

CHAPTER 43

⁴²⁷ *Quinquagesimarum autem die.* Although Egeria was acquainted with the term *pentecoste* (cf. chs. 25 and 41 and n. 301 above) to designate Pentecost, she here uses *quinquagesimarum dies,* "the feast of the fiftieth day." Bludau 166 and Bastiaensen 136–41 cite texts where both *pentecoste* and *quinquagesima* mean either the feast of the fiftieth day, as here, or the period of fifty days after Easter, that is, Eastertide.

⁴²⁸ *procedit omnis populus in ecclesia maiore.* Although it is used here in the active voice, I interpret the verb *procedere* in this passage in accord with the interpretation discussed above in n. 294.

[429] *omnia legitima.* Bastiaensen 83 ff. gives "usage préscrit, rite établi."

[430] *sed eadem adceleratur (adceleratus* in the Arezzo manuscript) *missa in Martyrium, ut ante hora tertia fiat.* In translating *eadem* by "on this day" I am following Löfstedt 66, who interpreted *eadem* as equal to *hac die.* The wording of this passage should be compared to that of the incomplete sentence immediately prior to the lacuna in the manuscript in ch. 25 (cf. n. 302 above). In both cases I have translated *missa* by "dismissal." My interpretation of the passage in ch. 25 was influenced by the wording in this chapter, for in each case the author is apparently making the same point.

[431] The importance of being at Sion at the third hour is explained by Scripture, Acts 2.15: "For these are not drunk, as you suppose, seeing it is but the third hour of the day." The mimetic dimension of these commemorative ceremonies was enhanced by a dual identity of place and of time. On the Christian pilgrim's vicarious reliving of the events of Scripture, cf. Intro. p. 18.

[432] The passage in question is Acts 2.

[433] The manuscript reading here—*ut omnes linguae intellegerent quae dicebantur*—was emended by Geyer and Bonnet (cf. CSEL 39.94), who inserted *audirentur ut omnes* after *linguae.* I have translated the text as thus emended. Bludau 163-6 rejected the emendation, and the Franceschini-Weber edition makes no mention of it.

[434] *postmodum fit ordine suo missa.* On the translation, cf. n. 421 above. It is clear that *missa* does not mean "dismissal" here, for, after explaining parenthetically why the particular passage from Acts was read, Egeria states specifically that the sacrifice was offered.

[435] The Latin text here reads: *Nam presbyteri de hoc ipsud, quod lectum est, quia ipse est locus in Syon, alia modo ecclesia est, ubi quondam post passionem Domini collecta erat multitudo cum apostolis, qua hoc factum est, ut superius diximus, legunt (legi* in the Arezzo manuscript) *ibi de actibus apostolorum.* The loose syntax tends to obscure the meaning of the sentence. In translating, I have followed Erkell 56 ff., who interpreted *lectum est* as a present passive equivalent to "it is stated," "one reads." On the interpretation of *alia modo ecclesia est,* cf. Bastiaensen 123 f.

[436] *Postmodum fit ordine suo missa, offertur et ibi.* On the

translation, cf. n. 421 above. In this passage, Egeria uses *missa* in the more general sense of "service" and reserves the more technical term *offerre* to indicate what precise service took place; for an analogous passage, cf. the wording of ch. 27 quoted in n. 332 above.

[437] *In Eleona*, an ellipsis for *in monte Eleona*, the Mount of Olives. Cf. above, n. 119 to the Intro.

[438] The Latin text reads: . . . *ita ut nullus christianus remaneat in civitate, qui non omnes vadent.* The construction is awkward and the syntax is faulty. Geyer (CSEL 39.94) proposed *christianorum* for *christianus.*

[439] The first station at the Imbomon marked a commemoration of the Ascension, as is readily apparent from the place where the ceremony was held and from the scriptural texts that were read. Cabrol 124 f. asserts that in the early Church Ascension and Pentecost were unified in a single feast celebrating the fifty days of Eastertide: "Jusqu'au quatrième siècle, la Pentecôte, c'est moins la fête du cinquantième jour que l'ensemble des cinquante jours qui forment . . . une seule fête. L'Ascension n'est pas indiquée comme une fête à part; elle est confondue dans la fête générale des cinquante jours de le Pentecôte." Regarding Dekkers' interpretation that this observation of Ascension on Pentecost Sunday afternoon resulted from transfer of the feast from its traditional day in the year 417 because in that year the Feast of the Dedication of the Basilica of the Nativity in Bethlehem fell on Ascension Day, cf. Intro. pp. 41 f. and n. 199 to the Intro. See also n. 423 above. According to Baumstark, *Liturgie comparée* 176 f., Pentecost in the 4th and 5th centuries at Jerusalem was both an historical commemoration and a feast summing up the whole economy of salvation. Cf. Intro. pp. 42 f.

[440] *tales pronuntiationes habent.* A. Ernout, *Aspects du vocabulaire latin* (Paris 1954) 213, interprets *pronuntiatio* as "subject matter" or "content." Bastiaensen 91 f. equates *tales pronuntiationes habere* to *sic pronuntiari*, "to be said in such a manner." Van Oorde 159 gives *argumentum* and *sententia* as equivalents of *pronuntiatio.*

[441] Cf. Mark 16.19 and Luke 24.50–53.

[442] Cf. Acts 1.4–13.

[443] *lente et lente.* This example of geminatio appears five times

in the text (twice in this chapter and once each in chs. 3, 32, and 35). I have varied the translation somewhat in each instance.

[444] *occurrent candele ecclesiasticae vel ducente.* Bastiaensen 164–9 discusses the passage in detail as an example of a tendency in late Latin, especially evident in liturgical texts, of combining a subject thing with a verb expressing an essentially human action. I have translated *occurrent* as equivalent here to *afferuntur.*

[445] *quae sunt de quintana parte. Quintana* as a substantive (scil. *via*) is defined in Lewis-Short 1514 as "a street in the camp which intersected the tents of the two legions in such a manner as to separate the 5th manipule from the 6th and the 5th turma from the 6th." The dictionary notes that "here was the market and business place of the camp." The word also came to have the more general meaning of "market" (cf., e.g., Suetonius, *Nero* 26). Eusebius, *Vita Const.* 3.39, states that the *propylaeum* of the Basilica of the Holy Sepulchre lay in the middle of market street, the *cardo maximus* of the Roman colony. Eusebius referred to it as the *agora.* According to the mosaic of Madaba, three great doors served as the entrance to the atrium of the basilica. Cf. also above, n. 116 to the Intro.

[446] These successive stations at the Martyrium, the Anastasis, the Cross and the late evening service at Sion do not correspond to any publicly established hours of prayer. The scope of the Pentecost liturgy confirms Baumstark's view that the feast was a celebration of the whole economy of salvation.

CHAPTER 44

[447] *de alia die quinquagesimarum.* On the sense of the phrase, cf. Bastiaensen 132 n. 1. Egeria makes no specific reference to the octave of Pentecost, nor does she mention, as do many of the Fathers, that this period also was a time for administering baptism.

[448] Egeria makes no further reference to a post-Pentecost fast. Cabrol 138 f. interprets her statement here not as a reference to a special fast associated with Pentecost, but as referring only to the resumption of the normal fasts interrupted during the Easter season. Mateos, *op. cit.* 247–53, describes a fast in the Chaldaean-Nestorian rite beginning immediately after Pentecost, and says that in the 4th century such a fast was observed at Jerusalem, Alexandria, and Antioch. Besides Egeria, Mateos cites

Athanasius, *Apologia de fuga sua* 6 (MG 25.652) and the *Apostolic Constitutions* 5. Originally lasting a week, this fast was lengthened at Antioch during the 5th and 6th centuries, and in the present-day Chaldaean rite it continues beyond the feast of Sts. Peter and Paul. C. Lambot, "Un *jejunium quinquagesimae* en Afrique au IV° siècle et date de quelques sermons de s. Augustin," RB 47 (1935) 114–24, cites the *Indiculum* of Possidius, where Augustine's Sermons 109 and 110 are listed as *per jejunium quinquagesimae*. Lambot states that the fast lasted one week, had no formal connection with Pentecost, involved at least two days of penance, and, from its title *quinquagesima*, would appear to have been of ancient origin. Lambot attributes the solemnity of the fast to its marking the resumption of the weekly fasting on Wednesdays and Fridays which had been interrupted during Eastertide. Bludau 168 f. cites the Canons of Hippolytus (can. 22) concerning fasts during the week after Pentecost to make up for the fasts not observed in Holy Week. Cf. also Jungmann, *Pastoral Liturgy* 238–51, on the treatment of public penance in the Roman liturgy during the octave of Pentecost.

[449] *tantum quod ymni vel antiphone.* In translating this phrase I have followed Löfstedt 302 f.

[450] Translating here the text as given in Franceschini-Weber (CCL 175.86): *clerici autem cotidie vicibus vadent de pullo primo.* The Arezzo manuscript has two partially erased words, *clerici autem*, after *vadent*, and Geyer (CSEL 39.96) emended the text to read: *clerici autem cotidie vicibus vadent; clerici autem de pullo primo....*

[451] *ut missa fiat matutina.* On the translation here, cf. n. 330 above. It is clear that the bishop participated in the full morning service; he came at the singing of the morning hymns, recited the prayer, made the commemorations, gave the blessings, and so forth (cf. ch. 24 of the *Diary*).

[452] On the Wednesday and Friday liturgy at Sion, cf. ch. 27 and n. 329 above.

CHAPTER 45

[453] Chs. 45–47 deal with the instruction of candidates for baptism. There is some logic in Egeria's placing these chapters after her discussion of Pentecost, for that feast marked the end of the period during which baptism was administered. Cabrol

143–63 interprets Egeria's text in the light of the *Catecheses* of Cyril of Jerusalem, and a detailed discussion is given by Bludau 170–82. On the preparation of baptismal candidates, cf. P. de Puniet, "Baptême," DACL 2.251–346; P. de Puniet, "Catéchumenat," DACL 2.2579–621; H. Leclercq, "Catéchèse, catéchisme, catéchumène," DACL 2.2530–79; Duchesne, *op. cit.* 292–341; Jungmann, *The Early Liturgy* 248–65; Weller, *op. cit.* 32–73; Baumstark, *Liturgie comparée* 211 ff.

[454] *ante diem quadragesimarum.* On the sense here, cf. Bastiaensen 132 n. 1.

[455] *Nam qui dat nomen suum, ante diem quadragesimarum dat et omnium nomina annotat presbyter.* Blaise 556 gives *nomen dare* as a technical term to designate the enrollment of the catechumens. Cyril of Jerusalem's *Procatechesis* (MG 33.333) confirms Egeria's statement that this enrollment took place on the Sunday of the first week of Lent. Bludau 171 indicates that the time appointed for the inscription varied: the Synod of Laodicea (A.D. 363) prescribed that it be completed by the end of the first week in Lent, while the *Ordo romanus* 7 (6th/7th century) set the Wednesday following the third Sunday in Lent for the enrollment of baptismal candidates.

[456] Cabrol 147 n. 2 believes that this was the throne of St. James, the first bishop of Jerusalem. Eusebius, *Hist. eccl.* 7.19, reports that the throne was still preserved in the 4th century. Bludau 172 mentions an inscription in the church of St. Martin of Tours stating that the throne could be found in the Church of Sion.

[457] Egeria's word for "candidate" here is *conpetens*, a technical term used for a candidate for baptism (except at Rome, where *electi* was used for the baptismal candidates). Surprisingly, Egeria uses the term only once, and then in reference to persons whose names had not yet been formally inscribed by the bishop. Bastiaensen 15 f. wonders if she was not using the term in its original sense of "someone who seeks": "En effet, il porte ce nom chez Egérie, quand il s'approche de l'évêque: l'inscription officielle en vue du baptême doit encore avoir lieu . . . et risque d'être refusée." Souter 65 equates *competentes* to "catechumens," translating the Greek κατηχόντες, but Mohrmann, *Die altchristliche Sondersprache in den Sermones des hl. Augustin* 91, states that, with a mass entry into the church, a clear distinction existed between the *catechumeni* and the *competentes*. Cabrol

144 and Bludau 171 agree that there were only two classes of catechumens, the *audientes* and the *competentes*. The Synod of Elvira (*ca.* 300) prescribed a two-year period in general, and a three-year period for pagan priests, in the rank of *audientes*. According to the *Apostolic Constitutions* 8, three years were required of everyone.

⁴⁵⁸ For "godfathers" and "godmothers," the text has simply *patribus* and *matribus*. Bastiaensen 17 ff. points out that since the candidates were adults, the sponsors were most likely not their parents. The technical term for godparents was *sponsores* (Cabrol 148 n. 1 gives as alternate terms *offerentes, compatres, fideijussores, susceptores, patres et matres*). According to Augustine, *Ep.* 98.6 (ML 33.362), parents were often the sponsors or godparents of their minor children.

⁴⁵⁹ On the *scrutinium generale*, cf. Bludau 173 f. and H. Leclercq, "Scrutin," DACL 15.1049. Egeria does not mention one important possible obstacle to baptism, namely, the profession of the individual concerned. Actors, wagoners, gladiators, soothsayers, and others had to renounce their professions before being admitted to the sacrament.

⁴⁶⁰ The formal enrolling of the candidate took place when the bishop inscribed his or her name. Generally, a liturgical ceremony was connected with the catechumen's being formally accepted as a *competens*: the bishop crossed each one with his thumb, laid his hands over him, blessed him, and gave him a pinch of salt, the symbol of wisdom.

⁴⁶¹ P. de Puniet, "Catéchumenat," DACL 2.2612, remarks that the institution of *scrutinium generale* was still in full vigor in 9th-century Carolingian churches. Baumstark, *Liturgie comparée* 212, attests the vitality of the *scrutinium generale* in Milan in the 12th century, and points to a *nomen dare* ceremony among the Nestorians after the 11th century.

CHAPTER 46

⁴⁶² *sine ratione fieri*. In translating this phrase I have followed Bastiaensen 168 ff. Bastiaensen suggests that *ratio* is used here not in the sense of "good reason," but in the sense of "explanation," "explanation of the mysteries," as in *rationem reddere*.

⁴⁶³ Bastiaensen 13 f. suggests that the rite of exorcism was performed by a *clericus* in the minor order of exorcist. Cyril of

Jerusalem, *Procatechesis* 9 (MG 33.348 f.), describes the exorcism of the baptismal candidates. On the rites of exorcism, cf. J. Fourget, "Exorcisme," DTC 5.1762–80.

[464] *mox missa facta fuerit de Anastase matutina.* The *de Anastase* clearly indicates that *missa* here = "dismissal." Cf. n. 330 above.

[465] Egeria clearly distinguishes a catechumen from a *competens*. Cf. n. 457 above.

[466] *primum exponens carnaliter et sic illud solvens (solvet* in the Arezzo manuscript) *spiritualiter.* For a discussion of these terms, cf. Bastiaensen 105–8.

[467] *hoc autem cathecisis appellatur.* Bastiaensen 112 sees in this clause a suggestion that Egeria became acquainted with the term *catechesis* only in Jerusalem. Egeria uses the term only in this present chapter, and she does not use the verb *catechizare* or any of the other nominal cognates, *catechismus, catechista, catechizatio.* Blaise 138 cites our author and Jerome as the earliest users of *catechesis* in ecclesiastical Latin. For a history of catechetics, cf. O. Bareille, "Catéchèse," DTC 2.1877–95.

[468] *tunc accipient simbolum. Accipere symbolum* and *reddere symbolum* are the technical terms to describe the reception of the Creed by the *competentes* and the later recitation of the Creed back to the bishop. Generally these ceremonies are referred to as the *traditio symboli* and the *redditio symboli. Tradere symbolum,* a phrase which Egeria does not employ, designates the formal transmission of the Creed by the bishop. On the *traditio symboli,* cf. Intro. p. 39 and n. 186 to the Intro.

[469] The explanation of the Creed lasted two weeks. Cyril of Jerusalem devoted his 6th through 18th *Catecheses* to instruction on individual articles of the Creed, but whether his catechetical lessons corresponded to those given during the 6th and 7th weeks of Lent at the time of Egeria's visit is open to question; on this point, cf. Cabrol 155–9. Bastiaensen 107 questions the meaning of a "literal" (*carnaliter*) and "spiritual" (*spiritualiter*) explanation of the Creed and suggests that the words here either are a carry-over from the preceding remarks on the teaching of Scripture or refer to the practice of prefacing the discussion of each article with Old Testament prefigurations.

[470] The text has *fit cathecisin,* though some editors—Gamurrini and Cholodniak—give *fit cathecisis.* On the use of the accusative with the impersonal *fit,* however, cf. Löfstedt 291.

[471] *qui ad audiendum intrant in cathecisen.* On the translation of *audire* by "to hear instruction," "to hear a sermon," cf. Bastiaensen 113 f.

[472] *Missa autem facta cathecisis hora iam tertia statim inde cum ymnis ducitur episcopus ad Anastase et fit missa ad tertia.* The first *missa* clearly designates the dismissal from catechetics, but it is unlikely that the second *missa* also refers to a dismissal, for the passage would then be redundant. In Lent a service was held at the third hour and Egeria seems to be saying here that, following the dismissal from catechetics, the bishop went in procession from the Martyrium to the Anastasis to officiate at the office of the third hour.

[473] On the *redditio symboli* ceremony, cf. Intro. p. 39 and n. 187 to the Intro. Egeria does not mention the solemn transmission of the *Pater Noster* to the *competentes.* For an example of a sermon delivered at the rite of the *traditio orationis dominicae,* cf. Augustine, *Sermo* 56 (ML 38.377–86; translated in P. T. Weller, *Selected Easter Sermons of Saint Augustine* [Saint Louis 1959] 198–214).

[474] *alloquitur omnes episcopus.* In translating *alloqui* by "to deliver a homily," I have followed Blaise 54.

[475] *ut potuistis tamen adhuc cathecumini audire.* In the immediately preceding lines the verb *audire* has been used twice in its normal sense of "to hear." Van Oorde gives *intellegere* for *audire* in this specific passage, and Bastiaensen 113 f. states that *posse audire* refers to the right of the catechumens to learn of the deeper mysteries of faith.

[476] Bludau 179 f. notices strong parallels between the bishop's discourse and Cyril of Jerusalem's *Catechesis* 18.32 f. (MG 33.1053–6). We possess sermons from other Fathers as well pertaining to the *redditio symboli* rite; cf., e.g., Augustine, *Sermo* 215 (ML 38.1072–6; translated in Weller, *Selected Easter Sermons of Saint Augustine* 215–22).

CHAPTER 47

[477] On the celebration of the morning liturgy during Easter Week, cf. ch. 39 of the *Diary.*

[478] The explanation of the mysteries to the neophytes took place in the Anastasis, whereas the instruction preceding baptism was given in the Martyrium.

[479] These discourses of the bishop would correspond to the five *Catecheses mystagogicae* attributed to Cyril of Jerusalem which were delivered during Easter Week and which treat of baptism, confirmation, and the Eucharist, the three sacraments administered at the Easter vigil service.

[480] Apparently the *disciplina arcani,* the practice of keeping from the uninitiated the full significance of the sacraments, particularly the Eucharist, prevailed in full force. Only after baptism was the full meaning of these rites revealed.

[481] Cyril of Jerusalem's sermons were often interrupted by applause; cf. *Catechesis* 13.23 (MG 33.800).

[482] *Vere enim ita misteria omnia absolvet* (*absolvent* in the Arezzo manuscript). On the translation of *absolvet,* cf. Bastiaensen 106 ff., who gives "révéler le sens des sacrements reçues."

[483] For a commentary on the problem presented by the use of Greek as the hieratic language of the liturgy in the East, cf. Bludau 182 ff. Bludau cites Eusebius and Epiphanius for evidence of the role of translators in multilingual regions of the Eastern empire. The literary language of the Christian community of Palestine in the 4th century was Greek, as can be seen from the writings of Cyril of Jerusalem, Hesychius, and Titus of Bostra. Jerome, *Ep.* 108.29, mentions that at the funeral of Paula Psalms were sung in Greek, Latin, and Syriac.

[484] *alii fratres et sorores grecolatini.* Van Oorde 84 gives *fratres in Christo,* a synonym for "fellow Christians," for *fratres.* However, Meister 381, Löfstedt 338, and L. Lorie, *Spiritual Terminology in the Latin Translations of the Vita Antonii* (Nijmegen 1955) 39, prefer the sense of "monks." Cf. n. 21 above.

CHAPTER 48

[485] *Item dies enceniarum appellantur.* There is apparently no connection between the subject matter of the preceding chapter and that of chs. 48 and 49, which describe a feast commemorating three events that would have been of particular significance for the church of Jerusalem: the consecration of the basilicas of the Martyrium and the Anastasis, the Finding of the Holy Cross, and Solomon's dedication of the first Temple.—The word *encaenia* would be familiar to a Latin Christian from Scripture (cf. John 10.22: *Facta sunt encaenia in Ierusolymis,* where it refers to the Jewish Feast of the Dedication, called in Greek

τὰ ἐγκαίνια, celebrating the re-dedication of the Temple by
Judas Maccabeus in 165 B.C., observed in Jerusalem around
the middle of December and commemorated in modern Judaism
as the Feast of Lights, or Hanukkah). Augustine explains the
word in his *In evang. Ioh.* 48.2: *Encaenia festivitas erat dedi-
cationis templi. Graece enim caenon dicitur novum. Quandocum-
que novum aliquid fuerit dedicatum, encaenia vocantur.* Egeria
uses the term *encaenia* only in the last two extant chapters of the
Diary, and only in reference to the specific feast being described
here. She may have understood the word only in relation to this
particular feast. In four of her five usages of the term it is in the
genitive plural dependent on *dies* in the plural (undoubtedly for
dies festi, or *festae*, since Egeria uses *dies* as a feminine). In one
case the word appears as a nominative plural referring to the
dedication of the two basilicas: *Harum ergo ecclesiarum sanc-
tarum encenia cum summo honore celebrantur.* For a discussion
of the word *encaenia* (*encenia*) in the *Diary*, cf. Bastiaensen
119–24.—On the probable date of the Feast of the Dedications, cf.
nn. 486 and 488 below.

⁴⁸⁶ The Constantinian Basilica of the Holy Sepulchre was consecrated in September of the year 335, and the event was described by an eyewitness, Eusebius of Caesarea (cf. his *Vita
Const.* 4.43–47; cf. also Socrates, *Hist. eccl.* 1.33; Sozomenus,
Hist. eccl. 2.26; Theodoret, *Hist. eccl.* 1.29). The probable date
of the consecration was September 13. Cf. Bludau 185–90.

⁴⁸⁷ *cum summo honore.* Cf. n. 308 above.

⁴⁸⁸ H. Chirat, "Finding of the Holy Cross," NCE 4.479–82,
cites the testimony of the *Diary* and states that "the finding of
the Cross must have taken place on September 13 between 325
and 334." However, can we reliably fix the day of the Finding of
the Cross on the basis of our pilgrim's statement that the dedication of the churches occurred on the date of Helena's discovery of the Cross? Egeria's remark may reflect nothing more
than a tradition popularly held within the radius of the influence
of the church of Jerusalem. Bludau 186 f. states that the
Nestorians observed the feast of the Cross on September 13, but
he adds that the other Syriac churches, influenced by Constantinople, marked the Finding of the Cross on September 14. Chirat
notes that the 7th-century Constantinopolitan *Chronicon paschale*
"gives as the precise date for the discovery Sept. 14, 320." We
may further note that in the same *Chronicon paschale* (MG

92.713) the consecration of the basilica is considered to have been held on September 13, but that the Cross was shown to the people for the first time on the 14th. Bludau cites several sources that indicate that the two events were commemorated annually on these successive days in various Eastern liturgies. The Greek church continues to observe September 13 as the Feast of the Dedication of the Church of the Holy Resurrection of our Lord and Christ, and, as F. L. Cross, ODC 698, states, "in the Greek Church the Feast of the Finding of the Cross was originally commemorated on 14 Sept., now the Feast of the Exaltation of the Cross. . . ." The present-day Feast of the Exaltation commemorates the exposition of the Cross in 629 by the Emperor Heraclius, following its recovery from the Persians, who in 614 under Chosroes II had carried it off after their capture of Jerusalem. The earliest reference to this feast at Rome dates from the pontificate of Pope Sergius in 691 (cf. Baumstark, *Liturgie comparée* 160). Apparently the present-day observance of the Finding of the Cross on May 3 can be traced to the apocryphal treatise *De inventione crucis Domini*, and the earliest references to it in the West are found in the Lectionary of Silos (*ca.* 650) and in the Gallican sacramentaries of the 7th and 8th centuries. Around 800, May 3 was probably being observed at Rome as the Feast of the Finding of the Cross (cf. F. L. Cross, ODC 480; Bludau 188 f.).

[489] Cf. 2 Par. 5–7. An account of the dedication of the Temple may also be found in 3 Kings 8. The dedication was in the seventh month of the Hebrew year, the month of Tishri, and was celebrated for seven days, from the 8th to the 14th day of the month. The ceremonies of the dedication preceded the Feast of the Tabernacles, which was annually celebrated from the 15th to the 21st day of the seventh month, concluding with a solemn observance of the octave day (cf. Lev. 23.34–43).

CHAPTER 49

[490] Theodosius (CCL 175.124) refers to the Feast of the Finding of the Cross, but his dating of the feast is confusing. He states that it fell on September 15 (*XVII. Kal. octobris*) and was observed for seven days, during which the Cross was shown (*per septem dies in Hierusalem ibi ad sepulchrum Domni missas celebrantur et ipsa crux ostenditur*).

[491] Eusebius, *Vita Const.* 4.43, had already remarked on
variety of nationalities represented at the original dedica
Adamnus (CCL 175.185 f.), writing around 685, long after
Arab conquest of Jerusalem, speaks of vast crowds that thror
the city for several days after September 12 (or 15, as thre
four manuscripts have it), but he makes no reference to a
or feasts marking the dedication of the basilicas, the Findin
the Cross, or the Exaltation of the Cross.

[492] Cf. chs. 25 and 39 of the *Diary.*

[493] At this point the manuscript breaks off. For the orde
stational churches during the Epiphany and Easter octaves
chs. 25 and 39 of the *Diary.*

INDEXES

1. OLD AND NEW TESTAMENT

2. AUTHORS

3. GREEK WORDS

4. LATIN WORDS

5. SUBJECT INDEX